Between the Masks

Culture and Education Series

Series Editors: Henry A. Giroux, Pennsylvania State University
Joe L. Kincheloe, Pennsylvania State University

The rise of new media and significant changes in media industries have brought about a major transformation in how knowledge is produced and assimilated. Today, TV, films, CDs, computer networks, and advertising all figure into the construction of cultural identities and social experiences—often in ways that were hard to imagine just a few years ago.

Surprisingly little academic study has been undertaken of these transformations in media, culture, and education. This new book series explores questions about the relationship among knowledge, power, identity, and politics in connection with issues of justice, equality, freedom, and community.

Race-ing Representation: Voice, History, and Sexuality
edited by Kostas Myrsiades and Linda Myrsiades, 1998

Between the Masks: Resisting the Politics of Essentialism
by Diane DuBose Brunner, 1998

Forthcoming:

Cutting Class: Social Class and Education
edited by Joe L. Kincheloe and Shirley R. Steinberg

The Mouse That Roared: What Disney Teaches
by Henry A. Giroux

Between the Masks,

*Resisting
the Politics of
Essentialism*

Diane DuBose Brunner

ROWMAN & LITTLEFIELD PUBLISHERS, INC.
Lanham • Boulder • New York • Oxford

ROWMAN & LITTLEFIELD PUBLISHERS, INC.

Published in the United States of America
by Rowman & Littlefield Publishers, Inc.
4720 Boston Way, Lanham, Maryland 20706

12 Hid's Copse Road
Cumnor Hill, Oxford OX2 9JJ, England

British Library Cataloguing in Publication Information Available

Library of Congress Cataloging-in-Publication Data

Brunner, Diane DuBose, 1949–
    Between the masks : resisting the politics of essentialism / Diane
DuBose Brunner.
        p.   cm. — (Culture and education)
    Includes bibliographical references and index.
    ISBN 0-8476-8895-X (hardcover : alk. paper). — ISBN 0-8476-8896-8
(pbk. : alk. paper)
    1. Identity (Psychology) 2. Identity (Psychology) in literature.
3. Identity (Psychology) in motion pictures.   I. Title.
    II. Series: Culture and education series.
    BF697.B79 1998
    191—dc21   98-23717
                                                                              CIP

Internal design and typesetting: Letra Libre

Printed in the United States of America

⊚™   The paper used in this publication meets the minimum requirements of American National Standard for Information Sciences—Permanence of Paper for Printed Library Materials,
ANSI Z39.48–1984.

For all the students who taught me much about performance, especially those named here whose words are used in this text: John, Ethan, Amy, Andrea, Danielle, Stacey, Essie, Keri, Michelle, Julia, Kristi, Jim, Larry, Christy, Marje, Debi, Steve, Tracey, Anne, Kristin, and Vanessa.

Contents

Acknowledgments

Because all writing is collaborative, this project, like all efforts, reminds me there are many who contribute and many to thank. Those most influential have been my students; some names are mentioned in the dedication and others have slipped by without mention. They have been my ardent teachers. My deepest gratitude also goes to Henry Giroux for believing in this project and for supporting it from draft to print. Another special thanks goes to Jill Rothenberg, a remarkable editor. Her close readings of the work in manuscript have been invaluable. A special thanks also goes to production editor, Scott Horst, to copyeditor Jon Taylor Howard, and to Rebecca Hoogs for aspects of marketing and cover design. I especially want to thank Jennifer Brooke for permitting me to photograph the mask for the book's cover and J. D. Small for his excellent photography. The mask is a story in itself. It is located in the Travelers Club, an international restaurant within walking distance of my house—a place where friends and cultures meet. My family and I have eaten in this restaurant for more than ten years, and during that time we've enjoyed not only the food but also all the different masks that grace its walls. The particular mask on the cover caught my eyes a few years ago when I began work on this project. Each time I'd notice the three faces in the one mask, I'd think about the expression I'd heard many times as a child—the denigrating phrase kids say about someone who is two-faced. As I've explored identity, I've come to see the body as the location of many faces, thus the mask that shows the many in the eyes of the one became an appropriate graphic. Finally, my family deserves a big thank-you for listening so patiently to all the thinking out loud that I've discovered is a necessary part of my work.

Introduction

My mask is control/concealment/endurance/my mask is escape/from my/self. . . . Between the masks we've internalized, one on top of the another, are our interfaces . . . to provide support and stability to collar, cuff, yoke.

—Gloria Anzaldua, Making Face, Making Soul, 1990, p. xv

Between my masks are shadows dancing an unquiet self. A clandestine outlier, I tear at the masks, struggling to make visible the diverse locations from which my voice and identity derive. Although I was raised "white" with Cherokee, French, and Scots-Irish grandparents, racial/ethnic difference is hardly all that constructs my identity. In me the location of culture and identity is not reducible to race, ethnicity, or gender any more than it is to the fact that family members picked cotton, cleaned, took in sewing and ironing, worked on the railroad, and repaired tractors.

We lived at the edge of town, the border between Lake City and what was called "colored town." A cemetery, a few houses, a church, and a park were the fringe areas that met the railroad tracks that separated both race and class in this small southern town. Though there were a few kids who lived on my street with whom I could play, our fun and fascination was in crossing those borders and doing what was forbidden. We were poor, living close to our neighbors across the tracks but separated by what adults imagined were maintainable borderlines, and a nearby park between the two areas became the doorway to unknown worlds. Like the writhing I'd do in church as I learned about forbiddens, this too made me writhe with eagerness to know what was so special that it was forbidden.

Fueled by a desire to resist taboos and to know what we were taught was unknowable, we often made our way into the cemetery where we engaged in the voyeuristic pleasures of crouching behind tombstones to observe the life fear taught us was off-limits. Seldom did anyone—they or we—venture across this invisible barrier, but a few times a child approached the tracks and was immediately called back by her or his mother. My mother would have done the same.

Fear of the unknown prevented us from speaking or playing, not the fear from knowing what the consequences of disobedience would be. From a distance, then, both "we" and "they" could only imagine lives that seemed to us as if marked by the signs that read "colored" and "white only" displayed at the soda fountains, diners, and over restroom doors.

In my lifetime doors have not been closed to me because of skin color, as they have to many of my black friends and colleagues. Though we were poor, I knew that *white* meant privilege. Much later, a college friend recalled traveling from Chicago to Biloxi and having to drink at a spigot marked "colored" while a "white only" fountain had bubbly water spewing up, its basin dripping with condensation from the cooler that chilled it. She told me there were times during their travels when they were turned away from five-and-dime lunch counters that displayed the sign "white only served here."

As a child I used crayons to draw the stories I observed from my vantage point—flesh for me, brown for them—and not just at the tracks, but everywhere our worlds seemed divided into an us/them. And I grew up wondering about the strangeness of a language for "white only."[1]

I return to those sites occasionally. Sometimes I sit on the park bench and talk with a grandmother who has brought her grandchildren to play in the park, and I almost think out loud, "Finally, you made it across those tracks."

There is no visible fear as we visit, and the children seem to play freely. In the 1950s this would not have been the case. Sometimes I'll visit my father's grave and look in the direction of what was once called "colored town," memorizing the past yet hoping to glimpse through the fully grown shrubs a mixing of relations that will be a sign that Lake City is no longer divided. Though the boundaries today may be less clearly marked and divisions are more subtle, in the cultural repository that is language distinctions remain.

In *Marxism and the Philosophy of Language*, V. N. Volosinov, a close associate of Mikhail Bakhtin, writes that all language is representative and has an ideological function;[2] it is a two-sided act (Volosinov, 1973). He writes further:

> Side by side with the natural phenomena, with the equipment of technology, and with articles for consumption, there exists a special world—the world of signs. Signs also are particular, material things. . . . A sign does not simply exist as a part of reality, it reflects and refracts another reality.

Therefore, it may distort that reality or may be true to it, or may perceive it from a special point of view, and so forth. . . . Wherever a sign is present, ideology is present, too. *Everything ideological possesses semiotic value* (p.10).

The signs of racism in my hometown were/are an uncomfortable reminder that language and ideology are connected. The ideological chain that passes between human consciousnesses is not only a material segment of reality (the "white only" and "colored" signs over washroom doors) but also a shadow that remains in human consciousness long after the physical signs have been removed. The process of social interaction that occurs in the space-time of the semiotic—the space of the ideological in language and the time of co-temporal in communication—is the space through which signs and their transitory meanings are carried forward into the future.

Julia Kristeva, a pioneer of the revolutionary theory of the sign, conceptualizes the semiotic as both spatial and temporal in its relationship to the social and political.[3] She further conceives of the semiotic as the place of meaning before meaning in which the flesh (body, dreams, desires) becomes word (the symbolic represents both the grammatical lexicon and the social order, the Laws of the Father)—a polysemic site; the semiotic is, therefore, relational, performative, and ambiguous (1986a).[4] Though language shapes and is shaped by the sociopolitical order, this two-sided contract between the semiotic and the symbolic that is prefigured in "speech performances," according to Volosinov, tends to be shaped by temporal relations of production (1973, p. 19).

Though Volosinov describes here a class relationship, it is not unmarked by race. Evidence of borders everywhere suggests class and race (along with ethnicity, gender, and sexuality) are co-constructed. The working poor were/are marginal in relation to those with money and power, the white working poor were/are often privileged in relation to people of color, and so on. It is, indeed, more than apparent to me that the travesties of race enacted on people of color in this society over the last 100 or more years passed me by because of my white skin. Though I overlapped racial borderlines,[5] I never had to sit at the back of the bus or drink from a spigot unless I wanted to.

On any given day I am privileged to be who I need to be even if that sometimes feels like a burden of representativity—a masking of the self I think I know but can't fully grasp, a self mostly known in the eyes of someone else. Sometimes I can be who I want to be, who I think I am, and/or who I might be—if only. . . . If, then, I am not just "who I am," it seems important to unmask the various sites that construct my identity. Despite having a material body that needs food, clothing, shelter, safety, and the like, identity and materiality are not separated in my consideration of who I think I am and/or need to be in any given moment because each bears directly on how well I am able to feed, clothe, protect myself, and so on. And how well I meet those basic needs or do not tends to figure positively and negatively on my identity, making me realize my own privilege and at once saddening me with the knowledge that walking through open doors, passing between many boundaries, is the bridge that links yesterday, today, and tomorrow. I am changed because of opportunities I have that my family did not, and it remains important, therefore, that I remember the fragments of my ancestry and our circumstances so that I am forever aware of how privilege and marginality marks, even scars, identities.

I do not intend this discussion to emphasize the sort of "identity politics" that Jenny Bourne discusses in her article "Homelands of the Mind." There she writes about Jewish feminism, in particular, and claims it fosters "an apolitical, amaterialist, and subjectivist point of view" (1987, p. 1). I tell this story only to locate my position within the larger framework of this book and to illustrate what I perceive to be a problem with the location of identity and whether or not it must be based on essence or what Frantz Fanon (1967) calls an "appearance" (p. 35).[6] The problem, it seems, lies as much with an unsatisfactory, perhaps undertheorized sense of "place" respective to the location of identity as it does with/in the politics of essentialism.

As evidenced in the title of this project, I perceive that "place"—respective to the tropes of performance and location (especially as regards identity)—always resides already in the gray areas between masks. In other words, performances of lived life range from writing, as an act of doing, to role-taking (Brunner, 1987) to dramatizing teachers' storied worlds (Brunner, 1994) to rearticulating gender by miming "killing" norms (Brunner, 1996) to staging deliberate acts of sexual identity-making/marking (Brunner, 1997a) to restaging the drama of the body (Brunner, 1997b) to experimental theater events; and all are "unmarked" (Phelan, 1993) as regards a specific tradition and political terrain. Two particular voices from performance theory articulate my intentions best: Richard Schechner and Jill Dolan.[7]

In his book Essays on Performance Theory 1970–1976 (1977), Schechner, a drama critic and director of experimental theater groups, explains why: "It is hard to define 'performance' because the boundaries separating it on the one side from the theatre and on the other from everyday life are arbitrary. . . . All studies in movement in art are studies of analogic phenomena" (pp. 44, 99). Schechner's comment, of course, begs the question: "But to what degree are studies of movement in life also art" (p. 99)? Schechner's work suggests these questions cannot be answered definitively because they depend on assumptions that are ideologically based.

Performance studies of biomechanics and kinesis bleed into studies of ceremony and ritual that bleed into studies of the theater as art. Each relies on systems of expression that are both analytical and intuitive. Thus "real" distinctions between theater and everyday life are difficult and, in Schechner's view, are arbitrarily imposed. His work and mine aim toward a "poetics of performance." He writes, "I find nothing disturbing about relating the finest achievements of human art—indeed, the very process of making art: the ritual action of rehearsal and preparation—to [instinctual] behavior. . . . Ritual action [in this sense] . . . employs the same means: repetition, simplification, exaggeration, rhythmic action, the transformation of 'natural sequences' of behavior into 'composed sequences'" (p 108).

Schechner (1977) provides an apt example of this conflation of theater and everyday life performance in a Vancouver troupe called The Performance Group (TPG). Their production of *Commune* was what TPG called a "real time" performance in which they invited audiences to come to the theater when the performers did. About twelve people came early and watched as performers set up the stage, did warm-ups, got into costumes, worked the box office, talked with the regular audience, disrobed at the end of the performance, and, finally, cleaned up and locked the theater (everyday life activities for TPG). Schechner says two performances occurred that night: one for the "real-time" audience and one for the "regular" audience, illustrating the lack of pure boundaries between theater and everyday life and exaggerating the spectator's role by making the "regular" audience part of the performance for the "real-time" audience.

From this and other examples, Schechner theorizes some of the reasons for what appears as a split between cultural manifestations of theater and performance. He says, "Words like 'script,' 'drama,' 'theatre,' and 'performance' are loaded, and none have neutral synonyms. My choice is either to invent new words, which no one will pay attention to, or . . . introduce regions of restrictive meaning into the more general areas covered by these words" (p. 38). For example, Schechner (1977) writes that the Western view emphasizes the drama-script dyad as oppositional pairs, but Asian, Oceanic, and African cultures emphasize theater-performance. Overlaps occur in all cultures:

> Wherever the boundaries are set, it is within the broad region of performance that theatre takes place; at the center of the theatre is the script, sometimes the drama. Just as drama may be thought of as a specialized kind of script, so theatre can be considered a specialized kind of performance. . . . Theatre doesn't arrive suddenly and stay fixed either in its cultural or individual manifestations. It is insinuated along a web of associations spun from play, games, hunting, slaughter and distribution of meat, ceremonial centers, trials, rites of passage and storytelling. Rehearsals and recollections—preplay and afterplay—converge

in the theatrical event [i.e.,] ritualized versions of gestures and sounds (pp. 39, 136–137, 157).

Moreover, drama critic Jill Dolan (1993) claims that the fields of cultural studies, performance studies, and feminist, gay, and lesbian studies have "creatively" borrowed concepts from theater studies to show that "the constructed nature of subjectivity . . . [suggests] that social subjects perform themselves in negotiation with the delimiting cultural conventions of the geography within which they move" (p. 419). I admit to the same. I strategically use these concepts to suggest "theatricalizing activism" (Judith Butler's term used in an interview with Liz Kotz, 1992)— overlapping the discourses of everyday life performance and performance as politics. Just as the theater marks particular historical sites for interventionist work, there are many other stagelike arenas (classrooms, dance floors, concerts stages, etc.) in which culture is performed and through which political interventions occur. These life performances, although existing outside the formal parameters of the theater, do not so much stand in opposition to the aesthetic aspects of theater as they draw attention to the theatricality of everyday life. The politics of gesturing and display refuse "notions[s] of inherent essentialist ontology, suggest[ing] instead a constructionist notion of identity as anti-metaphysical, emphatically material and historical, constantly refashioning itself in various contexts and configurations of reception" (Dolan, 1993, p. 419). Moreover, Dolan writes, "'Performativity' as metaphor . . . describe[s] the nonessentialized constructions of marginalized identities . . . [with] various conflicting combinations and intersections of these categories and positionalities" (p. 419).

Dolan's (1993) chief argument in her essay on geographies of learning deals with the likenesses and dissimilarities between performance and the performative. Descriptive of cultural behavior, performance and the performative are not the same, though they are not mutually exclusive, according to Dolan: "Performance is a genre with its own history, applications, and cultural uses" (p. 423). Performance connotes an event where "cultural products" are negotiated and dominant meanings are contested. Performativity, in its attention to identity and positionality, is also a term that has a particular history related to metaphors of location. That performance as a medium of expression should be connected at all to projects of positionality marks an opening onto pedagogical sites for disrupting and then reconnecting interdisciplinary methods of "other(ed) geographies, other(ed) desires, and bodies othered by what hegemony has refused to allow seen" (p. 421).

My own location in this argument seems simple and yet is complex due to the sorts of exclusions that Dolan recalls. English studies is not historically the site for pedagogical studies, especially performance pedagogy. Though the Theatre Department at Michigan State University (MSU) in East Lansing, where I teach, resides within the College of Arts and Letters along with the Department of English, the two are not inclined to interact where academic production is concerned. For example, the first time I needed a stage for an end-of-semester performance, I had to apologize for my encroachment on the Theatre Department's turf and reiterate that we were only pursuing experimental theater in my course on stories and performance. So while the explicit intent of my project is to suggest that identities reside between the masks and that this "in-between" is a "place" for resisting the politics of essentialism (Peggy Phelan, 1993, declares that "Being is performed in that suspended in-between," p. 167), the implicit intent is to suggest that pedagogical and cultural studies that borrow from performance studies and collide with English studies are also a "place" to resist the hierarchicalizing of canonical interests and promote interdisciplinary modes of academic production. My own interest in performance pedagogy, ethnography and performance, culture, and education vis-à-vis media, feminist, and multiethnic studies suggests some of the locations I perceive are in confluence. As sites of confluence that press and converge on the performance of everyday life in all its multiplicity and contradiction, that is, a "place" between the masks, Dolan's argument and my own challenge essentialist exclusions and absences, drawing on "the power of theatricality to describe and to change the way social identities are performed and received" (p. 421).[8]

In this book (see Chapter 2 for a detailed explanation), I theorize "place" as an opening "in between" (Bhabha, 1994, p. 2) space and time in which the "subject-as-[pedagogical] site" (Foucault, 1986) actively seeks to "undo the [essentialized] proper" (de Certeau, 1984). Place here is an uncontainable space-time, an altering aspect. Kristeva (1984) refers to this altering aspect as the thetic—where the slippage between signifier and signified occurs in the uncontainable place of the semiotic, a dimension between what is sanctioned or status quo and what is "illicit" or "uncivilized" (p. 113). For Kristeva (1986a) the semiotic is a space-time in which the body assumes the role of linguistic signifier. She writes, "The thetic [is] that crucial place on the basis of which the human being constitutes himself[/herself] as signifying and/or social" (1986a, p. 117).[9] This space-time gives rise to what Butler (1993) implies is the body's own literacy, when bodily foreclosures replace linguistic disclosures.

The space-time between performances is also uncontainable and thus permits alteration. Though I suggest narrative-performative strategies of displacement in theorizing place, *these strategies are meant as a critical bridging to a place from which to speak* (Bhabha, 1994), a bridging to a "place" from which to alter consciousness and the wider society. Homi

Bhabha is one of the leading postcolonial theorists writing today against the politics of essentialism. His work offers an explanation for why modern Western culture must recover from the grips of colonialist thinking. In so doing, Bhabha theorizes a notion of cultural hybridity, translating social difference beyond the polarities of Self and Other.

More than positionality, then, place reflects the space-time in which the subject regains agential control to authorize the narratives/memories that have been suppressed by authority. Though I primarily focus on identity in this text when theorizing place as an opening through which to resist essentialist habits of mind, my discussion of the politics of essentialism moves beyond an association with identity politics that positions humans with particular identifying characteristics/behaviors against one another (insider/outsider) and describes also the ways in which essentialist ideologies suggest a single perspective (a single "truth") with respect to any phenomenon or idea.[10]

In *Essentially Speaking* Diana Fuss (1989) raises the question of whether or not it is possible to base identity on anything but the physical and easily identifiable, for example, sex, race, nationality, economics (1989). In this text she voices concern for the relocation of identity from "within" (what I read as sexual, racial, etc.) to the locations "between" identities. I share her concern for the materiality of one's existence, yet I find the social constructions of identity so palpable as markers of identity that I perceive that the difficulty of their unmasking relegates most of us to living between the masks. I do not agree that locating identity between performances positions difference outside identity so much as it recognizes the constraints of social masking and reclaims agential control. In other words, I do not resist the notion that I am of a particular bloodline, yet simultaneously I do not perceive that is the extent of my identity. Moreover, it is not the idea of essence per se that I quibble with; rather I find deeply problematic the politics of essentialism or the way in which persons, ideas, and phenomena are reduced to a single perspective and then hierarchicalized.

As performance ethnographer and theorist Dwight Conquergood (1991) suggests, "Borders bleed, as much as they contain. . . . Inside and outside distinctions . . . blur and wobble. . . . The major epistemological consequence of displacing the idea of solid centers and unified wholes with borderlands and zones of contest is a rethinking of identity and culture as constructed and relational, instead of ontologically given and essential" (p. 184).[11] This project, therefore, aims to complicate any view of identity that suggests it is reducible to any single perspective, any absolute.

The psychoanalytic view suggesting that identity is a contingency of a "split-subject," I perceive, supports this notion. To quote Kristeva, "The *sub-*

ject of utterance is both representative of the subject of enunciation and represented as an object of the subject of enunciation. . . . The subject of utterance is dialogical" (1986a, p. 46). I perceive that Fuss is accurate in her assessment that such a position moves identity away from the notion of an "identity of things in themselves towards an analysis of *identity statements*" (1989, p. 103). Yet this is what I assume makes identity performative, process-oriented, stance-driven, and thus changeable. Identity is located not in specific constructions but instead between the multiple masks and performances, not merely the essence of a raced or sexed being or constructed in identity politics only. Both of the latter conceptions may be a valid means of expressing identity, yet each can also be a means of containment.

I agree, then, with the view that worlds exist in the "in-between," in the interstitial sites of collaboration and contestation (Bhabha, 1994, pp. 1–2). I do not perceive that the notion that suggests identities are multiple and shift between performances (or *identity statements*) signifies the lack of materiality; it garners instead social agency for the possibility of changing one's material reality. As my own story indicates, the world is often portrayed as black and white, yet most of us live in the gray. Moreover, it may be impossible to know or theorize the "real" person behind the constructed masks worn in the "theater of identities" (Kristeva, 1992, p. 147), so, in fact, maybe only the statements one makes provide any clue at all to one's identity.

Do I find this a pleasant state of affairs on the eve of the twenty-first century? Yes and no. I find it symptomatic of many of the social ills that plague this period, and I find notions of contingency and the provisional a refreshing possibility for undoing the fixed perceptions of the way the world works, or "ways of being in the world," as Clifford Geertz stated (1983, p. 155), for undoing the binary logic of insider/outsider, for undoing the proper (de Certeau, 1984).

Gaston Bachelard (1964), the French philosopher with extraordinary meditations on the relationship between space and imagination, investigates the spatial logic of inside/outside in *The Poetics of Space*. Here Bachelard sees curiosity as a playfulness leading to the further development of imagination. In his discussion of openings he suggests the performative. The opening of a casket, as in one example, performs the function of dissolving the dialectics of inside and outside.

In contrast, Laura Mulvey (1992), a feminist film critic whose work problematizes society's obsession of the slick and fashionable, writes that "the literal reality of spaces and images . . . [is as] elastic as the forms of metaphor and metonymy themselves" (p. 71). Though understated, both Bachelard and Mulvey employ concepts of temporality in their discussions of spatiality, for each renders the forward projection of time in the workings of curiosity.

Curiosity and the Liberation of Memory

Mulvey suggests that an "aesthetic of curiosity" resides in the theatrical pageantry of masquerade. Here ideological contradiction, the flesh incarnate, desire, and the "machine" all must be transformed in the moments of self-reflexive gesturing that occur between the masks. Performances depend on glossy masks that conceal and often render the subject idealized. The masquerade can exaggerate fetishes, seduce, overvalue. It is often invested with voyeuristic pleasures, yet this fragmented, forbidden place offers hope from the "blinkered vision of a single, anthropomorphic perspective" (Mulvey, p. 70).

In Mulvey's discussion of the "Pandora" topography, she writes, "While curiosity is a compulsive desire to see and to know, to investigate what is secret and reveal the contents of a concealed space, fetishism, on the other hand, is born out of a refusal to see, a refusal to know, and a refusal to accept . . . difference. . . . Curiosity describes the desire to know something that is concealed so strongly that it is experienced like a drive, leading to the transgression of a prohibition" (pp. 65, 70)—to the liberation of "dangerous" memories. Similarly and perhaps more emphatically, fetishism, like exoticism, divides, segments, *others*—it essentializes.

The dialectic of inside/outside has a special function in status quo ideology that perpetuates the politics of essentialism; inside/outside renders sameness "natural" and difference transgressive. Though Mulvey's analysis of the Pandora myth is from a psychoanalytic perspective as regards a Freudian "sight" of the female anatomy,[12] her analysis is also useful in understanding the topography of boxes or spaces, which are conceived as containers, in general, and thus the insider/outsider binaries of essentialism. In other words, masking the void displaces anxiety about what is unknown, perhaps even forbidden. It covers over what might parallel both desire and spectacle.

Mulvey embraces the complexity of time and space; she seems to understand that temporality changes the segmented, contained space. That is, opening as a verb with temporality changes what was as a noun conceived only as a space and in its closed state was enigmatic.

That said, however, it seems important to make problematic Western conceptions of time, conceived as linearity vis-à-vis the three-tense system of past, present, future. Widely contested for his theory of linguistic relativity, Benjamin Whorf (1997/56), who studied Chinese, Navaho, Apache, Hopi, Aztec, and Maya language systems, notes the limitation of the linear conception of time, calling it a scheme of objectification about duration.

Similarly, Conquergood (1991) describes the importance of rescuing the temporal as a postimperialist form of praxis. The way to rescue linear time from the one-way history of expansionist campaigns, according to

Conquergood, is through performance (i.e., word-deed, action-interaction) that prevents temporal reification. He says that the spatial suggests practices that divide and classify or compartmentalize, but the temporal depends on co-presence, utterance, and multivocality.

A logic that embraces the complexity of time and space suggests that everything is together in consciousness (Whorf, 1997/57). Mulvey's alteration, the opening that opens, can be said to include the logic of time-space and performance to which both Whorf and Conquergood refer, a logic that gives rise to the gesturing and display of difference. Performance changes what is linguistically and theoretically spatial into an expression of space-time.

Though Mulvey writes about curiosity as the space or threshold from which "secrets" are revealed—in what might be interpreted as a classical exoticist view—I find her discussion interesting and useful in terms of probing the idea of a space-time or place through which memories can be revealed. Because the liberation of memories (some of which are "dangerous" in that they threaten status quo interests) can lead to the transformation of both consciousness and action, Mulvey's example can also be read as peformative, oppositional culture work in spite of its complicated relationship to the binaries of inside/outside or open/closed. With respect to Mulvey's "play" on Freudian "sight" or surveillance (where "closure is constituted by the gaze"; Conquergood, 1991, p. 183), which does tend to exoticize women, her discussion of unveiling seems to involve uncertainty, whereas a traditional exoticist's view relies on a single "truth." What appears is not necessarily what is. Playfulness, then, is a part of Mulvey's unmasking through openings—not unlike seeing what lies between the masks. Exoticizing tends to sustain the binary logic of inside/outside, but openings, according to Bachelard (1964) and Mulvey, can displace the inside/outside dialectic.

In his book *The Predicament of Culture*, James Clifford (1988) discusses "curiosities" that exoticize human life. He tells the story of Victor Segalan, poet, novelist, archaeologist, and travel writer, whose almost obsessive desire to find himself in "the other" of distant lands made him complicit in the very forms of exoticism his strategies of displacement sought to undo. Clifford's essay on Segalan discusses the difficulty of moving into an alternate site that does not exoticize by polarizing self/other. Indeed, in Clifford's own words, Segalan's travel narratives construct an*other* of desire and fiction, despite the fact that his narratives are constructed in uncertainty.

The latter is what reveals for me the relational, alterational, and fully contingent aspect of displacement. I perceive it is as apparent in Mulvey's analysis as it is in Clifford's discussion of Segalan, for what exists between the masks is multiple and uncertain and thus confusing.

Trinh T. Minh-ha, a Vietnamese writer, filmmaker, and composer, discusses the "forced removal-relocation-reeducation-redefinition" and dehumanization of being an exile as she develops a discourse on displacement and its relationship to the exigency of creative expression on issues of ethnicity and femininity (1989, p. 80).[13] She weaves stories of her own struggles together with postcolonial theories, continuously intersecting notions of cultural hybridization and multiple identities. Through poetic, analytic, and reflective expression she challenges traditional wisdom as regards the role of women writers/artists in building a historic consciousness. In both *Woman, Native, Other* (1989) and *When the Moon Waxes Red* (1991), she makes clear the difficult nature of undoing *fixed* ways of knowing/thinking the world when she writes about the act of displacement:

> Displacing is a way of surviving. It is an impossible, truthful story of living in-between regimes of truth. The responsibility [for the displacer] is a highly creative one: the displacer proceeds by introducing difference into repetition. By questioning over and over again what is taken for granted as self-evident, by reminding oneself and the others of the unchangeability of change itself. Disturbing . . . one's own thinking habits, dissipating what has become familiar . . . and participating in the changing of received values—the transformation (with/out master) of other selves [in] one's self (1991, p. 21).

Insurgence that disrupts contained ways of knowing difference, then, is a particular instance of the performative.

Butler (1993) suggests performativity is the "relation of being implicated in that which one opposes" and the masquerade is that which makes possible the rearticulation of identity (p. 241). A theory of the politics of place, then, is a theory of displacement and seems a necessary part of theories of performance as regards identity.

Victor Turner's (1979, 1982, 1983) anthropological work on dramatic ritual is also central to my theorizing here. Turner suggests dramatic ritual is a reflexive, agential process that occurs at all levels of society and within all social relationships. His speculation differs considerably from researchers who fail to capture the notion of performance/process in their definitions of ritual. Turner writes that without the notion of process one misses the transgressive potential in ritual.

It is this transgressive potential that I perceive is so important in the drama of identity. Likewise, transgressive ritual can be a pedagogical opening onto the development of multiple displacement strategies for untelling essentialist hierarchies.

Turner's work is, perhaps, the first to translate the theory of symbolic interactionism for ethnographic studies in ritual performance. Not only does Turner identify performative rituals in social settings as a cultural phenomenon, he sees rituals as processes or forms of social drama that occur in everyday life. From social dramas researchers can study the wider (hegemonic) cultural symbols that metaphorically name experience.

I extend both Turner and Butler to suggest that the rearticulation of identity and difference occurs between the masks if unromanticized memories are liberated and deciphered through critical reasoning. My definition of *performance* is inclusive of everyday acts, that is, I see life as a performance in which constructed masks are made necessary because of the relations of production and the sociopolitical order. Like Anzaldua (1990), I perceive that the place of healing is in-between.

Though I agree with Butler's concept that performativity itself is what allows for constructions and therefore alternative articulations of identity, I perceive the role of performativity may be like the structuring of topography to which Mulvey (1992) alludes, that is, it marks a threshold from which to contest and/or perpetuate some phenomenon. What Anzaldua calls a crossroads (1987) or the "focal point or fulcrum, that juncture where the *mestiza* stands, is where phenomena tend to collide. . . . The work of *mestiza* consciousness is to break down the subject-object duality that keeps her a prisoner"(pp. 79–80). What interests me most, however, about Mulvey's idea is the notion of the opening through which secrets emerge (read: the liberation of memory).

The notion of structuring here is unlike a traditional reading of the word *structure* that implies "the continuity of ritual symbols and ritual metaphors" and more like Peter McLaren's (1986, p. 147) conception of "antistructure" (drawing on Turner's work). Antistructure is a space-time not unlike the semiotic through which alteration or the altering aspect of the thetic might occur. In McLaren's ethnographic study of educational symbols and gestures in a Catholic school, he writes that organized resistance was the provenance of the ruling-class students, whereas working-class students had to resist through illegitimate paths.[14] The latter was "located in the antistructure where contradiction and conflict" pushed students to be disruptive: "The antistructure of resistance was a dialectical theatre in which meanings were both affirmed and denied simultaneously" (p. 147). Place as theorized in this book is the theater in which resistance is performed.

Thus performances themselves are enigmatic arenas of contradiction, bordered by binary opposites like fear/safety, anxiety/ease, mistrust/trust, disillusionment/joy, sanctity/incivility, and so on. Performances may be "the representation of an event that takes place within the bounds of [dramatized] self-consciousness" or the ritualized performances of "proper" daily living (Bakhtin, 1984, pp. 214–215) or even the stylized performances that do not meet status quo code. In each instance, however, the contradictory space of the "box" and its relationship to the slippages between signifier and the signified (Mulvey, 1992) can be seen as analogous to performances and their relationship to the slippages between the masks through which dangerous secrets are revealed and resistances occur. As in the case of racism and the privileging of whiteness, the secrets that are betrayed when the gaps are examined relationally show a performance based on white supremacy.

Growing up white was a performance that privileged. Learning the secrets of my ethnicity/blood required opening many boxes, looking behind many masks. Understanding those secrets required my examining the tain of the mirror—not the surface but the underside (Gasché, 1986), the slippage between word and deed, signified and signifier, for resistance too is a performance.

The Pandora story is a cautionary tale about the dangers of curiosity; it is a narrative that registers sanction in the status quo. Pandora opens the box and "evils" escape. Only "hope" remains boxed, literally bound. Yet as the thetic space-time of meaning before meaning in the semiotic suggests the possibility of moving beyond the dogma of the sanctioned, so might curiosity lead to transgression. Mulvey adds her own cautionary word, however, and I concur: though curiosity leads to the desire to know, "it may not lead to enlightenment" unless what is uncovered is "deciphered" through critical reasoning (pp. 65–66).

Curiosity, then, and imagination can give wings to critical reasoning (McLaren, 1991) in the in-between. Though schools are pedagogic sites that are both social and institutional and therefore can be "simultaneously represented, contested, and inverted" (Foucault, 1986, p. 22), I theorize the "place" of rupture as between the constructed masks often worn in the performance of schooling. Critical teaching can, indeed, create dramatic moments in the classroom, yet I see these moments more as the mapping of an area from which to evolve. Maxine Greene calls such areas "openings" and teacher work "teaching for openings" (1995). Likewise, those "teachable moments" about which Eliot Wigginton (1986) wrote may be seen as "answerable events" theorized in Bakhtin (1990, 1993), and each in the performative arena of school can be seen as a rehearsal for revolution (Boal, 1985).

Between the masks, then, is where I see the potential for "true-real" change,[15] in general and especially as regards understandings of identity. The "true-real" in Kristeva (1986a) is "an area of risk and salvation . . . [that] gives enunciation a topology constructed by heterogeneous spaces" (p. 217); the true-real signifier is the body. The true and the real is precisely what is repressed in classical mimesis/mimicry/theater. Acting out, the antithesis of acting as imitation, holds the potential for disruption that Kristeva's true-real offers (Hart and Phelan, 1993). In the time-out, nonlinear, self-reflective *moment* that disrupts the progression of linear scripts—

in the worlds between texts—the sense of change here is similar to that suggested in the notion of carnival (Bakhtin, 1984). As in Bakhtin's rendering of the regenerative possibility of carnival, the moment of transformation ends unless a "true-real" break occurs.

Russian scholar Mikhail Bakhtin has been hailed as one of the great thinkers of the twentieth century (see his biography written by Katerina Clark and Michael Holquist, 1984). Bakhtin's work in language and literature (*Problems of Dostoevsky's Poetics*, 1984, *The Dialogic Imagination*, 1981, and *Speech Genres and Other Late Essays*, 1986), and its respective implications for human life in general, have won him a place in fields as diverse as semiotics and anthropology, communication studies and literary theory, social theory and psychology, and is important to my project because his work is, finally, about disrupting containment. Influenced by earlier theorists also in diverse disciplines (from Kant to Einstein), Bakhtin's fascination with medieval life and carnival culture as a particular space-time of connection and change led him to in-depth (dissertation) research of the books of François Rabelais (1944). Bakhtin later published his dissertation as *Rabelais and His World* (1965). Recently published manuscripts (*Art and Answerability*, 1990, and *Towards a Philosophy of the Act*, 1993) that were written between the years of 1919 and 1924, when he was imprisoned for trying to synthesize Marxism and Christianity, show his early thinking for the self-in-other/other-in-self concept of dialogism.

Opposed to containment of every sort, Bakhtin's theory of the word and the world as double-natured or two-sided is thoroughly rendered in his concept of carnival. Here carnival is not conceived as "narrow theatrical-pageantry," and it is more than "sensing the world as one great performance" (Bakhtin, p. 160). Bakhtin's concept of change in carnival is found in the "risk and salvation" to which Kristeva alludes:

> [It is the] sense of the world, liberating one from fear, bringing the world maximally close to a person and bringing one person maximally close to another (everything is drawn into the zone of free familiar contact), with its joy at change and its joyful relativity, as *opposed to* that *one-sided* and gloomy official seriousness which is dogmatic and hostile to evolution and change, which seeks to *absolutize* a given condition of existence or a given social order (p. 160) [emphasis mine].

Bakhtin's notion of change that does not create a new orthodoxy, is not monolithic, and does not essentialize is also my understanding of significant change.

In *Towards a Philosophy of the Act* (1993), Bakhtin says that love is the only thing that will keep us from continuing to *fix* or "absolutize" the world in a dichotomy of self/other. Love here is mutual respect that produces an intimacy that requires that we take time to (cognitively) know the particulars of one another's life ("maximally close"). He further suggests that fascination for these particulars is born out of curiosity for the other (who is always already a part of the self).

Because it is often easier, then, to reduce people and/or ideas to a simplistic perspective than to take the time to know someone/something, taking steps to resist the politics of essentialism is everyone's business. It should especially be the work of teachers.

Respective to the work of teachers and teaching, if resisting the politics of essentialism is more likely to occur between the "official" theatrical-pageantry of school (or the ritual performances of schooling; McLaren, 1986), then concepts of where teaching/learning takes place must be broadened, and teaching for openings or sites for risk and liberation needs to be a part of every teaching agenda (Giroux, 1994b). Teaching students to read the world as a text, then, is part of responsibly educating school children and youth (Gramsci, 1971; Freire, 1973). Teaching about issues of knowledge and power and about the politics of schooling and teachers' roles within that hierarchy, about relations of production and consumption, about the impossibility of consumerism and transformation, about the politics of representation and myth, and about ethical responsibility (both collective and individual) are a part of educating for a democratic citizenry that has both voice and vision. Such teaching requires a content strategy as well as a democratic process in the classroom. Critical theories and cultural materials combined with a critical pedagogy is the form and content that I find work best. But teaching for change is not limited to the above, for curiosity and imagination often gives rise to in(ter)ventions not yet conceived.

Important, then, is the self-reflexive, curious, and imagining social actor who can bring forth what Kristeva (1986a) might call "uncivilized" memories that poke holes in the originary narratives that suggest a monolithic, homogeneous, unified past (Bhabha, 1994). For unromanticized memories may light the way to transgressing status quo inscriptions of identity and difference. Thus the liberation of memory may be the most fierce secret disturbed in those unsanctioned openings between masks.

Mapping the Text

In this book I argue the notion that identity work can mark a rearticulation of old readings, questions, and valuations. A new theory of "place" in the performance of identity may help humans resist the tendency to look for essences. "What saves us," says Maxine Greene (quoting Maurice Merleau-Ponty), "is the possibility of a new development" (1995, p. 115). A theory of place that invokes struggle is as much about practice as it is about place (de Certeau, 1984). In the struggle against essentialist readings of culture, then, identity can be seen as "the effect[s] of social struggles between different communities over issues of representation, the distribution of material resources, and the practice of social justice" (Giroux, 1994, p. 61).

Taking various routes through experience in cultural texts like music, film, television, and especially multiethnic literatures can be an opening onto teaching against essentialist hierarchies. Indeed, cultural texts can be an opening onto the study of identity formations that traditional English curricula based on a logocentric Western canon may not easily engender. What I hope to foster in this text are border literacies that can help students negotiate their way between performances in order, as Anzaldua (1990) suggests, to "crack the mask and thrust out" (p. xv). How students make meanings and how meanings figure into the formation of nonessentialized identities, however, *assumes a political assessment of the ways in which cultures are represented.*

As teachers consider all the potential ways in which curriculum can be disruptive, it would be wise to consider the strategies, assumptions, and outcomes located within our own views. For example, how do my own strategies, assumptions, and desired outcomes reinforce hegemony even as I believe I am disrupting hegemonic order? How do the hegemonic practices of culturally commodified forms reinforce the invisibility of living between masks? How are these practices naturalized and through what images? How are they contested? How is resistance understood? Does this resistance jar sensitivities or engage imaginations in ways that may lead to transformed social practices? How are sites of desire also negotiated as sites of struggle? How important is it to crack the mask? What fears do I associate with the "risky business" of identity work, culture work? How is this work valued by my department, university, and society at large?

There is much to be done in cultural studies/theory, and the "looseness" that Angela McRobbie characterizes as necessary for cultural work to remain open to socially imaginative processes makes this work a lived practice (1992). Whether our teacherly stance is impositional, oppositional, or whether we position ourselves in accord with a student-centered classroom, how curriculum is taken up by students and how students reveal what they understand seems to depend on a variety of interdependent factors. Often, though, how students show what they know depends on whose glance tends to count most. How students will respond to social curricula is unpredictable, whether or not those curricula represent "official" school knowledge or expand to include cultural studies.

Many different curricular projects may be capable of binding interrogation with imaginative capacities to go beyond ideologies that perpetuate violence. Performance narratives may make visible the range of inscriptions (not fully constituted) that identities suggest, turning back injustice and apathy, mapping new terrains through memory and imagination. Pedagogic sites that serve as bridging places to critical reflective activity, then, may be our best hope for teaching against the politics of essentialism, for gaining complex understandings of identity, for complicating monolithic, fixed categories of identity, and finally, for awakening a whole range of imaginative possibilities that reveal new ways of being in the world.

As identity performs, acknowledging and making visible that which social masks have allowed to remain invisible, multiple constructions reveal identities that oppose the appearance of ideological *fixity.* In the latter instance recognition of the performative may help make apparent the dynamic *processes* involved in identity-making/marking, which can bring forth unknown landscapes in order to challenge the assumption that what is outside is representative of what is inside. This position neither denies difference nor suggests fixity. Rather the shifting terrain of performance suggests the relationship between difference and construction.

Relationship and positionality, then, are everything in my analysis. Fortunately for me, as a participating social subject, I am not fixed but continue to make myself, performing identity, making/marking against a range of cultural phenomena, again and again (Butler, 1993).

This text focuses on what I take to be important sites of interrogation for resisting the politics of essentialism. Four areas strike me as crucial: issues of "place" respective to agential social performance, issues of prescribed culture respective to the political economies of representation, issues related to the masking and unmasking of identity, and the problematics located in acts of cultural recovery.

Part 1, "On Pedagogy and Performance," includes a chapter on essentialism as a pedagogical site for disruption and a chapter that theorizes "place" in the performance of identity and suggests narrative-performative strategies that can be useful for untelling essentialist hierarchies. Part 2 interrogates the "mirrors of seduction" in music, film, and literature. My arguments are based on the premise that the seductive nature of representation makes it an important pedagogic site to make and contest meanings; representations tend to define the "order of things" and are perhaps the body's most important teacher (for example, teaching how to eat, dress, act, what to think, how to speak, and in general, how to be in the world). Part 3 describes in(ter)ventions that mark an interplay between language/culture/skin/voice as a borderline qua integrative "crossroads." Students' performance narratives show them either consciously or unconsciously giving voice to skin as they peel away layers that make visible diverse locations of identity.

In part each chapter theorizes the "antistructure of resistance." that is, the temporality and insurgency of critically reflective places that provide a matrix through which to not only discover hidden histories but also recover them. I make wide use of previous work in narrative inquiry coupled with de Certeau's (1984) notion of narrativity to "undo the proper" and Trinh's (1991) conception of narrative "untellings" to resist and rework marginality and privilege in stories of essentialism. The concrete strategy of narrative and performance-based inquiry may be an opening onto critical, reflective activity that can make visible that which often lies concealed in essentialist hierarchies. In all I suggest that doing theory is pedagogy, that is, using theories as tools for making meanings, circulating theories about how the world works in and through lived experiences to theorize/make sense of the world.

Pedagogy as activism offers no final answers. Instead narrative-performative inquiry in the service of negotiating a "politics of place" understands reality as process, possibility, and praxis in the "theater of identity." In this regard, I most often see my students performing between constructed masks and essentialized understandings of identity, sometimes for survival and sometimes because of unacknowledged assumptions. Finally, I suggest how particular configurations within circuits of power produce particular subject positions in order to secure specific forms of authority and how practices that rework and resist fixed forms of self-definition can mark "subjects-as-sites" of resistance (Foucault, 1986).

The Coda marks the finale in this performance piece against the politics of essentialism. "Critical Teaching and Theatricality in Everyday Life" is a strategic critique of crucial houses of knowledge—universities and English departments, specifically. The "play(ing)" off history, culture, and power (Hall, 1990) here is a "play(ing)" against a paradigm bequeathed by imperialism, that is, traditional English studies that have essentialized the transmission of culture in an attempt to reproduce the mental and material practices that ensure a particular vision of society. What's at stake here is a knowledge/power issue that essentializes literacy to practices of reading and writing that serves status quo interests. Critical teaching in crucial houses of knowledge (of which universities are only one) can bring together the literary, the historic, the theoretical, and the sociological through a pedagogy of narrative-performative inquiry.

Aligned with other culture work, then, my project begins with a self-in-other assessment that forecloses participation in and simultaneously interrogates wider political systems because resistance here is aimed at disrupting dominant narratives, presumably organizing culture and identity. As an educator seeking to understand the relational complexities of power, knowledge, agential reclaiming of public spheres, and the struggles that ensue, I've developed a discourse about disrupting containment, one that must be repeatedly interrogated. Though narratives like the one I offer here tend to be contested both within my classroom and the larger university, I perceive that all critical educators (myself included) must take the lead in willingly subjecting our own discourses about practice to what bell hooks calls fierce critical interrogations (1990).

With respect to discourse on practice, Pierre Bourdieu (1977) notes that even though talk is not the same as practice it is impossible to study practice without discursive activity. I would argue, however, that discourse can also be conceived as social action when classroom debate has empowerment as its agenda and proceeds by educating for public participation and freedom.

Reflective, then, of one direction in which educators might begin to move toward, cultural studies as a pedagogical site embraces curriculum theory, teacher preparation, policy, and the like. The challenge, of course, will be to find a way for dialogue to occur between people with opposing views (Mercer, 1994). Cultural material is filled with disturbing and instructive potentialities that can help educators modulate those conversations and the complicated contexts of schools today. Reconstructing relations of power within social configurations, the theoretical and pedagogical impulse of cultural studies in education marks a move toward the intertextual, interdisciplinary study of the "politics of place" and its representations.

Notes

1. For a list of forty-six ways white people are privileged, see McIntosh, 1988.
2. There is much dispute among translators and other Bakhtinean scholars as to whether the writings of Volosinov were actually written by Volosinov or by Bakhtin. Michael Holquist and Vadim Liapunov (editors/translators of *Art and Answerability*, 1990) suggest that Volosinov along with Medvedev were among Bakhtin's closest associates, and it is Holquist and Liapunov's belief that the manuscript published as *Marxism and the Philosophy of Language* (Volosinov) was written by Bakhtin and given to Volosinov to publish. (Bakhtin was imprisoned in Russia from 1919 to 1924 for attempting to synthesize Marxism and Christianity.)
3. Kristeva's work in linguistics, psychoanalysis, and literary and political theory is central to this project, especially for the way in which she theorizes the split subject as both self and other. Though she draws on Bakhtin's early work in dialogism, she extends these ideas to a lucid concept of intertextuality that relies not only on semantics but also on syntax, introducing a psychoanalytic element that suggests both the reader and writer are "subjects-in-process" (Guberman, p. 188). Her writing complicates the pyschic identity by suggesting it is always both the subject of utterance and the object of enunciation.
4. I borrow concepts of performance and the performative from theater studies. Historicizing of these terms appears later in this chapter (see discussion by Jill Dolan).

5. Henry Louis Gates Jr. (1987) equates crossing the color line with passing and both with passing on or passing away.

6. Other scholarship suggests the notion of essentialism as rhetorical strategy. For example, in *Bodies That Matter*, Butler (1993) discusses the matter of essence as a discourse from which women have been excluded as "the improper, the propertyless." Butler goes on to suggest that "biological essentialism" may be a "rhetorical strategy," suggesting the "feminine in language as a persistent impropriety" (pp. 37–38).

7. After completing a draft of this book, I learned about a body of scholarship that closely paralleled my own thinking. I have since added these voices from the field of performance studies/theater studies to my own (i.e., Jill Dolan, Peggy Phelan, Richard Schechner, and Dwight Conquergood). Their scholarship has helped situate my project more squarely within an existing discourse on performance. Although they did not inform my theorizing here, their voices have helped me to clarify my intentions respective to performance pedagogy.

8. See also other recent works on performance studies that address the interdisciplinary nature of performance and performativity: Conquergood, 1989; Schechner, 1985, 1988; Schechner and Appel, 1990.

9. See, for example, the discussion in Chapter 4 on Charlotte Perkins Gilman's narrator in *The Yellow Wallpaper* (1973). This narrator is constituting herself as both object and ego through the body's own literacy (the semiotic). The thetic, I perceive, is the basis on which she makes this transformation, both elaborating and going beyond the boundaries of social/textual experience.

10. Through no desire to essentialize essentialism, I protest the single perspective. Yet even in this contestation I must be honest and admit that my own rhetoric against essentialism oftentimes becomes essentialist. What I am saying is that I believe it is necessary to take a stand against essentialism and in that moment, that situation, I privilege my own thinking and therefore essentialize. This is not unlike the notion of strategic essentialism to which Gayatri Spivak refers (1990, p. 10–11). For example, in her discussion about "symbolic clitoridectomies as marking the place of women's desire," she says that in antisexist work there is the "strategic choice of genitalist essentialism." Not committing to anything would find me as much in complicity as arguing that I could refrain from all such positions, whether or not the position I take privileges a particular view. The point here is to be strategic, to become "vigilant about our own practice," as Spivak puts it.

11. A Derridean perspective of the arbitrariness of the sign suggests that what is significant to consider with respect to notions of inside/outside is the relationship between the two (Derrida, 1976, p. 44).

12. Mulvey's (1992) analysis suggests the opening of boxes or exposing of concealed spaces is analogous to the female anatomy that is constructed in absence— the absence of a penis. Following Freud's "theory of castration," Mulvey names the opening of the box as the "sight"/site of male anxiety and threat of castration, "indicat[ing] that the penis is not a necessary and ever-present part of the human anatomy" (p. 68). She suggests that if feminist criticism does not render "the mask of femininity, constructed as an object of desire and spectacle," as being generated by the appearances of male castration anxiety, then the image of woman as mask simply redoubles the idea of woman as fetish object (p. 69).

13. Vietnamese naming customs present the surname or family name first and the given name last. Trinh is, therefore, Trinh T. Minh-ha's last name. In spite of many bibliographies referencing her in the *M*s, observing the American custom of "family name last," I have referenced Trinh T. Minh-ha in the *T*s, in keeping with her own desires. She was present at an MSU film studies conference in 1997 in which she made that request known. See also her film *Surname Viet, Given Name Nam* (1989).

14. Though McLaren sets up a binary in his description of ruling classes/working classes, I assume that his descriptions aim to be true to the class dinstinctions that operated in the school under study. I also do not assume that framing a project in an antiessentialist perspective obliterates class distinctions in the wider society or the struggle with and against relations of power that difference creates. Antiessentialist perspectives do not disrupt difference; such perspectives can only suggest that social and even material difference is not necessarily fixed. It is, therefore, important to read class and other distinctions relationally and to understand that the inside/outside shifts and marginality and privilege occur differently within different spheres of influence. It is also important to note that physically crossing borders is not to say that one can so easily shed or even that it is desirable to shed, for example, one's working-class consciousness. If I seem to privilege working classes here (especially respective to issues of social change), it is because my own working-class background/consciousness has helped me understand much about the relations of power that exist between the classes that, for example, McLaren describes and where motivations for change tend to derive. I do not, however, believe that cultural revolution is the provenance of a single class or that any class is monolithic, as some inscriptions suggest; instead I believe in solidarity with people of many races, classes, sexualities, etc., joined in a common quest for freedom.

15. For Judith Butler (1993) what seems to be the "kernel" or "real" lies in the "vacillation between the two points," i.e., between the signifier and the signified (pp. 198–199). Recovery within the "real" involves the embodied act of denying the phallus by disallowing its continued domination in the lives of individuals. Denying the phallus means breaking the rule of heterosexist and sexist mythologies, and through foreclosure instead of linguistic self-disclosure, language that represents and violates is denied the power to define. The foreclosed body, then, is a radical alterity—completely, wholly not of previous possibilities. Instead of the self-other relationship that is the subject-object relationship, the self is in relationship to itself and its altered identity is other than what has been before. For Butler, foreclosure creates a relationship that can never be conceived in binary terms. Transformation marks a plus-plus relationship; it derails oppositionality based in linear logic—beginning/ending, birth/death, etc.; it celebrates the true-real. The reformualtion of kinship, then, is articulated in the true-real, according to Butler: denying the phallologic order redefines the "house" in alternative terms, not solely that of whiteness or heterosexual norms, and in all "its forms of collectivity" (p. 241). In *Telling the Other*, Patrick McGee (1992) defines the "true-real" as what escapes the false in language, and it is therefore free to signify a reality that is neither a subject nor an object. This conception is based in the notion that language violates reproducing the images that essentialize, that language

plasticizes the real body, objectifying the body as a discourse about it. Moreover, it is the plastic force of language that reveals the political in language, and the political reveals sexual mythologies that resign women and men to essentialized categories. Under the assumption, then, that the body's own literacies produce signifiers, the body that writes itself is not half of a subject-object, self-other, man-woman dichotomy.

Part One
On Pedagogy and Performance

Toward a Pedagogy of
Narrative-Performative Inquiry

Power is not a structure nor an institution but a strategy that "reaches into the very grain of individuals, touches their bodies and inserts itself into their actions and attitudes, their discourses, learning processes and everyday lives."

—*Michel Foucault,* Power/Knowledge, *1980, p. 39*

In *Seduction* Jean Baudrillard (1979) says people not only are aware of the mechanisms that seduce but also tend to let themselves be seduced. The "play" of appearances enables disguises that seduce. Moreover, the disguise that suggests cultures are inhabited by like-minded peoples enables nonmulticultural thinking within the same culture. But memory and imagination can disrupt this gaze, "re-membering" the fragmented parts (hooks, 1995, p. 64), not assuming an amorphous fluidity.

Essentialism thus is political; it is based on a strategy of power that deploys appearance in its seduction (Baudrillard, 1979; Foucault, 1980). Gloria Anzaldua writes that "mask[s mean] control, concealment, [and] escape." Hidden between the masks are "interfaces," or sites of reflexivity that can resist inscriptions that contain (Anzaldua, 1990, xv). Bodies are material, but they are not static. Consciousness, self-critical reflection, and interpretation lie between "what appears" and "what is" and therein can create openings that consider differences within the relations of power in which they circulate (Butler, 1993).

What *appears* in constructs of race (sexuality, gender, class, and so on) is ideological fixity. What is left out of *appearance* are the events that mark historical and derivational contexts. "A meaning-event," says Foucault, "is as neutral as death: . . . not a particular death, but any death" until it occurs within a particular context (1977, pp. 165, 174). Only when a mean-ing-event occurs in a particular historical context that is embedded in a par-ticular worldview does the word "death" as an event take on special signif-icance (e.g., the death of my father). In other words, it requires the performance of all those contextually related items to become meaningful.

My father's death, for example, has meaning, and the word *death* is now attached to that particular event when I think of loss. His death cre-ates all manner of associational inscriptions. For example, his absence marked the time from which my mother's Alzheimer's seemed to worsen—literally loss of his body and further loss of her mind. His ab-sence also marked an end to particular habits (annoying and loved) that began to presence in his loss.

Presence/absence are two sides of the same coin, then, the same sign if you will. How signs signify is always context-dependent and is what makes meaning slippery. In other words, all other instances of death may trigger memory of my father's death, but the word *death* will not refer par-ticularly to his death. The word *death* relates only to his death in that one event in time and space, and all else is memory. In and of itself, the mean-ing-event carries with it no specific reference that holds for all people. Yet abstracting meaning arbitrarily serves status quo interests and antago-nisms, justifying either/or categorizations that result in divisiveness: men to women, bosses to workers, white people to nonwhite people, and so on, leading to an essentialist narrative.

It is precisely, then, because no category of meaning-event contains 100 percent sameness that identities overlap. Not necessarily because white identities contain racial/ethnic mixes but because human identity can never be monolithic; its meaning-event is performative, not fixed.

Displacement is also performative; it is a meaning-event that must be considered within a context to be meaningful. And as an event it marks *action* that has a temporal quality (a continuous condition of time). A ped-agogy for resisting essentialism can also be a meaning-event that marks action over a course of time. Essentialist metanarratives that address uni-versal truths, universal ways of acting and being, are written in homoge-nous, serial time, according to Homi Bhabha (1994). Nevertheless, the dis-ruptive nature of temporality, says Bhabha, displaces the grand narratives of Western culture, imperial scripts that are always already reading us.

Respective, then, to temporality is the creation of a "place" from which to speak (Bhabha, 1994).[1] Despite systems of power-knowledge and their effects to greater or lesser degrees, Bhabha writes that the flux of time through which the boundaries of cultural containment become bridg-ing places—what he calls the intervention of the "Third Space"—is what gives "the structure of meaning and reference an ambivalent process, chal-lenging our sense of the historical identity of culture as an homogenizing, unifying force, authenticated by the originary Past" (p. 37). In this book I suggest such an intervention, and in this chapter I outline the reasons why a Third Space is needed.

Untelling Essentialism

Trinh (1991) writes that *untelling* the stories of privilege and marginality is a form of displacement that takes a long time. This sort of untelling is the basis for a pedagogy of narrative-performative inquiry. Repeated untellings mark acts of insurgent speech that can continually (over time) disrupt "common sense," complicating it by interweaving the discursive practices of interaction and action, considering every act and deed a performance (Bakhtin, 1993).

Raymond Williams's contributions to Marxist theory and his ground-breaking work in cultural studies and cultural analysis make his writings a foundational part of this project.[2] His concepts of the overlapping terrains of text and culture and of residual and emergent meanings and practices guide much of my thinking (1977). In *Marxism and Literature* (1977), Williams points to the problem of common sense when he writes, "The very powerful pressures which are expressed in political, economic, and cultural formations . . . seem to most of us [just] the pressures and limits of simple experience and common sense" (pp. 87, 110). This "simple" understanding of experience is what Trinh and I perceive must be complicated, interrogated, displaced. Essentialist categories that operate as givens, reducing whole cultures into boxes to be checked, are a form of violence. And beneath the lie of essentialism is a whole teleology of false dichotomies.

At the most abstract level, codes of meanings attached to readings of "whiteness/nonwhiteness," for example, suggest binaries like good/bad (Nietzsche, 1969). To take this essentialist reading into classrooms often means students' differences are coded good student/bad student (and often along race or gender lines), high achiever/low achiever, and so on. Even if the label "at risk" is an attempt to problematize the binary opposite of the high achiever—to suggest instruction impacts capability, when ideologies suggest the world is either one way or another, when readings do not include an understanding of the effects of power on performance—then an essentialist reading categorizes the student. And like remediation that never remediates, such labeling places the child in a zone of determinateness.[3] What is not recognized in this binary logic is the way in which locations mediate positions and result in identities—complexities that deal with the site-specific circulation of power.

The problematic here is the ideological nature of representation (Volosinov, 1973, p. 13) and how discursive practices are implicated in essentialist frameworks through the meaning-making activity of narrative production and reproduction. In other words, wider narratives about student ability are explicitly related to the circulation of power in schools, and how we imagine, represent, and see students within that powerful arrangement is affected by what we believe about the way the world works (Berger, 1977, pp. 7–11). So the stories we tell ourselves (about all sorts of things) are inextricably related to some larger ideological mapping.

In suggesting a pedagogy for resisting the politics of essentialism, I aim to trouble the categories that contain insider/outsider binarisms that do violence through racist, classist, sexist, heterosexist, and other attitudes and behaviors. Indeed, I do not assume the consequences of this complication will produce cathartic self-definitions or that attempts to crack the masks of essentialist politics will signal a romantic homogeneous past (Bhabha, 1994).

On the contrary, "the alterity of Identity" suggests that any unmasking is a continuous, social struggle of "sameness-in-difference . . . from which, in forked tongues, [multiply inscribed identities] communicate" (Bhabha, 1994, p. 54). Although the pedagogy I propose suggests strategies for cracking the masks of fixed categories of identity, I want to make clear that I simultaneously resist the "amorphous . . . leveling uniformity [of] melting pot theories" of multiculturalism (Foucault, 1977, pp. 188–189)— theories that do not dissolve the insider/outsider binarism but instead perpetuate it.

According to Raymond Williams, cultural "insiderism" (Paul Gilroy's term, 1992), or I might substitute "essentialism," was the outcome of the "greatest changes ever seen in . . . cultural production (1989, p. 33). The 1980s marked changes that resulted in "defensive cultural groupings, rapidly if partially becoming *competitively self-promoting* [emphasis mine]" (p. 33). Williams notes further that "endless border-crossing[s] . . . raised to a level of universal myth this intense, singular narrative of unsettlement, homelessness, solitude and impoverished independence. . . . Modernism, reflected in the early movements of surrealism, cubism, formalism, and constructivism, etc. . . . defined *divides* politically and simply—and not just between specific movements but even within them" (pp. 33–34).

From modernism, then, to the particular experiences of women, gay men and women, people of color, and the indigent, framed with/in a *post*modern climate, critical projects tend to remain attached to those *divides* through a binary logic even though discourse suggests value is placed on multiplicity. Still trapped by positivist thinking that cannot meet or answer the dilemmas that occur in classrooms or in wider society, it seems imperative, then, to find a language and action that cuts through the juxtaposition of extremes, freeing speech and thus action from histori-cal constraints. The defensive speech that often arises in classrooms dur-ing talk about sexuality or racial or gender oppression suggests to me what John Fiske, drawing on Pierre Bourdieu, suggests is the result of practices circulating in society without their meanings consciously entering social discourse and being discussed (1992). Indeed, I perceive that the best ef-forts of liberatory teaching will fail at forming alliances across differences if our projects remain rooted in a hierarchicalized language and logic that prevents the circulation of meanings about how power performs strategi-cally within relational contexts and how agency is a theory of practice.

How can we affirm and support one another in crises when we use a language of divisiveness? How can we equip our students for this task? How can our critiques produce more than contemptuous feedback? How can we do more than hinder the struggle for freedom? How can we under-stand the "not-fully constituted" identity (Laclau, 1990)? How can we be-come "attuned to each other's humanity" (hooks and West, 1991, p. 12)? Maxine Greene (1988) suggests being attuned to one another's humanity occurs when "individuals come together in a particular way, when they are . . . present to one another (without masks or badges of office), when they have a project they can mutually pursue. . . . [When there is] a com-ing together of those who choose themselves as affected and involved . . . [when there is] an opening of a space between them, an in-between, deeper and more significant than merely practical or worldly" (pp. 5–9).

Regardless of whether we assume people develop identities or find them, how identity formation occurs is much less important to me than how identity is signified in political practice. The latter, I perceive, relates to what I call the theorizing of a "place" from which to speak. Here, place does not depend on the essence of one's economic status or on one's sex or race; place depends on agency, authorial voice, and the shifting con-texts in which agential control is reclaimed. Materiality and identity are in-separable in this understanding as well as why identity is performative— that is, a matter of place or space-time and positionality/agential control.

As poststructuralists critique common binarisms like us/them, in-sider/outsider, and margin/center to render visible the multiple inscrip-tions of ego and identity, I am reminded of how important it is to maintain the radicality of those perspectives by paying attention to race, ethnicity, class, gender, sexuality, and so on. The vital role these critiques can play in disrupting ideological fixity that tends to impair vision and dominate dis-cussion around questions of race, poverty, identity, community, and the like need not lapse into what Kobena Mercer calls a "populist modernism" (1994, p. 236) or what Paul Gilroy calls "ethnic absolutism" (1992, p. 196).

Because cultural reproduction is a strategy that structures visibility in public spheres through a regulatory representation, Mercer suggests "our access to such spaces is rationed by the effects of racism (1994, p. 236). Drawing on Gilroy's work, Mercer writes that "simplistic dichotomies of margin and centre, left and right, or black and white, are no longer adequate (and probably never were) as a means of making 'good sense' of the bad times we find ourselves in at the end of the twentieth century." Although many doors are now open for the children of my black friends, racism is as insidious as ever before.

It is especially true that racism prevails in terms of the essentializing position of "insiderism." Like the insiderism of "white only" privilege, a new kind of insiderism develops within racial and ethnic cultural affiliations that may have begun as a collective mobilization in response to racism. The danger of "white only" insiderism or any racialized insiderism is that it tends to suggest that the ideological structuring of society is fixed, thus regarding culture as the "final property of different 'racial' subjects or ethnicities" (Mercer, 1994, p. 237). In this context Gilroy notes the difficult "resonance between race, ethnicity, and nation" (1992, p. 196).

Here I am not disputing the importance of mobilization in wider spheres of influence. I am not disputing the value of unions and other organized groups. I am arguing against forms of alliance that become new platforms for containment. When alliances become place-holding positions for enunciation—a problem of speaking for and speaking to (Fuss, 1989)—I understand this to be what Mercer calls "the new racism" by people on the left (and to "insiderism," generally, I would include classism, moralism—any regulatory form). Quoting Gilroy, Mercer writes: "A commitment to the mystique of cultural insiderism and the myths of cultural homogeneity is alive not just among . . . racists but the antiracists who strive to answer them. The rampant popularity of these opinions . . . culminates in a reluctance to debate some racial subjects because they are too sensitive to be aired and too volatile to be discussed openly" (pp. 237–238).

And with respect to sexual issues and activisms—for example, gay/lesbian activism—Fuss argues that "being gay" does not constitute activism. She suggests that it is problematic to attach the political to all that is personal because it both limits revolutionary potential and in some cases has created an "inward-looking, self-righteous 'politics'" (quoting Bourne, 1989, p. 101). Fuss argues that subjects who do not move beyond "projects of self-discovery and personal transformation . . . re-privatize social experience, to the degree that one can be engaged in political praxis without ever leaving the confines of their bedroom" (p. 196).

I too perceive it is important to move beyond self-definition, especially when personal self-discovery is romanticized and is considered on par with political praxis in wider arenas. Indeed, much that is said and done in the name of freedom produces little more than contemptuous criticism.

I assume developing a political terminology that is inclusive is needed and necessitates a "patience for uncertainty" (Brunner, 1994) in order to resist the kind of paralysis that tends to take over when we fear the unknown. Raymond Williams makes clear that if we are to break out of what remains a fixity in postmodernism then "we must search out and counterpose an alternative . . . [that] may address itself to this by now exploitable because quite human rewriting of the past" to conceive a "*future* in which community may be imagined again" (1989, p. 35).

If we are to take Williams's charge of community seriously, then we must counterpose by displacing the binary codes that tend to result in perceptions that margin/center are static. I assume, therefore, we must, like Trinh (1991) suggests, learn to ask, Marginal in relation to whom? What? When? Where? The narrative that reduces human actors, ideas, and phenomena to essences hinders the bridging of "sameness-in-difference" (Bhabha, 1994, p. 54).

As for Williams's charge for community, I do not perceive he was referring to the sort of community that Chandra Mohanty (1994) calls a "harmony culture," where "empty pluralism" merely allows "alternative perspectives." Community, in Mohanty's view (and mine and, I perceive, Williams's), is a space for "epistemological standpoints that are grounded in the *interests* of people and which recognize the *materiality* of conflict, of privilege, and domination" (pp. 146, 162). If we are to take the charge of community seriously, then a critical pedagogy to resist the politics of essentialism is needed.

Thus, the consequences of the sort of cultural overlap to which Mohanty and Williams address issues of community suggest the need to make visible various inscriptions and ethnicities respective to the revision of multicultural knowledge in order to untell the old stories. As Trinh comments, "Differences should also be understood within the same culture, just as multiculturalism as an explicit condition of our time exists within every self" (1991, p. 107).

Bakhtin's conceptualizing of self-in-other and other-in-self frames my perspective on performance and pedagogy in the study of culture (1990). The context for this project, then, is interrogation of the multiple relationships that make/mark my own identity performances and coursework in which students interrogate representations of identity through a variety of cultural scripts and narrative/performative activities. Students are most often elementary and secondary teachers-to-be and experienced teachers of secondary and community college, or they are prospective university teachers. I depend on an interplay between critical theory, culture studies (of which public education is one culture), and critical pedagogy: in my English Department this program is called Critical Studies in the Teaching of English.[4] Overlapping discourses—as much a set of intentions as a set of practices (Giroux, 1994)—of everyday performances (life), of political performances (positionality), and of staged performances (theater) are presented in the shifting and intersecting emphases with/in my teaching project. The critical practice I describe here depends on contemporary critical theories and simultaneously is an attempt at responding to and problematizing the postmodern. In other words, as Della Pollock and J. Robert Cox (1991) suggest, "critical theory . . . must be understood within the intellectual and practical history of its formation . . . [and it] must be engaged *critically*" (p. 171).

Film, television, music, multiethnic contemporary literature, and performance events provide the stage for such critique. Cultural materials circulate through courses as both an opportunity to study the politics of representation through the "mirrors of seduction" (Baudrillard, 1979) and to study what I perceive is a cultural nexus in "the arts," a threshold through which dominant meanings and practices can be simultaneously contested and perpetuated. These moments in art reveal the artist's ability to disrupt contained ways of being/thinking, even as they are reproducing culture as commodified objects/icons. In this manner, culture studies becomes an important pedagogical site of both resistance and desire; it teaches students about themselves through the study of representations, identity, and materiality; it teaches them how to proceed as culture workers toward the transformation of school and society.

Thus, related to the study of representations that figure in the formations of identity is the idea that the body is a highly political terrain. It is political by virtue of social regulation and because identity is not simply a measure of one's own uniqueness but rather of the social negotiations one makes in time and space. Accordingly, the cultural body is not only a "whole" body but also a collective body that remains an agential site of both desire and resistance. Because social forces circulate through the body, all constructions of identity are at once co-constructions, rendering a textualized body (Benstock, 1991) or a body/text (Kristeva, 1986a) with layers of determinacy and indeterminacy related to class, race, gender, sexuality, and so on.

Culture studies requires, then, critical theories and a critical pedagogy in order to fully capture its revolutionary potential to unmask constructed identities. The critical pedagogy of narrative-performative inquiry I discuss here is for sense-making of both identity and practice, for strategizing with students possible ways forward, for disrupting ideological fixity and resisting the politics of essentialism. After an interrogation of the "machineries" of representation (strategies of power for maintaining dominant culture), the body (power, as in Audre Lorde's [1978] concept of the empowered body), and recovery of the past (history), the balance of this book develops the particular strategy of narrative theater as a "play[ing] off history, culture, and power" (Hall, 1990, p. 225).

I have developed my line of thinking from a study of representational performance and a critical reflection on identity[5] through a pedagogy of narrative-performative inquiry (Bakhtin, 1990, 1993; Boal, 1985, 1995; Butler, 1990). In resistance to essentialist politics I focus on the performative, identity-making/marking role of cultural materials in the recovery of different and overdetermined histories that intersect sexually, ethnically, and so on. I combine structuralist and poststructuralist with feminist, Marxist, and postcolonial thinkers who fuse ideology critique with the study of representation, claiming the dissociation of the sign from the significer makes any possibility of a stable system of meaning unlikely and the absolutism of any fixed position unjustifiable. My theories of identity formation are reworked largely from principles that suggest identity forms in relation to what it is not (its "lack" according to Lacan [1977]; opposition according to Foucault [1982]; another according to Bhabha [1994]). Combining multiple critical perspectives to produce strong readings with a semiotic method of analysis, then, tends to make more readily transparent demonizing representations with racial, ethnic, sexual, gender, and class biases. (This critical multicultural/multiperspectival approach is discussed at length in Brunner, 1994; Giroux, 1994; Kellner, 1995.)

Finally, I borrow from the field of human geography to translate theories of space, place, and identity for education in the study of culture (Aberley, 1993; Shields, 1991). Human geography theorizes an axiological mapping of identity in relation to the tensions between space and place (location/positionality/agency).

A number of cultural critics discuss identity formation as related to the negotiation of cultural knowledge and school knowledge (Frith, 1992; Giroux, 1994; Grossberg, 1986, 1988; Ross and Rose, 1994; McLaren, 1993; McRobbie, 1992). These discussions seem to move beyond a purely sociological perspective toward what I perceive to be an understanding of the social body in the psychoanalytic view of the subject; in the postmodern tradition, their discourses subvert distinctions between high and low culture,[6] reforming what I take to be cultural criticism drawn largely from the Frankfurt School of social theory (see, for example, Adorno [1946] and Horkheimer and Adorno [1972]). Although, as Kellner (1995) suggests, classical Frankfurt School philosophy relies heavily on dichotomies of mass and high culture, high and popular art, it is the school most likely to develop "theoretical models of the relationships between the economy, state, society, culture, and everyday life" (p. 32). Following Frankfurt School philosophy in the latter sense, then, these critics have "produced methods to analyze the complex relations between texts, audiences, and contexts" (Kellner, 1995, p. 31) that morph into power and knowledge issues (Foucault, 1980).

I too am attracted to the Frankfurt School but recognize its limitations, as do others. With Antonio Gramsci (1971), I imagine resistance and opposition produce struggles that can assist in the formation of new alliances to promote hope, even liberation. Yet beyond orthodox Marxism, I resist grand narratives, totalizing discourses, and essentialist constructions.[7]

Similarly, and more strongly, then, I reiterate that the contradictory nature of the study of culture and cultural materials requires the flexibility to see a broad spectrum of methods for the analysis of relationships of production, consumption, and domination that is inclusive of text, audience, and context—a triad that connotes performance here. In other words, studies that are cross-disciplinary will be served best by methods that are cross-disciplinary. Examining belief systems within representations, myths, and narratives is most commonly associated with identity work and with the current project. Moreover, though it has been argued by Fiske (1978) that literary analysis fails to account for production/consumption/domination issues within media, I argue here as elsewhere (1994, 1995) that within a broader, more inclusive framework of analysis that includes political economy and ideology critiques, strong social readings can be produced through literary analysis, especially a feminist analysis of text; combined, these methods retain the linkage between form and content.

I assume that within the multiple inscriptions of the social body there is the agency to empower oneself to be a "border intellectual" (Giroux and McLaren, 1994), reading cultural texts and making meanings that rely both on desires, which Foucault suggests are learned (1985), and on resistances that can displace hegemony. Thus, my perception of social actors and the theories I apply suggest hybridity and a multiperspectival approach.

In addition to perspectives drawn from the Frankfurt School, I include here several connected but slightly different conceptions that theorize identity respective to the negotiation of self-other. For example, Jacques Lacan's (1977) psychoanalytic view of identity suggests that the self or subject develops from a lack. When the self looks in the mirror and meets her or his own eyes, the result is the creation of the "I." When the self looks for confirmation of self in society but sees instead other than self, a lack is formed.

Hierarchical othering occurs when self is capable of dominating that which does not produce same-self images (Bhabha, 1994). Bakhtin's (1993) view of the negotiation of self-other conceives of a self that is complicit in constructing the other, as in Lacan's view. However, Bakhtin posits a socially responsible "I"—a "non-alibi Being" that is answerable for his or her construction. He perceives this develops from a systematic construction of knowledge toward "architectonic" wholeness (the building of wholes here is dynamic respective to humans rather than static, as he perceives the architecture of buildings to be). Bakhtin's (1990) position merges theories of radical constructivism, deriving from the Kantian notion that only what can be perceived can be known, as well as more recent theories of social construction (see, for example, von Glassersfeld, 1976, 1984, for psychologically based constructivist theories; Kuhn, 1970; Vygotsky, 1962, and Bruffee, 1986, for social theories; Kelly, 1970, and Polanyi, 1958, for psychosocial theories).

Moreover, relative to the body's positioning amid circumstance, then, Bakhtin says that "in dancing, my exterior, visible only to others and existing only for others, coalesces with my inner . . . organic activity. Everything inward strives to come to the outside, strives to coincide with my exterior. In dancing, I become 'bodied' in being to the highest degree. I come to participate in the being of others . . . the *other* dances in me" (1990, p. 137). He is transgressively mapping silences that point to ambiguities, contradictions, hybridities, to the untellable, to the unquiet self.

Because the body is one of many sites for pleasure and is the site for movement, it may be less easily colonized than the mind, according to Leslie Gotfrit in her essay "Women Dancing Back: Disruption and the Politics of Pleasure." She says the way music works in that intersection of pleasure and resistance to domination is through the "genuine physicality of sound waves vibrating. . . . [It works through] its 'real' ability to make us feel" (1991, pp. 175–178, 184). Like Bakhtin's assertion of the fluidity between self-other in the embodied act of dancing, Gotfrit perceives these are rare moments in which the mind and body are one—when both creative expression and resistance to the divisions between self-other are embodied.

From these perspectives, then, I theorize the notion of multiply inscribed and constructed identities that are dynamic and never fully constituted and the disruption of essentialist codes of identity that appear *fixed*. I theorize the "place" of culture work in relation to English department curricula; the social/political representations that are made concrete in performative acts through which culture is dramatized; and strategies for teaching against dominant cultural representations. Strategies here imply negotiations one makes in the construction/care of self (Foucault, 1988).

Again, the strategy I refer to is a critical pedagogy of narrative-performative inquiry, that is, I begin where the student is, strategize with the student ways to proceed, and always connect the personal struggle to learn, grow, transform consciousness, and so on to wider political processes and social movements.[8] Narrative-performative inquiry can work against dominant meanings and practices because it requires a range of curricular contexts. Here a critique of identity, difference, and power is crucial, for it is not merely the act of invoking difference in curricular materials and discussions but the way in which difference is engaged: it is the strategic way in which students and teachers engage difference and power both in the classroom and in wider spheres of influence.

Educational Significance

At this moment in the history of Michigan public schools, opportunities to engage difference and power are gravely jeopardized. In its rhetorical stance, at least, the state's strategy for dispensing with a multicultural agenda in schools is not unlike the conservative ideologies of the religious right. Marketing cultural conflict is now the state's key platform, where a manufactured crisis plays out the attack on public education.

Samuel Bowles and Herbert Gintis, in *Schooling in Capitalist America* (1976) and "The Crisis of Liberal Democratic Capitalism" (1982), foreshadow the current manufactured crisis in public education in Michigan. Bowles and Gintis extend views of institutional sources of crisis to the state as the central mediator in cultural conflict. For them the state is more than an agent of social control; the state is integral in the manufacturing of crises so that it can offer solutions.

Thus, I perceive that current attacks on public education are part of a wider reaction to the groundswell of change agendas respective to public education in the last decade. Though what I will suggest in this section sounds very conspiratorial, what I mean to suggest is the same as Gramsci (1971), who put it best: what is occurring in Michigan education is really the interconnecting network of many strategies at once, simply creating the impression of conspiracy—what Marilyn Frye (1983) says is a "network of systematically related barriers" (p. 5).

Conflict over both the content and the processes of educating children and adults in Michigan has prompted those on the "inside" to create strategies to deflect changes that would promote a multicultural revision of knowledge in schools. This counterstrike might be thought of as a "corporate offensive"—what most of us in this state know as privatization. By putting into effect regressive funding measures that no longer attach funding to particular communities (in the name of equalizing school funding), the state has successfully created a system for marketing education as competing business sites. These sites, which would otherwise have no funding base because they are private, are known as "charter schools." (Though my analysis is strictly local, it applies, I assume, to current federal strategies as well.)

According to Philip Wexler, privatization is an advanced form of capitalism. Wexler says that privatization redraws the boundary between "polity or person rights and economy or property rights" (1987, p. 58). It offers a discourse of legitimation because person rights are now applied to economic practices located in the state (e.g., the sales-tax funding of public schools in Michigan). The public/private partnership, with greater emphasis on the private, is double-speak for historic transformation in the discourse and site of cultural conflict. This dialectic creates a new logic that masquerades as the transformation of practices of capitalist production to a more democratic form of state government. The mystifying separation between political and economic democracy, according to Wexler (1987), has always been the vehicle of ruling-class ideology in the United States (closely paraphrased, pp. 58–61).

Moreover, and continuing to apply Wexler's analysis to Michigan's situation, the opposing languages in the discourse of privatization have as their central tendency two dynamic parts of an internally contradictory structure that is in the process of solution. One is the language of the free market, or individualism in America; the other is the language of morality. Respective to the free market are the attacks on "big government," and its opposing language emphasizes social integration more than individual choice. The latter values faith and loyalty, order and continuity; it is against all forms of cultural modernity as revealed in the Bible (e.g., it campaigns against abortion, homosexuality, evolution). It focuses on the reclaiming of family ties and religion in the name of morality and decency (closely paraphrased from Wexler, 1987, pp. 62–63).

Although this public/private discourse is not easily attached to public education, in Michigan it is now seen: schools are under threat of receivership for low test scores, and there is the strategic placement of successful business leaders as advisers in universities, community colleges, and public schools. At the community-college level, there is a move underway to hire thirty-five business consultants and five educators to do a needs assessment (i.e., to examine whether or not curricula match the business community's needs).

On one hand there is the press toward the defense of the patriarchal family and "family values," fundamentalist religion, faith, and the like; on the other there is the press toward extending the market to all social relations, which allows the commodification of human resources to flourish. Though neither side claims to represent particular interests, it is important to recognize the central tendency of internal conflict in the manufacturing of a crisis. This historical internal strife—market commodity exchange and family-religion integration—is what creates the need for structural reorganization, mobilizing groups of commodity actors.

One of the first signs of school crisis is the pervasive attention to inadequate performance and to the withdrawal of institutional forms of commitment—what Wexler (1987) calls a crisis of legitimation and production. The mounting of a strong campaign against public education in Michigan especially began during the administration of Gov. John Engler, who first took office in 1990 and won reelection in 1994, with the anti-school campaign starting soon thereafter.[9] Legislation was passed in an attempt to relieve the state of any burden for educational progress. Simultaneously, bills proposed the removal of environmental and bilingual education requirements. Likewise, proposed legislation threatened to ban multicultural education in the language arts. Bills were rescinded that required administrators to be certified; simultaneously, bills were passed allowing anyone with five years' experience to teach their subject area without certification.

Shortly thereafter newspapers began to print articles attacking public schools, discrediting not only teachers but teachers' unions. Headlines like "Public Schools Are Killing Our Kids" were followed by articles related to the future funding of schools in Michigan. There was talk of cutting adult education and limiting funds for K-12 instruction.

As noted earlier, a ballot proposal (Proposal A) was floated to equalize monies available in all schools, followed by a drive for charter schools. Although Proposal A met with some success, closing the gap on funding in poorer districts, it simultaneously paved the way for Michigan to promote segregated, often religious-based charter schools that would otherwise enjoy no local tax revenue.

The rhetoric of "insiderism" has stressed outcomes instead of process, basic skills in isolation, phonics instead of reading for meaning, control not choice, obedience to authority not empowerment, conformity not thinking, monoculturalism not multiculturalism. An obsessive anxiety over standardized tests has further marked the current view that schools are failing.

As Wexler (1987) notes, despite a slight upturn in SAT scores across the nation, the discovery that some 23 million Americans are functionally illiterate makes the perception of school failure an even greater crisis (closely paraphrased, pp. 65–66). Yet I perceive that this fascination with crisis is an early phase in a much larger process that will lead to the total institutional reorganization of education that would dismantle the infrastructure of schools.

The attack is twofold: it attacks curricula and budgets. In other words, the aim seems to be to change the content of schooling, and the market-commodity tendency in this movement is to withdraw federal spending on programs for minorities, women, the handicapped, and others. (One school in the Lansing area felt such a crunch that it had to plan a shutdown day in 1997 to shave $125,000.) The anti–big government strategy in this fiscal reorganization involves reducing, decentralizing, and disequalizing. This amounts to cuts in funding of state education programs and conveniently puts education in the hands of the state, which, as Bowles and Gintis (1976, 1982) have said, can produce crises and offer solutions.

Wexler (1987) suggests that "the movement for 'quality in education' hides the reconstitution of education as an object of commodity exchange" (p. 71). In order for commodity exchange to work, there must be a "set of markets capable of accommodating the commodity"; once education has been redefined as a marketable outcome-commodity, it is necessary to work toward "appropriate distributive structures" (p. 71). The obvious choice is to transform what was a public service sector into a private service one. When schools were funded by property taxes, it was less likely that privatization could or would occur. Now, however, under restructured funding, there is nothing to prevent turning public schools into sets of private businesses. Private schools are important in this reorganization process, not for their number but for their capacity to demonstrate a "better way"—the future of U.S. education. The move to privatization is just one means of establishing so-called educational choice. "Choice" in this instance, however, amounts to the transformation of public schooling into competing educational businesses—and thus will engender cultural conflict.

Foucault (1972) says power is a strategy more than a structure or institution. Attacks on the curriculum have come from the left and the right. Leftist critics attack the sorting process of schooling as social class reproduction; rightist attacks on the curriculum are aimed at censorship. Meanwhile, the state's solution to this internal crisis is the reprogramming of school finances, a preface to the very clever strategy of further commodifying schooling by marketization. Hidden in the binary logic of public/private, privatization is the irrational hope of the ideologically restored, more privatized, free-market individual.

In the act of untelling essentialism, a revised view of culture that displaces the binarisms of insider/outsider—not a multicultural agenda that simply shifts the margin to the center—must make its way into classrooms and the curriculum. But classrooms are only one venue. Those on the "inside" at every level of society must also understand the importance of a revised view of culture. This will require, as Trinh (1991) suggests, a multicultural revision of knowledge.[10]

If my strong position on this matter labels me essentialist, then as Gayatri Spivak (1990) states, "I must say I am essentialist from time to time" (p. 11). Strategic essentialism may be necessary when difficult situations warrant taking a stand with particular ideological perspectives. Fortunately, I can admit my project has never been about consistency; unfortunately, however, this is one of those irreconcilable contradictions that locates me in my argument and makes me complicit in what I rail against.

Strategic essentialism may be seen as a method of positioning oneself, according to Jill Dolan, through a point of departure, a stance, "a strategy that locates one's personal and political investments and perspectives across an argument, . . . stopping the spin of . . . postmodernist instabilities long enough to advance a politically effective action" (1993, p. 417).

Points of Departure

My job, I perceive, as important as any set of instructional materials, is to disrupt the easy maintenance of the status quo, to reveal its fakery at all levels, to shake up what appears to be cemented foundations, and to strategize with students ways they might resist essentialism in wider spheres of influence—ways that may eventually affect policy. Such strategies allow for the kind of positionality that Dolan (1993) refers to and can simultaneously allow one to argue that the subject is nonessentialized and emergent from a historical perspective.

Though I teach a largely white population of students, many of them—and not just white students—easily accept that white America is the norm, and some work hard to maintain it. That students do not readily notice this insult to their intelligence as the subtle sway of hegemony is, according to Bhabha (1994), quite literally a conflict in judgment on the part of the subject: "whiteness" becomes a metaphor for what already operates as the "illusion" of privilege, and in its abstraction it is substituted for a metonymic sign of privilege. A "metaphor cannot be taken at its word," writes Bhabha; "it is the process of substitution and exchange that inscribes a normative, normalizing place for the subject" (1994, p. 51).

Normatively, then, "whiteness" as a feature of "American-ness" can be thought of as a posture being performed; in the words of today's youth, "whiteness" is a poser. It operates most effectively on the "play" of appearances. Not apparent in this sleight-of-hand, however, is the relationship that powerful melting-pot theories of culture mount in presumed ideological *fix*ity. What appears fixed in the melting pot construct, however, actually remains loose within dialectic frameworks (i.e., inside/outside), according to Foucault (1977), and therefore creates circulation of power as well as circulation of differences. Dialectics, then, "appear as the successful subversion of the Other . . . [when instead they] secretly assist in the salvation of identities" (p. 185).

Yet appearances can lead to bipolar opposites that spin "false" stories (Foucault, 1977, p. 185), promoting racism and ethnocentrism based on a belief system of white supremacy and the like. With Kristeva, I perceive the roots of these discourses to be mythological—"a giant at once civilized and backward" (1992, p. 146).

Often unwilling to circulate a critique of "whiteness" in and through their own bodies and in the contexts of their lived experiences, many of my students render invisible their own relationship to privilege, marginality, and various ethnic affiliations. They fuel the "machine" that represents out of a mythological framework. (For a critique of whiteness in the film *Grand Canyon*, see, for example, Giroux, 1994a, pp. 29–55, including those constructions of whiteness that mask ethnicities.). Again, it is not difference per se but rather how it is engaged that renders curriculum both a site of desire and resistance for teachers and learners.

The dynamics of cultural recovery, then, the performative aspects of cultural self-discovery, can reconnect the subject with community to move society, simultaneously addressing how every act performs within the circulation of power and "how every action is an answer to a question, even if we are not aware of it" (Postman, 1988, p. 27). After one assesses where a student is in relation to her or his understanding of "the 'play' of history, culture, and power" (Hall, 1990, pp. 222–223), strategies that work to transform consciousness then begin, as Paulo Freire suggests in *Education for a Critical Consciousness* (1973), with an examination of the political economies of representation through studies in literature, accounts of history, advertisements, newspapers, media news, film, television, music, and so on.

This book, then, is one attempt at untelling the narrative of essentialism. Essentialist identity politics fail to account for differences in relation to the circulation of power and therefore create a cultural prescription on the body instead of viewing identity as both process and performance. The essentialist narrative is convincing, with its easily referenced "norms" and labels. Again, I am suggesting that action and interaction make knowledge, as the literacy of the body signifies, reading the world and being read by the world. This view muddies an essentialist perspective; I hope it makes apparent the politics of essentialism.

In the following chapter I theorize the role of "place" in undoing the proper. I also suggest narrative strategies for performative bridgework.

Notes

1. See Chapter 2 for an in-depth discussion of "place."
2. Raymond Williams was a professor of drama and fellow at Jesus College, Cambridge.
3. For a thorough example of the way in which reducing phenomena and human behavior to a single perspective can result in both obvious violence (e.g., racism, harassment, child abuse) and more subtle violence (e.g., school policies, teaching methods, labeling, etc., that tend to give preference to the interests of administrators, teachers, and even parents over those of children), see, for example, Epp and Watkinson (1997), on "systemic violence in education."
4. Interestingly, critical pedagogy is now especially something in which students planning to teach literature at the university level seem very interested.

5. The research framework for this project is not empirical; that is, the turning-back to course materials and to the relations, actions, meanings, etc., in specific contexts did not come about as a result of a planned research project. Rather, it is what the history and philosophy of science scholars call reflexive research or *reflexivity*. Reflection and critique of one's own practice as a teacher and the subsequent writing after reflection and critique, known as reflexivity, has been a common practice associated with the Science Studies Unit of the University of Edinburgh since the 1980s. According to the director of Michigan State University's Human Subjects Review Board, projects based on reflexivity do not require informed consent because they were not planned at the onset of particular classroom activities but are the result of teacher reflection on practice that evolves into a project (see, for example, Barnes, 1985; Bloor, 1988; Latour, 1987, 1990).

6. A footnote in Jill Dolan's essay "Geographies of Learning" (1993) notes that cultural studies, conceived by some as popular culture, has the reputation for studying "low art"; she attributes this to its origins in media studies. Her point seems to be that performance studies, which tends to focus on everyday performances, stands in relation to theater studies, which tends to focus on theater performance events, in much the same manner respective to high/low status. Crediting Gramsci's notion of hegemony and resistance, she perceives that cultural studies methodology is useful for theater studies as regards the destabilization of the high/low binary. Dolan perceives that theater studies is misrecognized by some as "anachronistic, humanist relics of artistry rather than as sites at which oppositional cultural work is frequently conducted" (p. 423). Her goal is the inclusive remapping of the historical application of theater studies to recognize and recast these exclusions.

7. Henry Giroux (1994a) notes the important contributions by poststructuralists who argue against essentialism and the "illusion of a universality." Nevertheless, he offers this caveat: "To reject all notions of totality is to run the risk of being trapped in particularistic theories that cannot explain how the various diverse relations that constitute larger social, political and global systems interrelate or mutually determine and constrain one another" (p. 258). Radical politics, according to Giroux, "must *narrate*, not under the guise of universal truth but in order to understand current practices and also to provide a model of intervention and change" (pp. 258–259).

8. Linking education to social movements is often overlooked in critical teaching. This aspect of critical teaching, however, makes the educational process part of a wider cultural struggle. One example is grassroots teacher organizations like the nearly thirty national and international offices of the Institute for Democracy in Education, where concerned teachers meet on their own time to strategize on behalf of democratic schooling/educating for socially liberatory purposes. In still wider spheres of influence are the organizations for labor and youth that embody a growing alignment of persons who have mobilized to fight current economic trends and political violence on workers. Participation at all levels assumes that every act or deed is a performance and that identities shift and position themselves differently in different spheres of influence. Culture work moves in and out of spheres of influence and becomes a performative activity that is a specific peda-

gogic act of resistance for examining the political economies of representation in local and wider arenas of interest.

9. Some of the information presented here about Michigan and its governor comes from Constance Weaver vis-à-vis a group of concerned educators in the Lansing area (Michigan for Public Education) who have been tracking the following issues and action items: charter school accountability, vouchers, school reform in the state, the role of the governor and the state's board of education, privatization, and Lansing's Edison Project. Visit MPE's web site at www.ashay.com/mpe; the group also distributes pamphlets and a newsletter.

10. Although my analysis suggests that the current state of education in Michigan is under attack by regressive funding, privatized schooling, and school-business partnerships and names these measures as symptomatic of a larger social problem, I wish to underscore that my deepest concern lies in the way I perceive these administrative foibles impact a multicultural revision of knowledge. I respect the fact that many parents send their children to charter schools out of frustration with the larger system. I understand the desire for quality education for one's child/children. I have even at times thought perhaps the most efficient way to make change, speaking as an educator who gets frustrated with the difficulty of change in a large system, would be to start my own school—a charter school. But the reality is that doing so marks one of those cosmetic changes that skirts the deeper issues rooted in greed and power. It is difficult to have the patience for uncertainty (Brunner, 1994) that is required if one participates in change and simultaneously realizes it is not just a slow project but a lifetime effort. Widespread social change must accompany school change, and that is a struggle that requires more than local action; it requires participation in wider public spheres. And it requires ongoing analyses of the political economies that drive education so that concerned individuals will enter strong protests when those in power *sell-out* education.

2

Theorizing "Place" in the Performance of Identity

In *Inquiry and Reflection: Framing Narrative Practice in Education* (1994), I called for narrative practice as a site of resistance to the grand narratives already scripting cultural practice. Resistance here marks an "untelling" of the old stories, to use Trinh's words (1994), or an "undoing" of the "proper place" to borrow from de Certeau (1984). I did so believing that examinations of self could reveal holes in the metanarrative framework always already suggesting status quo readings of culture that *appear* fixed. I perceived personal narration could highlight the multiple inscripting of a life lived not in isolation but in community, a multiplex self working with/in larger communities of struggle. Not the confessional, but rather narration that examines self against society—vacillating between self-in-other and other-in-self (Bakhtin, 1990)—I perceived could highlight the gray areas of life seldom revealed in everyday performances. In the unearthing of ideological assumptions and the unmasking of hidden histories, I perceived that local narratives could disrupt, shift, and reshape universal narratives, especially if the narrator were engaged in critical self-reflection. In this way, I conceived of the individual narrator as a "shape-changer," to borrow from Anzaldua (1988, p. 30), and narrative practice as a means for resisting "residual culture" and invoking "emergent culture" to use Williams' terms (1977, pp. 121–135). I perceived narrative practice as a shuttling back and forth, a both/and construct, never a polarization of personal and public discourse. Interweaving discursive practices, I perceived, could mark an overlap of textual forms that bleed into cultural spaces and influence processes. Both/and discourses, as I imagined, never suggested an "anything goes" policy but rather a political strategy for disrupting the power of authorized, unitary narratives by breaking forms to break norms (Benstock, 1991, p. 22).

Deliberate acts of expressing what is inside involve memory, imagination, and circumstance and extend de Certeau's claim that a "politics of place" is the basis for strategies that theorize what I refer to as "materiality" and "identity" and is the rupture of what he calls the "proper place" (de Certeau, 1984, p. 55). De Certeau says that all practice is guided by an economy of the proper place that takes two forms, both equally important even if unarticulated: the first is material need and maximization of circumstances that provide for such need. Likewise, "development of the body, both individual and collective," is a part of this place. Here de Certeau describes the proper in terms of hegemonic practice: materiality toward the accumulation of wealth and the (reproductive) body as a site of fertility for the accumulation of heirs (p. 55). Moreover, de Certeau makes problematic Bourdieu's (1977) hierarchical positioning of place over practice, whereas in de Certeaus's own "politics of place," practice is equally fundamental.

Displacing the Proper

Bourdieu suggests place as *habitus,* the practical, situated context in which hegemonic practice occurs. Moreover, he suggests that assessing that situated context is a first step in disrupting it. De Certeau (1984), in contrast, describes his strategy in terms of memory *and* circumstance; he calls it performative and names it a strategy for "undoing . . . [the] proper place" (p. 82). Both Bourdieu and de Certeau outline a theory of practice and suggest strategies for rupturing hegemony.

Place and practice, then, are necessary in the emerging theory of place in this book. Here *place* is much more than location or even social position in terms of homogeneous categories of identity. Place is marked by the struggle to disrupt hegemonic practice; therefore, it is both spatial and temporal. Agential control and (authorial) voice are constituents of place in this context—how persons position themselves in different locations and situations within which power circulates.

Bourdieu's notion of practice, which aims to disrupt hegemony, occurs through a critical pedagogy that stresses involvement in social movements; de Certeau's is through performative acts of "narrativity." It is my intent in this project, then, to theorize place as a space-time of both/and: both the body/identity with agency/voice and critical practice/critical performance—a combination that reflects positionality/(authorial) voice and the mediation of structure and agency through a critical pedagogy of narrative-performative inquiry that intervenes in local and wider processes.

Conquergood (1993) defines narrativity as "a way of knowing, a search for meaning, that privileges experience, process, action, and peril" (p. 337). That is the sense of narrativity that reflects my reading of de Certeau as well as my purposes here. Undoing the proper through acts of narrativity requires an understanding that "knowledge is not stored in . . . [narrative acts but] is enacted, reconfigured, tested, and engaged in imaginative summonings and interpretive replays of past events in the light of present situations and struggles. . . . Active and emergent, instead of abstract and inert, narrative knowing recalls and recasts experience into meaningful signposts and supports for ongoing action" (Conquergood, 1993, p. 337).

Mapping the displacement of the "proper place" or the dislocation of boundaries also demonstrates a new working of Peter Hulme's (1980) "geometrical metaphor." According to Hulme, a geometrical metaphor is "a central axis about which both planes swivel free of one another" (pp 55 56) to form new connections. Hulme's metaphor refers to recent postcolonial theories as regards erasing or shifting boundaries with respect to rethinking the Western literary canon; his logic is similar to Bakhtin's theorizing of the hybridity of overlapping languages and discursive forms.

Particularly in regard to the emphasis on performance to displace the architectural constraints of "the proper" disciplinary foci, Hulme's metaphor relates well to the examination of the interdisciplinary axis of performance studies as it rotates between English studies, pedagogical studies, cultural studies, and, of course, theater studies. These connections mark a place from which to experience and critique cultural production: "performance studies," according to Dolan (1993), "widens the range of locations, and suggests that all of culture is in some ways performative" (p. 431). Moreover, Dolan says that "intentionally performative moments . . . [allow us to] 'dramatize our collective myths and history [and] present ourselves with alternatives'" (quoted in Zarilli, 1986, p. 372; Dolan, 1993, p. 431).

It is difficult to entertain notions of "the proper" without invoking Bakhtin's concept of the "carnivalesque" (1965). In his published dissertation about the double-sided nature of medieval life drawn from the writings of François Rabelais, Bakhtin describes the "undoing" of the proper in that ambivalent space he calls *carnival*. The *proper* of medieval times (i.e., the official, monolithic, serious, hierarchical, dogmatic, fearful, pious) is hardly different from conceptions of the modern *proper*. The carnival in medieval times was seen as the profanation of all sacred things, and much that would be called "popular" today might be considered analogous.

Interestingly, there are intersections in today's culture where the official and the popular collide. Take the case of Newt Gingrich, who as Speaker of the U.S. House of Representatives ran into troubles with the Select Committee on Ethics for allegedly breaking laws regarding the use of tax-exempt charities for party politics (Alter and Isikoff, 1996). Consider also Pres. Bill Clinton's money scandals associated with campaign contributions from a Chinese-American entrepreneur; or his campaign opponent in the 1996 election (Fineman and Hosenball, 1996), Bob Dole, with his connections to Richard Nixon and the Watergate tapes (Alter and Isikoff, 1996). And then we have the example set by thousands of mostly white men (and a few of their sons), who gathered in Pittsburgh's Three Rivers Stadium in July 1996 to pledge their allegiance to "God's army" of Promise Keepers. Looking like sports fans out for a ballgame but instead donning caps with slogans like "His Pain Your Gain," nearly 50,000 members of the Religious Right filled the stadium, creating a spectacle that could have easily been mistaken for a rock concert.[1]

Though each of these intersections marks an interesting blurring of officialness and popularism, they lack one common element in Bakhtin's (1965) rendering of carnival: they lack the positive regeneration in which subject-subject relations are formed. They do not "undo the proper" or even displace it. In each the discourse of the Other is continued through subject-object, fact-value, true-false binarisms. There is always someone who is above the law, someone who is beneath it. Promise Keepers are "Godly" in part because they believe they are "right" and in part because they are "white."

Carnival, then, is more than a space; it is also a moment. Conceived as a series of contingencies in which human actors choose themselves, the space-time "place" of carnival is, as Maxine Greene (1995) put it, "more than [a] dance or [a] laugh; [it is the] release . . . of energy that will permit 'familiar contact with everybody and anything'—custodians, caretakers, bureaucrats, managers" (p. 63).

Lacking the binary association, however, of today's high culture/low culture construct, Bakhtin (1965) saw carnival as the confluence of what was present in every human. Bakhtin argued that either/or constructs like high/low culture did not exist except in its appearance and through its discursive practices (Butler [1993] also argues that the masquerade depends more on appearance than on what is). In other words, the power of one group to the other was maintained both by appearance and a discourse of domination and devotion. By skillfully arguing against tradition in what might be considered an even greater assault on official and academic politics (in Stalinist Russia during the 1920s and 1930s), Bakhtin mounted his campaign against otherness by suggesting that the ambivalence and sacrilege of carnival existed within us all.

Drawing on the premise of architectonics (Bakhtin wrote about this idea during the 1920s: the building of wholes through a systematic organization of knowledge about self-other that disavows any split between life and culture), Caryl Emerson (1995) writes (quoting Bakhtin):

> An ethical and creative subject must engage in the far riskier, more humbling, present-tense practice of "participative" thinking. To do so requires

that I actively "enter in" to the other's position at every moment, a gesture which is then followed *not* by identification but by a return to my own position, the sole *place* [emphasis mine] from which I can understand my "obligation" in its relationship to another. Only then will I nurture an "I" of my own. (p. 412)

Emerson goes on to say that we do not easily come upon wholeness in the wider context. Rather, wholeness is found in response to what we make of the world. The responsive act empowers us to *"initiate a whole in ourselves"* that forges identities rather than accepting how others imagine us. The "I" here is a socially responsible "I" accountable for all that she or he says, does, and makes of herself/himself. It is not a victimized "I" nor a blaming "I." It is not an isolated "I" but an "I" that connects and recognizes responsibility, even obligation, in that connectedness. The responsive act, then, I allude to here is possible between the masks of theatrical pageantry that are performed each day as rehearsals for revolution (Boal, 1985).

Thus social accountability is, I assume, necessary in theorizing "place" in the struggle that is the drama of identity. Displacing the proper place is necessary for renewal when renewal marks the dislocation of cultural, social, and political "boundaries of home." The proper here is an official site, the "safe" or even unsafe space that gives haven but can promote stasis, a site that lets the comfort of white, middle-class life affect one's ability to see poverty, suffering, and pain. Indeed, finding comfort in one's own home or private life may be intolerable if that privacy becomes an excuse to keep out the world. The price of being at home in one's home is often alienation.

In Doug Aberley's (1993) collected volume of essays titled *Boundaries of Home,* Canadian ecologists Doug Sheriff and Eleanor Wright describe an evolving vision of place that values the entire ecosystem. Another project reports the community that evolved when "every local person [was seen] as an expert" and asked to share how she or he "valued" place. In this regard Aberley writes: "As a collective entity we have lost our languages, have forgotten our songs and legends, and now cannot even conceive of the space that . . . is connected to the womb of all human endeavor[s]" (p. 2). And even though this project speaks of a remapping of ecological location, it is simultaneously about the "joyful relearning of what has been taken, lost, or forgotten" (p. 2); it is also about the liberation of memory. This work does not appear to be just another policing of homogeneous culture, just another romantic embrace with a homogeneous past; instead it is a remembering that suggests that "people of many origins who find themselves newly planted in city or in country are asserting their aspirations for political and economic regimes" (p. 2).

Here the concept of *home* or *place* is, I perceive, close to that noted in Giroux's discussion of the theoretical, historical, and ideological borders that mark "homelessness" as "a site of struggle over the politics of representation, the exercise of power, and the function of social memory" (1994, p. 143). Likewise, place that is space-time is more than location; it is also positionality and agency. In this book, as in de Certeau (1984) and Giroux (1994), place must constantly be reinvented, transformed, critiqued, remapped in what is an *act* of "storytelling narrativity" (de Certeau, p. 120).

Storytelling narrativity invokes both performance and the performative in its tropes of identity, location, and positionality. Following Butler (1993), the performative in narration functions as a relationship of self implicated in the other and often in relation to something one opposes. Students place their personal stories side-by-side, first to make apparent their "sameness-in-difference" (Bhabha, 1994), second to begin the critical work of resisting the wider narratives that have scripted their individual and collective lives. The latter can make apparent diverse locations of culture that may have been invisible prior to this inquiry. De Certeau calls this activity a "spatializing [narrative] operation" that implies a "representation of places" in a "local order" that has been "interlaced and then slowly dissociated in literary and scientific representations of space" (de Certeau, 1984, p. 120).

De Certeau's example of the spatial story is the "tour" or "travel story"—stories that structure "journeys and actions [and] are marked by the 'citation' of the places that result from them or authorize them." From the "maps" offered in travel stories, de Certeau says we can compare our personal stories against history (1984, p. 120), in what I have theorized as the disruptive site of personal narrative when read against grand narratives (1994). Dolan (1993) claims that "traveling across or within geographies to be with people in other, often 'othered' spaces, looking, intentionally, pleasurably, meaningfully" is what makes performance and the performative unique as an inquiry that displaces (for her within theater studies, as for me within English pedagogical studies) (p. 431).

Narrative inquiry, then, is a strategy for resistance. When inquiry and reflection show the ways identities shift and overlap as they resist boundaries of cultural containment, then as a strategy it may help map or structure sites necessary for rearticulating identity and difference. Because local and wider processes slide together in examinations of identity, narrative that presents the "slippage" in complexities of self helps to break down the easy opposition of self and other and examines location in relation to position and each in relation to constructions of self/selves. The slippage between performances can be an opening onto "responsive acts" (Bakhtin, 1990) that reflect "sameness-in-difference" (Bhabha, 1994, p. 54).

Bhabha's concept can be compared with Bakhtin's (1993) discussion of the subject-in-object relationship. Bakhtin posits from the Latin *subiectum* the notion of "thrownness" or the internal trajectory of throwing identity from self to other and back, a continuous encircling of self-in-other. This conceptualization of self is not depicted as an innocent bystander but as a "non-alibi Being" that owes its development from all that surrounds. The interrelatedness of self-other and deeds, acts, or performances in the construction of identity (all of which Volosinov says are ideological because they represent; 1973, p. 13) is taken up in this book.

The idea that identity shifts in different performative situations is nothing new. Examination of this phenomenon respective to the particular knowing and doing that students perform, however, may intervene in the *taken-for-grantedness* that accompanies much teacher work. Yet I do not aim to suggest that focusing on identity in performance narratives marks the "place" of rearticulation—it is merely a bridging. In other words, I aim to suggest narrative-performative strategies that I think can assist in the bridging to a place from which to resist the politics of essentialism.

This project extends previous frameworks and focuses on the "reflexive" examination of students' performance narratives in English courses.[2] Performance narratives are both storytelling segments of class discussion (often elaborated from journals) that perform a particular function in the course, revealing the student's practical situation, and narrative segments cut and pasted for the purposes of producing a collective script to dramatize. Dramatized, collective scripts can have a more transgressive potential because they show the student "thinking through the body" (Gallop, 1990). Yet I do not mean to suggest here that particular performances— school performances—have any greater role to play in the articulation of identity than any other performative counterpart, and I do not perceive performance per se as the "place" of resistance. Rather I attend to the gaps, openings that reveal imprints—the body's secrets, openings from which reflective activity may occur.[3]

The *masquerade*, in general, as I and others (e.g., Butler, 1993) have construed it is, indeed, a site for the construction of multiple identities. Yet the performative may not always produce enlightened resistances: *the masquerade is only a crossroads from which transgression might occur.* Wearing the mask, covering up, screening is far too often associated with performances that are ritualized, stylized, and therefore not transformative. In his study of "making Catholics," for example, Peter McLaren shows the "root paradigm or cultural model for behavior" in a Catholic school as a performance that is richly symbolized. Meanings drawn from such cultural symbolism represent a tendency at work: "Even the most idiosyncratic thoughts and gestures are rarely of one's own making but rather belong to the culture" (pp. 180–181).

Thus it is difficult for me to accept that identity rearticulates on a wholly transformative front in daily performances. Instead I perceive that the resistance one makes between performances through critical self-assessment/self-reflection may carry forward into daily life in measured amounts, always protective of the masks worn in what Kristeva refers to as the "theater of identity" (1992, p. 147).

Critical educational strategies, then, are useful in helping to construct a critical site for negotiation and therefore resistance to the politics of essentialism. Action and interaction can produce a knowing that becomes a bridge to linking "sameness-in-difference" (Bahbha, 1994), that is, performance narratives can be regenerative in their abilities to *awaken* students to the ways in which their histories, cultures, ethnicities, and the like overlap—indeed, to show how they are self-in-other.

Narrative-Performative Strategies

In this chapter I have suggested the role that narratives, placed side-by-side to create collective scripts, can play in creating critical sites for the rearticulation of difference—a rearticulation that I assume can be regenerative if it displaces strict hierarchical order. Kristeva's (1986a) description of the avant-garde as a displacement of the proper is what I perceive is also the power of performance narratives that disrupt by suppressing the authority of "official" texts/scripts. She writes:

> [The avant-garde] includes all genres (short stories, letters, speeches, mixtures of verse and prose . . . a kind of political journalism of its time). . . . The scene of the carnival, where there is no stage, no "theatre," is both stage and life, game and dream, discourse and spectacle. . . . It is proffered as the only space in which language escapes linearity (law) to live as drama in three dimensions. . . . Here the text is elaborated as *theatre* and as *readings* (pp. 49, 53–54, 56).

In *Crimes of Writing,* however, Susan Stewart (1991) reminds us that the problem in narrative is the problem of social representation and thus of containment. Indeed, the problem with inclusive forms like those Kristeva alludes to is still the politics of representation, for even dreams/nightmares/visions are marred with "everyday" understandings suggested by dominant codes. Displacement or the break in logic that might "undo" particular codes comes through the body. Yet as McLaren (1986) notes, the body is schooled to act/react in particular ways that may elude the intrusion of critically restaging the drama of identity. Without an internalized turning out of the refugee within, freedom from the mask does not occur, and indeed it may make more necessary the forms of concealment masks offer.

Disruption is visceral; it is both emotional and physical; it re-members the fragmented moments of lives lived from one performance to another (hooks, 1995). On the one hand, fragmentation, as Mulvey (1992) suggests it, is useful in that it "allows heterogeneity and flexibility to be valued over a single critical perspective" (p. 70); on the other, remembering requires a "gathering" hand (Berthoff, 1978) to reform, refocus, and finally to displace mythic notions of "home" and the proper. Turning out the proper marks a transformation of place through exile-like border-crossings where the crosser "does not respond to the logic of convention but to the audacity of daring and to representing change, to moving on, to not standing still" (Said, 1994, p. 64).

Mapping travel stories—narratives of change, of places, and the influences that authorize them, as de Certeau suggests—is one method of undoing or displacing the proper, that is, narrating the personal as a pedagogical site for the disruption of universal narratives. Since the "personal" narrative, however, is often synonymous with "confessional" forms of autobiographical writing, it is important to begin the process of displacing the proper by dispelling the myth of "individualism."

In *Releasing the Imagination* Maxine Greene (1995) writes with reference to life stories that "my life story" is not just the story of "my self." Although it may be a means of identifying the self, the narrative itself cannot escape "the shaping influence of contexts." She writes, "I cannot exclude the contexts of my gender, sibling and maternal relationships, political and professional phenomena, and even aging and decline" (p. 74). To shape a life is to place it within a context, to imagine its direction, to see it as a "quest," suggests Greene. She adds, "Seeing our lives as quests opens the way to our seeing them in terms of process and possibilities . . . an experience which gradually clarifies [as it] . . . proceeds by dialogue" (p. 75).

Dialogue, as Bakhtin (1981) suggests, then, is the life or spirit in language; more than any other linguistic feature, dialogue shows the body in language production. This may be especially true in narrative. Contrary ideas and identities figure narrative texts as if the "word" embodied "flesh."

In this way narratives form what Kristeva (1986a) suggests is "an exploration of the body, dreams and language" (pp. 49, 53). It is from this notion of embodied narrative that I articulate narrative-performative strategies.[4] Moreover, Kristeva argues that although the *personal* text may be an identity-marking body/text, it need not necessarily be read as identification that is *identical* to the author of the narrative. Rather she says that autobiographical writing is as fictive as much as fiction is drawn from personal experience. Because experience is social, what is personal cannot be separated from what is public; therefore there is no narrative that is precisely personal.

The complex relationship, then, between personal-public makes "narrativity," to use de Certeau's words (1984), a mapping strategy for "undoing the proper." The performative-narrative strategies in this chapter are mapped from reflections on teaching practices over the past five years or so that have included journals, autobiographical portfolios, narrative excerpts combined in groups and scripted for performance as narrative theater, and much discussion on literature and other performative cultural materials such as film, television, music, and the like. Having noticed a pattern that addresses the gap or "slippage" between word and action, signifier and signified, I have focused on students' rescripting for performance what is suggested as an awareness of prescripted identity. But because what students voice is often different from what they perform, the semiotic relationship between words and action is highly problematic and is, therefore, what I find most interesting. In other words, what students voice is often a resistance to considering themselves anything but individual, and what is often made visible are the scripts that we have rendered problematic in our discussions of the several media—print and electronic.

To be more explicit, students will often criticize the particular attitudes and practices that have become what they perceive is the "text" in the class (Fish, 1980), yet they perform the cultural scripts that are still deeply embedded. Both situations are widely apparent in their dramatic actions and yet not so blatant in ordinary classroom interaction. Sometimes this practice is ritualized and sometimes it is slightly more transgressive, but nevertheless it is still ritual. Because I do not assume learning circumvents the body but rather circulates through the body, I perceive these "identity rituals" are a part of learning. Examining with students the gaps their identity rituals reveal creates a possibility for further critical inquiry, critical knowing—what I perceive is the basis for critical practice that acts in the wider public to disrupt hegemony, to displace the proper.

Though everyday practices may be more about circumstance (i.e., materiality), in "narrativity," which is about the "dwelling" place of materiality and identity, or "wealth and the body," as de Certeau puts it, "the art of memory and circumstance . . . intervenes . . . taking on different masks and metaphors [in its] undoing of the *proper* place" [emphasis mine] (1984, p. 82). My impetus, then, for concretizing performance through pedagogical theaterlike rehearsals (Boal, 1985) is the revolutionary potential of self-conscious, critical activity created by the aesthetic of curiosity (Mulvey, 1992), though I assume identity is a drama (Butler, 1993) even when it is not made concrete through strategies such as I describe here. Of that place of undoing then, Augusto Boal (1995), the Brazilian educator whose working-class theater presents a literacy of the body, writes:

The aesthetic space possesses . . . properties which stimulate knowledge and discovery, cognition and recognition: properties which stimulate the process of learning by experience. Theatre is a form of knowledge. [Here] one can be without being . . . the past becomes present, the future is today, duration is dissociated from time, everything is possible in the here-and-now, fiction is pure reality, and reality is fiction (p. 20).

My own students' responses to staging their narratives have tended to be like Boal's notion that within the aesthetic fiction is reality and reality fiction: "After all, it's only acting, and acting is different from real life," they will say.

The literal staging of performative actions creates a site for wearing a different mask. Within the complex of practices that occur during these performative rehearsals that have as their goal the further structuring of a site for critical negotiation, then, the "juxtaposition of . . . dimensions [that] concern time and space, . . . state and action . . . [and suggest] different 'orders' [are] all the more present because less visible, . . . *passages into something else* through 'twisted' relations" (de Certeau, 1984, p. 84). It is, then, this sense of "passages into something else" that marks the purpose of my teaching intervention in the critical work of resisting essentialism between the masks.

Not unlike Boal and de Certeau, then, Herbert Marcuse (1978) argues that artistic intervention "subverts the dominant consciousness, the ordinary experience. . . . [It] protests [social relations] and at the same time transcends them." From this perspective, Marcuse further suggests that sometimes circumstances are so miserable that only through memory and the imagination can one change one's "petrified" reality; this is a central component of revolution. Indeed, for Marcuse, "A major prerequisite of revolution is . . . the fact that . . . radical change must be rooted in the subjectivity of individuals themselves, in their intelligence and their passions, their drives and their goals" (pp. 3–4). Again, according to Mulvey (1992) the aesthetic of curiosity is felt as a drive. Embodiment and the potential for transformation seem to mark narrativity as a site of desire and resistance and suggests its appropriateness for the study of identity within a pedagogy against essentialism.

It is not, then, the importance of the personal story or the public script as a separate construct but the integral relationship each bears on both the self-other complex and wider contexts to untell the metanarratives of culture that is germane to this discussion. The transformative potential of narrative practice lies in the possibility that personal stories (when they *show* a multiplex self with/in community) may disrupt universal myths that make culture *appear fixed*. In other words, a revised view of narrative practice goes beyond simply placing stories side-by-side; it also circulates various readings of lived experiences that show self acting with and against culture and then examines performative scripts against directive if not prescriptive texts as an act of transforming consciousness and claiming agency, rendering fixed meanings and identities problematic. This revised view, leading to a pedagogy against essentialism, makes wide use of the co-relational function of words and actions in the construction of knowledge/social (body/border) literacies.

When narratives of self read against metanarratives, reworking universals to reveal the ritualized mythological provenance that seems to guide practice, narrativity can show the ways identities shift, slide together, and overlap, readying the moment between performances when displacing old boundaries through transgressive rituals bypasses accepted practices. *Displacement* is key here and is a practice that defers and prevents the creation of a new orthodoxy.

Gayatri Spivak explains this notion of displacement, after the method of deconstruction put forward by Jacques Derrida (1976). She writes, "The peculiarity of deconstructive practice must be reiterated here. Displacing the opposition that it initially apparently questions, [deconstruction] always defers . . . [and] marks a shifting limit rather [than] the desire for complete reversal" (1988, p. 103).

Spectators/Spectacles/Subjects

If "all history is myth," as Claude Levi-Strauss (1963) suggests—a creation of the human mind—then displacement of ordered relationships would, it seems, mark a "place" from which to write new myths, part of the work of displacing the "proper." A logic that places the self-in-other collectively within a new framework, a countersphere, for understanding position and subjectivity in relation to place and space may invoke new perceptions of history and its relation to Beingness. From a subject position, mythmakers are historymakers, participants and not merely spectators.

In *Lipstick Traces* Greil Marcus (1989) discusses situationist Guy De-Bord's spectator/spectacle connection: here the spectator seems merely a marker of ideological reproduction, watching history as it is made in the spectacular. The spectacle, in contrast, is "*capital* accumulated until it becomes an image" (Marcus quoting DeBord, p. 99), an accumulation of "advertisements, entertainments, traffic, skyscrapers, political campaigns, department stores, sports events, newscasts, art tours, foreign wars, space launchings" (p. 99). As described by DeBord (in Marcus), spectacles represent "democracies of false desire. . . . The spectacle dramatized an ideology of freedom . . . an inner spectacle of participation, of choice. In the home one could choose between television programs; in the city, one could choose between the countless variations of each product on the market" (p. 99).

Augusto Boal (1985), like DeBord, suggests the defenselessness of the spectator role: "Empathy," he says, "functions even when there is a conflict of interests between the fictitious universe and the actual one . . . [yet its] subjects and themes [are] selected from among the values of a competitive capitalistic society" (pp. 114–115). Boal suggests *spectator* is a *bad* word! He says that the spectator's role needs to be liberated from passiveness; the spectator must also be a subject—what he calls a "spect-actor." Because "the spectacle [as in DeBord's sense] is a preparation for action," theater in Boal's sense as drawn from a "poetics of oppression" is a "rehearsal for revolution" both by actors and spect-actors (pp. 154–155).

In *Theatre Audiences: A Theory of Production and Reception*, Susan Bennett (1990) also tries to rescue the audience from passivity by insisting that politicizing the theater as a cultural institution may move the audience to resist the traditional spectator role. Bennett's work suggests it is the cultural institution of the theater that norms audiences' bodies toward passivity and that audiences must learn to resist this hegemony. Bennett claims the marketplace is what determines for audiences their relationship to art/theater, suggesting there is a political economy at work in audience receptivity.

When particular works of art/theater are mystified, canonized, given a certain authority, they appear in representation as a naturalized part of the status quo. So with respect to the formation of the subject as audience or spectator, "representation implicitly constructs a particular viewing subject to receive its ideological meanings. . . . Subject-object formation is itself an ideological enterprise" (p. 41).

"Undoing the proper" (de Certeau, 1984, p. 120) in performance, as Bennett (1990) suggests, is a matter of nudging the audience to resist. Performance group's like Richard Schechner's have, for example, worked to radicalize the consciousness of audiences by returning to "the model of theatre as ritual . . . encourag[ing] spectators to participate in the performances on physical, emotional, intellectual, and sometimes sexual levels. . . . [His] aim was to [have audiences] join in the collective unconscious, articulated in the visceral, present moment of the performance space" (Dolan, 1988, p. 43). What is revolutionary, then, is the unmasking of ideological representations that reveal superstructures that "reify all human relationships" (Boal, 1985, p. 154).

And what is required for revolutionary unmasking is for the subject to place herself/himself within an unfinished version of history, a *place*ment that restores the capacity for social action. Although "playing" in school may not be an adequate substitute for social action in the wider context, it can impact the sort of dislocation and placelessness that marks the spectator as someone who only thinks or acts in her or his place (i.e., as to know one's place or position in society). The latter is a hierarchical sense of place that suggests socioeconomic positioning instead of authorial voice, authorized subjectivity, the subject of one's own experiences. A new "politics of place" as de Certeau (1984) suggests does not reestablish the old subject-object relationship but instead suggests subject-subject relationships, a possibility wherein human dignity is spared through active participation more than through passive reception. Although we may not assume that social and economic structures and their underpinning ideologies will radically change, how one positions oneself within such a matrix may mark some progress forward. Reconceptualizing history as myth that can and must be considered and rewritten, I perceive marks a necessary perceptual change.

Auto/biomythography

Borrowing *biomythography* from Audre Lorde's *Zami* (1982), the form that most readily offers the possibility for memory and imagination to reveal diverse locations of culture is what I am calling here *auto/biomythography*. Here performance narratives have as their primary function the reconceptualization of history from the recollection of what may be perceived as "dangerous" memories because they are not the homogeneous myths of a common culture. Despite the nature of myth to universalize and thus stereotype, as Lorde's narrative suggests, I perceive the notion of "myth" added to forms of narrative inquiry can be a code-breaking genre. Adding *auto/* to Lorde's *biomythography* further illustrates how we architect the self with/in communities of difference and likeness and how biography is also a self-in-other/other-in-self form. Myth infused with autobiography suggests, I think, a point of contingency. It suggests the inscriptions already always present because of universal narratives, and it suggests the fictive possibility of recreating self/selves. The latter especially announces the impossibility of narrating a precise identity.

Interweaving vignettes that are autobiographical, biographical, and mythological can begin a remapping that may structure or map the groundwork and conceptual frame from which to articulate new relationships that do more than blur distinctions; through social imaginations auto/biomythography may oppose old dualisms. Auto/biomythography may be seen as human resignification, not resignation. In rethinking public sites through which to reclaim the material conditions that organize experience, I perceive self in community can forge political and cultural practices that alter social realities.

Displacing the masks of conformity admits the role of self in any transformative act. As Herman Melville's Ahab in *Moby Dick* suggests, facing the prison inside us in which we are confined is a step toward liberation (cited in Metcalf, 1991, p. 65). Conformity and tradition make cracking the mask and thrusting out particularly difficult (Anzaldua, 1990).

Auto/biomythography aims at cracking the mask, and because it involves human agency it moves beyond what various literatures show occurs through transcendence or even metamorphosis.

Following Ernst Cassirer's (1946) example in *Language and Myth*, metamorphosis is the outstanding characteristic of the mythical world, but it is problematic because it relies on magic, not the subject's own agency or critical capacities, to bring social change. By a sudden metamythic turn, everything may be turned into everything. Yet as Ovid's (1955) *Metamorphoses* shows, it is through "the magician's powerful herbs" that Medea is capable of rejuvenating Jason's father. Linking the earth as the source of magical herbs and hailing the winds, mountains, and "all spirits . . . of the night" inscribes a double marginalization on the "natural" world, making it the "preternatural." Since "mother earth" is one of the masks women have been called upon to wear, suggesting powers of change occur only by magic is yet another double inscription of powerlessness (pp. 192–198).

Such originary narratives are unitary and rely on hierarchical notions of position. A new mythos, however, that attempts to subvert this system may, indeed, be possible under different perceptions of place in space-time, body in identity. Such conceptions may deepen William Blake's point: make your own myth or be enslaved by another person's myth (Blake cited in Corngold and Giersing, 1991).

Understanding autobiography in the context of mythmaking is important for several reasons. First, it diffuses the idea that autobiography is the precise personal story of one's life; autobiography suggests instead a collective representation of a self in a world. Additionally, placing autobiography in the context of mythmaking changes the confessional nature of self-authorization. Though autobiography may have the capacity to situate one within a historical context, it tends also to focus on one's plight as the victim rather than the change-maker; it tends to focus on the self-contained life as if lived in isolation, not with/in community. Mythmaking relies on more than self; a new mythos can rely on self-in-other/other-in-self. More to the point, mythmaking relies on the human capacity for extraordinary thinking.

To use an example shared with me from a student's reading of *Godel, Escher, and Bach*—a title that refers to interwoven dialogues about Godel's, Escher's, and Bach's different works to construct a metaphor for the disruptive project of showing interrelationship (the golden braid)— Douglas Hofstadter (1979) says that human perception's tendency is toward dualistic thinking, that is, toward imposing divisions or drawing lines that lead to the creation of separated systems that divide the world into hierarchicalized parts, each with its own rules. (Thus autobiography typically falls prey to this dualistic thinking as well.) By showing readers the figure-ground worlds of Escher, Hofstadter demonstrates his idea by forcing readers to jump from one perception to another, forcing readers to abandon earlier perceptions. Birds and fish merge and alternately become background for each other, making it impossible to observe the birds except by blocking out the fish and vice versa. But once identified, the objects move and the figure-ground separation is complete.[5]

Seeing worlds within worlds is the biographer's or autobiographer's job, but the human tendency is to do as reader's do when observing Escher's birds and fish—to frame them and separate their elements. Essentializing identity, then, is a part of this human tendency, but particular strategies can help recast earlier perceptions.

Auto/biomythography may be such a strategy, for it depends on the dissolution of borders. Additionally, auto/biomythography, what I have called performative narratives here, depends on "architectonics," to use Bakhtin's (1993) term. Architectonics refers to a constant building toward wholeness and emphasizes self-in-other/other-in-self as opposed to unity; additionally, it is organic as distinguished from architecture.

Both Bakhtin's (1993) idea of architectonic building and Hofstadter's (1979) notion of the golden braid suggest the need to resist categorizing, making possible an open-ended and constantly overlapping system. Each realizes, I perceive, the problem of reductive essentialism and stresses the need for code breaking. Architectonics, and by extension auto/biomythography, requires breaking conventions and rules in order to step outside how one is already always perceived.

Yet the self-confessional, so common in much autobiography, is what Bakhtin suggests is an "axiologically solitary relationship to myself . . . [where] the axiological position of the other is absent" (pp. 142–143)—a closed system. Further, "confessional as self-accounting comprises only that which I myself can say about myself (in principle, of course, and not in fact)" (p. 141). Bakhtin suggests autobiography has the potential to produce a self-conscious/self-critical self-in-other/other-in-self reflection (to show "this bodied other within ourselves [as] our mother," giver of life) when "I perceive myself within a collective . . . so long as my life . . . is interpreted, constructed, and organized (with respect to all the constituents it shares with the world)" (p. 153). Moreover, according to Bakhtin, the other in me that helps author my life "is not fabricated by me for self-serving purposes," and I am not "produced through the agency of the other . . . reducing the other to a means (it is not the world of others that is within me, but I am myself within that world as a participant in it); there is not parasitism here" (pp. 153–154).

Again, even though the potential to displace old myths through a form of cultural mythmaking born out of nonlinearity and thus nonhierarchical social ordering may exist, it is not easy for the colonized mind to switch its thinking so drastically. And not by any stretch of the imagination can we say that narrative by itself is the same as social change. However, the degree to which individuals see themselves as both *shaped* and *shaping* their communities may have an impact on the proliferation of narratives to unmask the grand narratives that order representation, categorizing identity. The problem, as Sheila Rowbotham (1984) describes it, however, is that one's potential and need to become—to succeed—is difficult because it is mixed with the partial acceptance of a preexisting order that may hinder the realization of one's goals. Yet the potential of this narrative strategy may lie in an enactment of mythmaking and with the terrible consequence of living out someone else's myth.

Greene (1995) writes of the sort of remembering to which I address with notions of auto/biomythography. Recalling the shapes of the past and drawing a future from the not yet, the unspecified "light of what might be," she says:

> I have lived inside a whole variety of ideologies and discursive practices . . . [yet] when aspects of the present are infused by materials originating in the past, there is always a re-viewing of the past, even as the new experience (enriched now) comes to consciousness. . . . The sadnesses of the past somehow alter, as the present experience is transmuted and enlarged. . . . Looking back . . . I realize what it means to say that I have lived one possible life among many—and that there are openings even today to untapped possibilities (pp. 74–77).

Like democracy and community itself, Greene's narrative is always in the making. It is a constant search for "justice, regard for human rights, respect for others" (p. 66). Her concern is to find ways to make education a public site in which students can become more fully aware of themselves and open to the world. That too is my concern—to break free of the mundane, of fixity, and to focus on what might be.

Perhaps, then, the greatest good that may come from the narrativization of experience is the possible nurturance of social imagination—imagination that extends beyond creativity in any general sense but leads us to imagine, indeed, to reconceptualize new situations/images for wider communities. The liberation of memory is the goal of this narrative-performative strategy and bridges the place from which to rearticulate identity and difference, unearthing ideological assumptions that reveal learned complicities in the perpetuation of essentialized identities. In the process of attempting to map new myths, we may develop what Greene (1988) calls a "consciousness of possibility" or an ability to articulate the obstacles that stand in the way of our reaching desired goals, to see those obstacles as problems that tend to be socially rooted, and to pose alternatives in a public arena.

In suggesting auto/biomythography as a potential terrain for mapping new myths, I am reminded of Nadya Aisenberg's comment relative to the sort of myths (which I describe earlier in this chapter) that especially mask designs and desires to change one's life and dwelling. Extending the idea of a person's feeling of placelessness in an environment of alienation emerging from domination (Heidegger, 1993), Aisenberg writes that we have lived by the *old* hero's journey, which is narrow and neglects concerns with community, negotiating human relations, and difference. The uncharacteristic form of auto/biomythography may lead to a release of the futuring capability of all humans. And in this place, the static images that categorize identities may be rearticulated into a dynamic, uncertain identity that is a *body-full dialogic bricoleur* (Levi-Strauss's phrase for the mythmaking collagemaker, 1963), knowing finally what it is like to weave a "web of human relationships" (Arendt, 1958, p. 183).

Chapter 3 begins the section on interrogating the "mirrors of seduction." I examine the representations in music that can seduce as well as simultaneously create a place to contest dominant codes.

Notes

1. Reported on the Cable News Network (CNN).

2. See note 1 in the Introduction for a brief discussion of "reflexive" research as sponsored by history and philosophy of science.

3. In Bakhtin's (1984) discussion of Dostoevsky's *The Double,* he articulates the importance of gaps (slippages), moments that develop as crises between performances in which interior dialogue emerges and begins to formulate changes, new ways of thinking, being.

4. For a further discussion of embodied narrative, see also Brunner, 1994, p. 17.

5. Lynn Chrenka, one of my doctoral students, shared this discussion with me on Douglas Hofstadter's book.. She read *Godel, Escher, and Bach* in my two-semester Bakhtin seminar (1996/1997), not as required course material but as additional reading that would help her understand some of the nontraditional thinking that Bakhtin's theories proffered.

Part Two
Interrogating the "Mirrors of Seduction"

3

Musical Elaborations[1]
of Identity

Bakhtin (1993) states that what can be known from performance is the circumstance in which acts are performed; we know less about the performer of any act than about the social order organized by the drama. How, then, do cultural representations that work in and through the mind and write the body with multiple inscriptions complicate the continued negotiations that must occur in the care/construction of self (Foucault, 1988) and subject positioning?

Inscriptions on the body, as de Certeau (1984) suggests, "place the (social and/or individual) body under the law."[2] From this perspective, "a body is itself defined, delimited, and articulated by what writes it." Bodies are marked by punishment, by marriage, by childbirth, by "all sorts of initiations (in rituals, at school, etc.), . . . into living tableaux of rules and customs" (de Certeau, 1984, p. 139). Inscriptions on the body serve two functions: the body becomes a text and the law becomes flesh. Yet de Certeau adds that tools are needed in order for such inscribing to take place. Knives, needles, and other such apparatuses scar and tattoo bodies, but they do not necessarily "copy" the body in precisely the way cultural representations do. Copying "makes the norm legible"; it renders the body a social space for social order (de Certeau, 1984, p. 141). This relationship between social rules and the body renders identity inauthentic—a copy, according to de Certeau. So what is my intent in raising issues related to the body and performance—specifically music and identity—and what consequence can such an investigation bear on inscribed identity? Moreover, what is my intent in arguing against essentialist identity politics if the body in relation to social codes is merely a site for punctuating and then confining already branded identities?

My intent is this: to show that *everything*, especially the visibility of ethnicity within a dominant culture, is a matter of "seeing" within a context (Berger, 1977). As Phelan (1993) suggests, I want to use "visibility to highlight invisibility" (p. 96). Whether someone perceives that the first leaves to fall in autumn are more compelling than the last ones is a matter of seeing, a matter of experiencing that creates impressions, feelings, images, and so on. The rational subject is not without feelings, and seeing implies this negotiation. Moreover, seeing that is more than looking implies a value center and worldview in every interpretation—what subjects each act of knowing and doing to a relational context. The "visibility/invisibility continuum" suggests that "location and identity are never *only* related to what can be seen" in one's field of vision. Perceptual knowing involves ideological apparatuses that affect "the endless theatre of everyday life" (Phelan, 1993, pp. 98–99).

Since music creates impressions, feelings, and images it is an especially interesting site for transgression, as Edward Said suggests in *Musical Elaborations* (1991). Because the form and content of music "quite literally fill . . . a social space . . . by elaborating the ideas of authority and social hierarchy directly connected," even when music appears to follow a particular order, it can be seductive; it is "able to attach itself to . . . var[ied] rhetoric[s], occasion[s] and audience[s]" (Said, 1991, pp. 64, 70). It is particularly important, then, for teachers to take up the contradictory issues invoked in lyrics to help students understand the partiality of forms of cultural representation that can serve as a system of social articulation that writes the body. It is simultaneously important as a means of disrupting the social scarring of the law turned flesh.

Anzaldua (1990) offers a cautionary word, however: she compares artistic representations with political activism that "tr[ies] to outshout a roaring waterfall." She says, "In as much as we build culture as we inscribe in these forms," we also inscribe tradition (p. xxiv). Although I am interested in the art form of music itself as having the potential to simultaneously subvert and perpetuate the dominant order, critical feminist, Marxist, and postcolonialist analyses can open critical sites for interrogation of the content of music as well.

References here to "popular" music are not intended to suggest cultural "populism" or that it is necessary to distinguish high from low art forms respective to potential sites of resistance. For transgression, like anything else, must be examined in a relational context. Music, when compared to other pieces of the time, can be disruptive because of its dissonant chords, for example, like "Peter and the Wolf" by Sergey Prokofiev. In fact, Prokofiev was known as the Russian bad boy.[3] Here, however, I wish simply to limit my discussion to the particular music favored by some young people, that is, what might be considered "youth" music as is most commonly seen on Music Television (MTV).

I refer to "youth" in this context as Dick Hebdige (1983) does. I am referring to the particular set of circumstances and struggles in which young people experience their lives, drawing meanings and values. It is not my aim here to essentialize youth as if some homogeneous group but to suggest some of the various means by which music may impact identity formations of young people.

Through particular tropes (often ones that mark an opposition to the status quo), music can and often is one means young people use to construct identity. Take the metal phenomenon, for example. Musicians like those in Metallica created an image and a sound based on their working-class origins. Music that matched the violent whir of metal clanging against metal addressed wide public concern over plant closings, job layoffs, homelessness, and the like. Metallica appealed to working-class youth who understood what working on the line meant; they had been raised in homes in which parents often worked several shifts. In Michigan, home of General Motors, Metallica enjoyed particular fame. Their themes were the themes of the workplace and of working class concerns, themes broadcast nightly on the news.

Resisting tradition, the band collected no royalties on albums cut from live performances. Initially, they vowed never to make videos for the "corporatized" industry of MTV. Today young people perceive that Metallica has "sold out."

In a recent undergraduate media-culture course I read Kellner's *Media Culture* (1995) and discussed issues of consumerism around the commodifying of the entertainment industry. After that I showed the students Metallica's newest video, "King Nothing." The class met for three hours during one night each week. It is a 400-level special-topics course in the English Department. Students are primarily undergraduate English majors and minors; there were four graduate students. Many represent the first generation of children from working-class families to attend college.

Prior to viewing "King Nothing," we discussed the current status of Metallica (the band had made a number of changes during the early 1990s). The band that was at one time the site of intersecting cultures, making a class statement about the violent nature of the competitive U.S. marketplace mentality and its effects on the working class, by now had become a power broker in the game it initially resisted. The band hired a "mainstream" producer and recorded a half-dozen new songs along with a ballad, "Nothing Else Matters." The 1991 album, *Metallica,* consisting of shorter songs, fewer chord changes, and themes taken from James Hetfield's current adult life, gave the music industry its first number-one metal album in history (personal communication, Juchartz).

"King Nothing" is a fire-and-ice video with paper crowns and nursery-rhyme lyrics: "Jack and Jill went up the hill / Jack fell down and broke his crown"; "Star light, star bright, first star I see tonight, wish I may, wish I might, have this wish I wish tonight"—with a resounding chorus with the message to be careful what you wish for, because it might come true. After viewing the video with my students without discussion, I asked them to divide into three groups. I gave each group a question; I wanted them to formulate a position and be prepared to discuss it before class ended. The questions addressed the notion of consumerism and transformation: How much influence did MTV wield in subverting Metallica's assumed counter-hegemonic practice? How much did Metallica influence its own demise as a hard-hitting heavy metal band? To what degree did the band already function as a cultural commodity?

The responses were interesting. Responding to the first question, one group discussed whether or not this video was supposed to mark a come-back for Metallica, who had since "going more commercial vis-à-vis MTV," turned out the first number-one metal hit in history but was no longer seen as a counterhegemonic band. They laughed, wondering if Metallica thought this video would "do it," perceiving a certain "lame-ness," to use their words. The group's general position was that although MTV had helped the band grow in popularity and did operate under a competitive, capitalistic model, the bottom line was that Metallica's own desire to "make it big" subverted its original counterhegemonic intent. Students also agreed that MTV did have significant power to set the agenda and message for the public and that once contractual agreements were made bands might have few options but to follow the dictates of pro-ducers and directors.

The group taking on the second question responded more angrily and nearly immediately said Metallica "did itself in." One student, who seemed to have been a fan in their earlier days, was grossly disappointed in the band for not "sticking to their words" respective to not making music videos. They thought "greed" won out when they knew the band could see how many people had become an instant success once MTV began to "pick up their tunes."

The third group (answering the question regarding the degree to which Metallica was a cultural commodity prior to MTV) responded mostly to issues of image and identity. One student in this group remem-bered a cousin having a "Metallica Kit" that contained "authentic" Metal-lica items. For example, there was a reproduction of a torn sheet of paper, a written statement denouncing the making of videos. There were autographed photos and posters. From the kit one might presume to learn the tropes of heavy metal identity.

The same student brought up Pat Boone's recently released collection of metal covers. She commented that Boone seemed to have perceived that becoming a metal musician was simply a matter of wearing a leather vest and getting a tattoo. She wondered if the new video by Metallica was, indeed, a response to having understood something about co-optation.

In general, the group thought it was impossible to produce artistic media without being commodified, regardless of the intent. It suggested that regardless of whether Metallica had begun to make videos or not the message of the working class was lost in the double-tongued application of subversion and consumerism, in contesting job layoffs while participating in and thus perpetuating a capitalistic market economy of goods and services. The "Metallica Kit" was just one example.

What I found most interesting about this conversation was the way students perceived identity as fixed, that is, that Metallica could not change and still be Metallica. Reifying Metallica's image, students seemed unwilling to concede that people change and messages change—all without the consent of fans. Though students may have understood that Metallica's identity performed a particular function in a particular space and time, "selling out" meant buying in instead of the recognition that hegemony, at least according to Gramsci (1971), meant a process of lived experiences in which there are many paths one might choose.

In *Marxism and Literature* Raymond Williams (1977) discusses the ways in which political literature or other artistic work contest social practices and phenomena (of the sort Metallica once represented). He notes that a "structure of feeling" or a "process, often indeed not yet recognised as social but taken to be private, idiosyncratic, and even isolating" (pp. 132–133) circulates within particular contexts. Contested practices may have been a part of Metallica's own "originary narrative," but as its projects slid "into a narrative war between authentic youth culture and corrupting commercial interests" (Grossberg, 1994, p. 42) Metallica and its music soon bore no resemblance to its earlier referents, as it had turned the tools of social inscription against itself. Attempting to meld seamlessly the "intensity and heaviness of metal with the romantic sincerity of pop" (Walser, 1993, p. 13) under the inscription of commercialization, Metallica, without its metal tropes, was no longer perceived as heavy metal, suggesting to identity-seeking fans everywhere that authenticity is merely a series of tropes to put on and take off. Here, bell hooks's (1992) warning seems appropriate: she reminds us that not all negotiations, even if they short-circuit the system, are actually subversive.

Similarly, and perhaps more emphatically, the political agendas in alternative bands like Rage Against the Machine[4] construct a like notion of authenticity that appeals widely respective to "originality and self-expression, [and] on music as a means of defining one's identity" (Frith, 1992, p. 174). Moreover, "at stake here is not authenticity of experience, but authenticity of feeling: what matters is not whether [the musician] has been through these things himself[/herself] (boredom, aggression, ecstasy, despair) but that he[/she] knows how they work" (Frith, 1988, p. 98). Identifying with the band, then, becomes self-referential as the identifying subject connects with the band's oppositionality, suggesting to that subject the possible authentic positioning of her or his identity.

Lyrics like those in Rage's "Take the Power Back" in *Rage Against the Machine* (1992), for example, seem to appeal widely to youth who feel disenfranchised by school. The song implicates education in the politics of representing a culture: "In the right light, study becomes insight, but the systems that dissed us teach us to read and write. / So-called facts are fraud. / We gotta take the power back. / Eurocentrics every last one of 'em, see right through the red, white, and blue disguise" (Rage Against the Machine, 1992). Studying the codes of "right" and "Eurocentrism" and the "the red, white, and blue" disguises can be an opening onto understanding what appears to be authoritarian strategies of power (see also Marcus, 1975).

But perhaps of equal importance is the question, Will any of the new alternative bands bring back the truly transgressive potential that used to belong to rock music? For consumerism works against more than just the transformation of self and the struggle of identity; it works against the opportunity for music to be transformative in the old sense, when rock and roll (and more so later rock) was first conceived to be a form of "social revolt" (Marcus, 1989, p. 53).

In "Theses on the Cultural Revolution," Guy DeBord (cited in Marcus) suggests that by the mid-1970s rock had become the "shiniest cog" in the established order (Marcus, 1989, p. 53). All that appeared to matter to young fans was having a transistor radio to listen to their music; not the music but the radio that played the music helped young people get through the day. Consumerism had "damned rock 'n' roll as a . . . monster of moneyed reaction . . . as a weapon against itself. . . . In 1958, even in 1968, a simple rock 'n' roll performance could open up questions of identity, justice, repression, will and desire; now it was organized to draw such questions into itself and make them disappear" (Marcus, 1989, pp. 56–57).

As in the Metallica example, it is important to interrogate the cultural affiliations and relations of power that are masked behind the privilege of producing and performing music. Larry Grossberg suggests that even among alternative musicians there is simultaneously a fear and a rejection of commercial success (1994, p. 42). Though groundbreaking lyrics have linked Rage Against the Machine with the Black Panther Party and Students for a Democratic Society in the 1960s, the American Indian Movement, and the Zapatista Movement in Mexico, how much influence does the music industry wield in subverting the band's assumed counterhegemonic practice? Because the band perceives that it is "seizing . . . mediums of communication and using them to inform young people about things that affect their lives in drastic proportions," will a countermessage occur as the band becomes more of a cultural commodity (Chuck D, 1996, p. 45)?

In a magazine interview with Rage Against the Machine, bandmember Zack de la Rocha says the message behind the band's album *Evil Empire* is a protest of the 1980s Reagan administration's "massive disinformation campaign about the movement in Latin America, and in particular its relation to the Soviet Union, which [Reagan] described as 'the evil empire.'" De la Rocha continues: "When you consider the atrocities we've committed in the late 20th Century, . . . [the title] directly applies to the United States. . . . Image-wise, we got this Eagle Scout–looking white kid who's smiling 'cause he's in control, but if you look real closely you'll see that there's fear in his eyes as well" (Chuck D, 1996, p. 44).

Despite this message, identifying with an oppositional band is not the same as critiquing the social forms that lead to disenfranchising particular groups or peoples. And it is not sufficient to think that authenticity resides in a series of tropes, that is, that one can put on a particular identity simply by putting on the accoutrements of that identity. It is important, then, that teachers help students recognize the narratives that particular music and musicians deploy. For in mapping this musical terrain students come to see more than the "tools" that work on the body; they come to see themselves.

An oppositional reading of the cover of *Evil Empire* might lead a student to ask what is masked behind the code of "whiteness"; a traditional reading might reinforce white privilege. Both readings, however, mark a caesura, a discontinuity, a hinge that bridges, suggesting, as Bhabha (1994) might, an intervention that renders both readings problematic. From this "presencing" bridge, Bhabha suggests, students can begin to question their own ethnicities in order to gain an understanding of the complex and cultural locations that have provided them with a sense of voice, place, and identity. White students, in particular, can begin the process of understanding how their own identities are not beyond ethnicity, history, privilege, or struggle.

Assessing the practical situation of students can begin the process of self-discovery, helping students discover that they do, indeed, live between various masks of identity. By examining the universal narratives that are always already scripting experience, memory and imagination may help invert perceived and socially situated conditions. Though all interpreters of music and other literatures have the potential for constructing meanings and identities that differ from the status quo, Bhabha (1994) warns that the "claim to selfhood . . . gives rise to the process of doubling . . . between Self and Other" in an attempt to *contain* difference (pp. 52–53). Claiming selfhood, then, is often simply a means of containing the perceived other. Resisting self/other dichotomies, as Bhabha (1994) and Bakhtin (1990, 1993) suggest, can be an opening onto the imagining of a self-in-other/other-in-self relationship, a subject-subject relationship instead of a subject-object one. Identities that oppose such dichotomies may form in negotiation of perceived new, nondichotomous realities (that exist both spatially and temporally); subjects may then resist, rework, and replace identities that serve status quo interests.

I perceive teachers can help students interrogate dominant narratives in music in the service of forging an identity outside the traditional script. Issues of containment, inscription, uncertainty/certainty, contradiction, double-languaging, and the double-bind can all be found within the scope of music (Said, 1991); they are also issues that must constantly be raised if the interrogation of popular materials is to have any impact on dismantling the universal narratives about identity, culture, and power.

If one of the most important tasks facing us today is revising curricula so that diverse voices can be heard, then it is all the more important that we resist revisions that offer a version of difference that is "benign variation" or "empty pluralism," as Chandra Mohanty suggests (1994, p. 146). It is not enough, then, to simply bring "the arts" into the classroom; when interrogated as a site of both resistance and desire, multimedia arts can serve to further the strategic critique of difference in relation to power. Curricular revisions must help students identify sites of contestation that can lead to the transformation of dominant meanings and practices in order to avoid essentializing difference. The examination of power relations could then lead us to ask whose habits of intellect are essentializing? And what habits? And for what purposes? Who stands to gain the most? Who controls when essentialism contains? Who loses control when difference is not contained?

This project shows identities performed between the masks, suggests how much appearance seems to be valued, and reveals complicity in identity politics that essentialize difference. Though masks make it possible to avoid looking inward at the multiple inscriptions that make and mark identities, Anzaldua suggests the need to examine the masks, struggle beneath, work to crack and thrust out—to make face (1990, p. xv). I perceive the recognition of complicity in the process of essentialism is perhaps a first step in the multicultural revision of knowledge that Trinh (1991) suggests is the *un*telling of the story of essentialism. She writes, "The story of marginality takes a long time to be untold" because it is a simple story (p. 21). Yet I perceive that it must be untold because of the narrative that implies a one-size-fits-all approach and because of the one that develops a "trope of 'authenticity' [that] is used to define . . . who does and does not belong" in a particular community (Mercer, 1994, p. 243).

The "Machinery" of Representation

I first encountered this notion of the "machinery" of representation in de Certeau (1984). His application particularly appeals, as he refers to this machinery as a "norming" of the body. With respect to the means by which bodies are regulated, de Certeau writes of fashion and food as "instruments through which a social law maintains its hold on bodies and its members . . . makes them conform" (p. 147). "Making the body tell the code" is how "tireless inscriptions" reproduce on the body, according to de Certeau: "It makes itself believable by saying: 'This text has been dictated for you by Reality itself'" (p. 148).

Indeed, seductive representations instruct in the matter of "seeing" and suggest who and what counts. What counts and who decides and what structures our reactions that enable seduction must therefore be addressed in order to begin to help students understand that representations, in general, contain part of a common stock of assumptions about the way the world works, the way "things are supposed to be," ways of being that are socially acceptable. Such imagery can dominate identity construction or it can be contested. Liberatory practices can help mediate the identity-making/marking process against dominant representations.

Giroux (1994a) suggests the need for a pedagogy and politics of representation in order to study various machineries and how they function within formations of identity to construe difference. He draws on Abigail Solomon-Godeau to argue, first, that forms of representation are contingent and must be identified as such; and second, that it is not enough to simply acknowledge complicity of representations that do violence. By teaching students the critical tools necessary to examine the strategies of power or machineries in which hierarchical representational systems dominate, teachers can move students beyond naive self-representation toward an understanding of the ways in which power circulates within cultures of difference. Rearticulation of categories of difference that considers positionality, receptivity, and reciprocity in the making/marking of identity returns agential control to students, teachers, and other culture workers. Third, Giroux argues that "representations are always produced within cultural limits and theoretical borders, and . . . [are] implicated in particular economies of truth, value, and power" (pp. 48–49). The seductive and partial nature of representations suggests that teachers ought to do more than simply analyze the structuring principles and paradigmatic roots of representational systems; they ought to help students learn how to identify, contest, and rewrite such representations.

I argue here, as in previous work (Brunner, 1994), that although literature and the various media are ideological because language itself is ideological, they are nevertheless interpretative fields that are never singularly voiced. Because identity is often assumed as a set of fixed images temporally and spatially bound in categories instead of as a process, part of the work of interrogating the machineries of representation involves a shifting in perspective toward what Bakhtin refers to as "novelesque thinking/production"; the drama of identity is both dialogization and carnivalization—always a two-sided act and always regenerative. There is no one-voiced drama, as there are no singularly voiced works of art— literary or multimedia. The machineries of representation show us this multiplicity in the mechanisms of voice that seduce the identifying body. Embedded, then, in the rewriting of representations is an understanding of the constructive function of what McLaren (1986) identifies as gestural display and symbolic meaning. What this means for identity work is that linking gesture and symbol to the ideologies or structuring principles of the ritual system suggests how they both inscribe and are inscribed.

As hooks does in *Yearning* (1990) and in *Outlaw Culture* (1994), I argue two important roles for "the arts": first, as teacher of the body, that is, how to eat, dress, act, what to think, how to speak—in general, how to be in the world—through defining representations within a particular "order of things"; second, as a site for the interrogation of dominant representations contained and naturalized within the traditional order. As I (Brunner, 1994) and others (see, for example, Giroux, 1994a and b, 1996a and b; Kellner, 1995) have examined film and television elsewhere, in this book I examine what I perceive is a transgressive location in music and its impact on identity formations.

I presume ambiguity welcomes transgression. And music is, in general, ambiguous and therefore inscribes transgressive potential. Despite the potential for mass-produced images to represent dominant interests, these images, especially in music, can call forth a range of imaginative potential. If what students, especially, experience in music is part of a complex of desire and resistance, then the paradoxical nature of this complex marks it a pedagogic site for multiple inscriptions. In other words, music may participate both in the perpetuation and revision of social codes, both in the formalization and reinvention of cultural boundaries.

I perceive, then, that music texts as well as students of those texts can be what Foucault (1986, p. 22) called a "subject-as-site" for disrupting and, finally, for rearticulating the meanings and practices of traditional dominant culture. Despite the ways in which the music industry appears to commodify music and artists (Adorno, 1946; Frith, 1978; Grossberg, 1988; Ross and Rose, 1994), I argue here that music can be a cultural nexus through which dominant ideologies may not only be perpetuated but also contested. And music may be an especially important form of insurgent speech for challenging representations of identity that lead, for example, to homogenous understandings of "whiteness."

Moreover, Frith (1992) suggests that music plays an important role in the construction of identity, because it functions as a site of pleasure. Since the process of identifying self usually begins by identifying with an*other*, media images of musicians are often seductive to young people, suggesting meanings and practices that are taken up and often reproduced in the identification process. As music creates within the listener a context for particular emotions (Frith, 1992), it "re-members" or brings together the fragmented parts of life (hooks, 1995, p. 64). Moreover, in the classroom and beyond, Larry Grossberg (1986) suggests, music can add consistency to an otherwise shifting terrain; in other words, music may help a student locate herself or himself, finding a center from which to grow. Though I perceive music has a profound impact on a young person's identity, I want to reiterate that I assume an active role for interpretation in making meanings and in constructing identity, as I likewise perceive meanings are contingent and identities not fully constituted. Since "full identity is never achieved," it can never be fixed (McRobbie, 1992, p. 723).

In the identity-formation process, then, social imagination can give way to identity constructions that resist monolithic, status quo representations of self and world—what McLaren has called "border identities" that form in opposition to official, rule-governed scripts (1993, p. 220). Border identities conceive of boundaries as alliance-making bridges, imagining a set of circumstances both spatially and temporally different from lived experience.

Curricular efforts that embrace the strategic critique of identity, difference, and power should consider hooks's words: "'the arts' is one of the most powerful . . . realms of cultural resistance, a space for awakening folks to critical consciousness and new visions" (1990, p. 39). Because artistic media include both dominant codes and opposing ones, it is a crucial house of knowledge where difference in wider political processes can be examined. As such, then, music may be viewed as a particular opening on which to write new subjectivities not born out of domination. Foucault (1982) suggests that we form identities in relation to contradiction; therefore, the contradictory nature of music can become a particular cultural threshold on which to struggle.

Thus in this chapter I argue that despite the commodification of music and artists by the music industry, as a popular art form music is a cultural nexus through which to perpetuate and contest dominant ideologies (see, for example, Frith, 1978; Ross and Rose, 1994). As such, music is one of the most transgressive machineries of representation: it literally fills the space, both of consciousness and subconsciousness (Said, 1991); therefore it is an important site for the interrogation and possible disruption of dominant representations contained and naturalized within the traditional order (Adorno, 1946; Frith, 1978; Grossberg, 1988; Ross and Rose, 1994). As a site of desire and resistance, then, music can be an especially important text if teachers wish to challenge dominant representations of culture. Having said this, however, I wish to reiterate that I am by no means suggesting that students do not already make meanings all the time. Instead I am suggesting that the discourses that give rise to the meanings students already make may be in need of interrogation.

Teaching the Popular

When teaching the popular, I assume first that students must be taught to read the popular (Fiske 1989). Reading the popular is a particular lens or framework for reading the world (Freire, 1970). In my own practice I focus specifically on reading the world in the popular when I teach media-culture courses. Cultural theories suggest reading methodologies that focus on production and consumption, audience response, and social myth and representation.

What follows are two classroom examples: one that betrays the "secret education" (Dorfman, 1983) that students receive while being entertained and that needs problematizing; the other shows what students can see when applying three different critical lenses to examine a gangsta-rap video by musicians whose meaning-events are often considered to be violent. In both instances, discussions led to questions of power and the possibility of negotiating meanings in order to subvert *taken-for-grantedness* (Greene, 1978, 1988).

Imagery in the following music under question, though not usually considered violent, may be read as symbolically violent.[5] Although I am not suggesting a one-to-one correspondence between representations and popular practice, I would argue that the degree to which these images tend to represent what some students suggest is "just the way things are" is a part of a cultural/ideological complex that may indicate how deeply embedded the attitudes are that guide practice (thus the difficulty in disrupting contained ways of being). Symbolic violence that lies beneath the surface of actual, physical violence is a subtext—a hidden killer, as Butler's "killing ideals of gender" suggest (1993, p. 125). Killing representations of gender occur both in the lyrics under question and in students' commentary. Although the images represented in the music I discuss here and students' language about that music may suggest a dominant social discourse, I contend that this music can be a site through which to rupture dominant attitudes. Kellner (1985) argues that media culture has become the dominant culture.

In my own exploration of transgressive sites for teaching/learning, I have sought out moments where I perceived dominant representations may do violence. In examining representations in music, I have especially assumed it is important to study the language codes through which dominant ideologies are expressed in song lyrics (i.e., particular language, its cultural understandings, and how it works in and through society to achieve particular goals). Yet because I also perceive creative acts signal both desire and resistance, music is an ambiguous site through which dominant images may be simultaneously interrupted and/or reinforced. Butler suggests, for example, that the same culture that makes possible the containment of dominant ways of being also creates a site for disruption (1993, p. 125).

The undergraduate class from which this discussion grows is a 400-level special-topics literature course in the English Department. Students mostly come from white, middle-class families, and some are from working-class families, being the first generation to attend college. The class averages approximately 45 students majoring in a variety of subjects, including English, journalism, advertising, political science, philosophy, women's studies; about half are education majors. For English majors this course may be used to fulfill the department's requirement for a course in women's/ethnic literature. Readings are contemporary works of fiction by women and other ethnic minority authors.

Each time I teach the course I vary the readings (one book and related critical selections per week), but the topics for inquiry always relate to social/political issues that surround representations of identity (the three-credit class meets twice a week for one hour and twenty minutes). I begin class with about ten minutes of information from critical sources not among students' readings, then we move to informal whole-class or small-group discussion, depending upon the book and sensitivity of topics for discussion. I require students to keep a journal of all readings, and I require two mini–research projects and a final paper or exam. There is wide choice over projects, and students can elect to take the final or write the paper.

In the particular semester under question, I included with my syllabus a large number of ideas for projects,[6] because I wanted to encourage students to examine the popular culture outside books (e.g., films, television, advertising, music, MTV, and toys). I asked students to explore representational imagery in whatever form they chose. Most chose to write their analyses from popular films and television sitcoms, several chose to examine advertising in magazines read by women, one or two education majors chose to watch particular cartoons, and some included posters with their writings. One student (a white, middle-class young woman who planned to teach high school English) xeroxed photographs of album covers and used song lyrics and descriptions of scenes from MTV to explore what she termed "violence" against women in popular music. Her project caught my attention for several reasons, but one in particular had to do with what seemed to lie just beneath the surface in this student's own reporting of what constituted violence. Although pictures of her album covers contained graphic violence, some of a sadomasochistic nature, the lyrics she chose were less explicit. Some of the lyrics did provide vivid images of violence against women, but others only implied a kind of violence my student could not readily name. In conference I asked her to talk me through what she was thinking when she included some of the selections, but it seemed the reasons, though obvious to her, were as of yet "tacit," that is, she could not yet articulate what she seemed to understand (Polanyi, 1966). Given the fragile nature of students' social positioning within classes, I am not surprised that this student was reluctant to name that which seemed less intrusive. Her visual narrative thus began explicitly with photocopies and the naming of violent images and moved to something unexplainable but present.

The cover page of the project depicted an album cover by Guns 'N Roses (1985) that seemed to work even harder to visually exploit women. The album cover portrays a woman who is literally bound and gagged, her features distorted and her body contorted into a shape that makes this sexualized female subject into a monstrous or grotesque image.

My student's reporting style, that is, counting negative images from a half-dozen song lyrics and music videos, created an oppositional site or an opening for interrogating representations of sexuality. In *Black Looks* (1992), hooks writes that through feminist analysis and intervention we might come to recognize the inconsistencies and contradictions embedded within mainstream images of women; we might begin to understand how these dominant representations work, and through such cracks or fissures we might glimpse the possibility of a world outside the order normally seen.

This project had created that crack or fissure through which to examine representations grotesquely displayed. The project reminded me that women's sexuality, at least according to Eurocentric traditions, has largely been a matter of denying what Audre Lorde calls the true "power of the erotic"; that is, instead of representing women's sexuality as a form of empowerment, women are still often cast in positions of submissiveness, their eroticism "plasticized" and sensationalized. Lorde writes: "The erotic has been made into the confused, the trivial, the psychotic, the plasticized sensation. . . . It has been confused with its opposite, the pornographic" (1978, p. 2). Because the misnaming/misuse of eroticism into pornography is what the cover page suggested to me, I wanted to check my understanding against that of the other students in my class.

As sexist mythologies have taught, students often saw women as deserving of their situations and often saw no need to problematize the text of lyrics in this particular student's project. When women were represented as what bell hooks calls the "embodiment of the best of the female savage" (though she was referring specifically to black women) (1992, p. 72) or as the lyrics in the project from "Slice of Your Pie" by Mötley Crüe (1991a) put it (a "kitten with a whip"), students saw this as "just the way things are." One student said, "Some women like those labels." Additionally, when we discussed the lyrics from Mötley Crüe's "Sticky Sweet" (1991b) (her walk "should be a crime"), another student yelled, "Yeah, some women don't just like it; they ask for it." No student saw these representations as a part of a dominant way of organizing men's and women's lives or as a social construction of gender that serves dominant interests and reinscribes male privilege. No student readily saw the power relations embedded in such images. No student seemed to understand the violence suggested in the naming of women as chattel or commodities, for instance when they are stamped "U.S. Grade A . . . Guaranteed" in the Van Halen (1991) song "Good Enough" from their album *5150*.

Violence was projected onto sexualized personae in these lyrical representations, and students' interpretations suggested yet another representation—one that is dominant, prevailing, and seems to celebrate what hooks refers to as the embodiment of production and consumption (1992, pp. 61–77, 133–143). The subtext of the lyrics and videos, not unlike the subtext in the films hooks critiques in *Black Looks* (1992), became a visual narrative as the camera focused on body size and body parts and on achieving a look of desirability (pp. 61–77, 133–143). And not unlike the Guns 'N Roses (1985) album cover, the sadomasochistic imagery of the music video "Where There's a Whip There's a Way" by Faster Pussycat (1992) depicts a woman strapped to a rack, eyes glowing, as the "dehumanizing master" goads the strapped woman into a kind of confessional.

Exploring issues of violence against women in particular songs also led to examining problematic associations of identity and difference in students' interpretations. For example, in a song titled "Baptized by Fire" by the rock group Winger (1988), lyrics tell the story of a prostitute who trades "flesh for gold." As the class discussed sexual images, what seemed to become obvious to most students is that even though we can critique the images in the song none of us had had particular experiences like the one in question (i.e., prostitution).

David Crownfield raises these questions in relation to the central problem in our discussion, that is, identity and difference. In *Body/Text in Julia Kristeva* (1992), Crownfield asks, "Can my identity be informed by, modeled in relation to, the life of another whose experience is incompatible with my difference, my gender, my anatomy, my sexuality, my politics?" (p. 141). My students' reactions, I perceived, had suggested that sexual difference—whether in music or in their own interactions with one another—translated into difference in relation to power. In other words, their reactions seemed to suggest that the meanings one ascribes to the language one uses depends on relations of power and on how power circulates within particular locations and positionalities—student to student, student to teacher, student to parent, and so on (Kristeva, 1986a).

The relationships of difference signaled in our classroom and in the language of the heavy metal music in one student's project portrayed sexual images (including images of violent sexual behaviors) that may have reflected popular practice. I did not, however, perceive it had to shape practice and thus identity. Indeed, sites of cultural collision, where anything can happen, do not have to "norm" bodies, as de Certeau suggests (1984, pp. 147–149), but can instead be a crossroads, untelling the codes (Anzaldua, 1987, p. 80).

According to Shari Benstock (1991), the female subject may subvert the dominant order by "short-circuit[ing] systems of cultural repression" and by placing herself in the dominant role (i.e., reversing her subordinate, nonsexualized position, for example, like the female subject portrayed as prostitute in the song by Winger). But the powerful roots of her female agency remain locked in a phallic economy that brings her role under subjugation and returns the male's role to that of the privileged conqueror (the female subject in the Winger lyrics is both hunter and whore) (p. 96). In other words, as hunter the subject subverts the dominant order, but her objectified status as whore suggests she is still operating within the phallologic order of male privilege and female subordination. Here the subject's own exploits literally bind her to the erotic exchange for which she both receives currency and serves as currency—"flesh for gold"—the left hand defying the system, the right hand encoding it. As Benstock further suggests, short-circuiting the system leaves no place to negotiate sexual difference in relation to power. And hooks states explicitly: "These celebrations [though they may short-circuit cultural repression] . . . do not successfully subvert sexist (/racist) representations" (1992, p. 64). In several instances, lyrics portrayed the female subject in what appeared to have subverted cultural repression by inverting the role of domination (for example, some lyrics portrayed women as a "kitten with a whip" or the prostitute who traded "flesh for gold" or as a highly sexualized female seductress whose walk "should be a crime"). But as hooks explicitly states in *Outlaw Culture*, "women's liberation was never about trying to gain the right to be dicks in drag. . . . We [should] insist that we want an end to domination. . . . [When the] desiring woman still reflects man's desires, the mirrors of patriarchal imagination cannot have been shattered" (1994, p. 22).

Echoing hooks (1990), Julia Eklund Koza (1994) argues that teachers need to subject all "official" representations to strong critical investigations. She writes especially about the place for black voices known as rap music and suggests teachers should decide if and to what extent rap music should enter the curriculum.

In the media-culture course, I showed "Vapors," a Snoop Doggy Dogg (1996) video from the *Doggfather* album. The viewing, brief group discussion, and summaries occurred at the end of a two-hour discussion of methodological tools for assessing media culture (readings were from Kellner, 1995). After viewing the video, students divided into three groups to do distinctly different critiques: the first group examined text and audience, producing a production/reception analysis; the second group produced an ideology critique, examining belief systems against representational images; the third group examined counterhegemonic effects in the video, looking for sites of resistance and possible change (they were asked not to place a value on the perceived change).

"Vapors" shows Snoop as a changeling, moving from the slickly dressed gangster in charge to the hip member of a culture dressed in flannel and low-slung khakis or wearing a T-shirt with the numbers 1 2 3 on the front to a suit on Wall Street. His story is one of change, of social agency, of things being not what they seem. Although the words are difficult to understand, the video tells its own story as it fades from one venue to another, with Snoop taking on different and sometimes unexpected roles. Students in each group thought that the video suggested he was taking back his life.[7]

The first group thought the video might send a positive message to youth. Because Snoop had been known for drugs and violence, students thought this video suggested a reversal. The cityscape in which it was filmed depicted scenes of cultural production that moved between the ghetto and the business district. The third group thought this negatively valorized capitalism, money, and power, yet they thought it positively portrayed Snoop's change. The first group noted, however, that Snoop moved between extremes as if he thought the only way to prove himself was to take on the discourse of the opposition. In other words, they said he seemed to think it was legitimate to turn greed for money and power into an acceptable business arrangement. Several in the group voiced an alternative opinion, however, that suggested he may have been satirizing Wall Street. The first and third groups seemed to understand that the social scripts are written for the extremes and wondered why Snoop had not reinvented himself apart from these extremes.

The second group of students mentioned Snoop's slide between extremes, as did groups one and three. The second group, however, added an interesting angle from an image that seemed to represent a cross as the city hovered over Snoop in one scene. Since myth and narrative are also what students were looking for respective to belief systems, they wondered if the cross might signify that Snoop thought the city, the music industry, and society in general had sacrificed him, his family, and his career with the negative press of a little more than a year ago. They thought such a symbolic gesture might be a plea on sentiments relative to forgiveness and a career comeback.

During the summary of this discussion, the first and second groups thought if such a symbolic gesture was intended, then it might suggest that Snoop knew how to appeal to audience morality. In general, however, each group summarized that the word "vapor" signified the fluidity of identities and an appeal for audiences to see that people can change. As for messages to youth, students also thought this was instructive and showed agency.

Each group, however, seemed perplexed at the possible readings that might be made relative to Snoop's initial resistance to the status quo through drugs and violence and his apparent turnaround toward the status quo. They wondered why resistance couldn't have taken another form—why it had to be drugs or the status quo. They wondered why power was so important that it had to be in each construction of self. Only in the scenes where Snoop wore flannel and khakis or the 1 2 3 T-shirt did he appear to be simply a member of a community, although some students read this as gang clothing and saw it negatively. Students thought the video could have gone further in showing young people that there are other choices and that taking charge of one's life and making changes is in itself a powerful strategy.

Of course, students also thought the video showed the circulation of power among what were perceived to be marginal groups. When placing this power, however, in the context of the wider cityscape, students said the group's power seemed minimal.

In each of the two classroom scenarios presented here, discussion raised questions about the potential for music or other art forms to give its audience a virtual experience (Rosenblatt, 1978). Other questions were also raised: How are sites of pleasure negotiated as sites of struggle? How is this resistance understood by young consumers? What are the ways in which language encodes dominant narratives? How do particular acts suggest naturalized views of culture, that is, are they already a part of a constant hegemonic *process* in which one's lived experiences become a part of that process (Gramsci, 1971)? And, finally, how do such views work within a culture?

We could have examined another issue in the Snoop video: the relative effects of MTV on the issue of authenticity, which Frith raises in *Music for Pleasure* (1988). I had hoped the first group would have addressed this issue, given my instructions to examine production/consumption respective to text/audience.

Central, then, to turning back oppressive structures like sexist representations of women or racial stereotyping is resisting "epistemic violence" or knowledge that violates. Co-optation and corruption are useful terms for understanding how this works respective to the impact music seems to have on identity-making/marking processes. For any rhetoric that depends on a binary logic and the strategic circulation of power is, therefore, part of a naming, calling symbol system that "brands . . . with a red-hot iron . . . the mark of the . . . Law," rendering bodies "no more than [a] graph, . . . a signifier . . . [to] decipher" (de Certeau, 1984, p. 140).

McLaren (1993) suggests this violence comes to us in the form of "society's treasured stock of imperial or magisterial narratives"—rule-governed scripts that are "already reading us" and on which we have assumed our identities are based (p. 205). Lyrical phrases, like those previously discussed in the music project related to students' understandings of sexual mythologies, show the potential for language to encode representations that do violence. As de Certeau suggests, language tells the code and norms it through the body (1984). But serious attempts at interrogating such language and representational imagery can provide another lens for seeing issues of power, ideology, culture, identity, and difference.

Resisting imperial narratives, then, may result in the person Maxine Greene (1978) describes as having a "committed rationality" (p. 22). For Greene (1988), this is a person who chooses herself or himself and is wide awake to the world and its possibilities—a person who sees a field of possibles and determines a way to negotiate the obstacles in her or his path (p. 5). Whereas Greene's philosophy suggests independent agential control and Williams (1977) suggests changes are a result of social experiences or movements toward new meanings and practices—those wider process to which Gramsci also alludes (1971)—I perceive that both mark social agency within organizations, like MTV, that wield powerful strategies.

Artists/musicians, then, are positioned in the place Benstock (1991) refers to as overlap between textual spaces and cultural spaces—between what Williams (1977) called residual and emergent meanings and practices. Thus an examination of the machineries that represent in music and would essentialize culture may offer one venue for stretching the imagination beyond hegemonic ideologies that perpetuate sexism, racism, and classism. It may, indeed, awaken a whole range of imaginative functions—not the least of which may be the social imagination fully necessary for surfacing new possibilities for ways of being.

In Chapter 4 I explore masks of identity in film and literature. Additionally, I problematize theatrical constructions of identity that render the self a "player" in an image-making drama.

Notes

1. *Musical Elaborations* is a book by Edward Said, 1991.

2. In *Woman, Native, Other* (1989), Trinh encourages women, especially, to write their own bodies.

3. Personal communication with piano teacher/composer Jeffrey Kleinsorge in July 1995.

4. A big thank-you to Leah Smithey, my great niece, for providing me with a notebook full of information about Rage Against the Machine.

5. I use the term "symbolic violence" after Julia Kristeva (1986b), who names the condition in China whereby the symbolic order violates through representations of gender/sexuality. She is writing of the "underground" in China where women, young people, artists, poets, etc., escape the "repressed content . . . of all that monotheistic capitalism has crushed in order to make itself identical and impermeable to crisis." "Whoever is on this side is fed up," she writes, is a "voice without body, body without voice, . . . cut off forever from the . . . changes that streak sleep, skin, viscera: socialized, even revolutionary but at the cost of the body; cut-off, swallowed up . . . under the symbolic weight of a law (paternal, familial, social, divine) of which she is the sacrificed [the law that] supports . . . the murder, of the body"(pp. 14–15). Henry Giroux (1996a) writes of the long cinematic tradition of "symbolic violence" that "attempts to connect the visceral and the reflective. It couples the mobilization of emotion and the haunting images. . . . Symbolic violence does not become an end in itself; it serves to reference a broader logic and set of insights" (p. 62). These definitions seem to complement one another.

6. For a list of the project options included in the course syllabus, see Brunner, 1992.

7. According to a *Newsweek* article (see Samuels, 1996), Snoop began writing *Doggfather* while on trial for murder; he was awaiting what might have been a verdict that would impose the death penalty. Respective to the "glamorized violence" in his music, Snoop is quoted as saying, "Should I not talk about something because it isn't nice or it isn't what you want to hear?" (p. 80).

4

Masks in Film and Literature

"I'll be your mirror" does not signify "I'll be your reflection" but "I'll be your deception. . . ." In forming a web of appearances seduction both sustains the hypothetical power of desire and exorcises it.

—Jean Baudrillard, Seduction, 1979, pp. 67, 87

Identity-consciousness is a relatively modern invention. In the past particular roles within a given community formed identities and political affiliations accordingly. As per Williams (1989), the emergence of Modernism brought more social than psychological changes as borders were erected between usually traversable terrain. Alienation, confusion, homelessness, shifts in schools, styles, and fashion in short produced narratives of discontinuity and therefore seems to have promulgated the sort of self-referentiality incorporated in a postmodern identity-consciousness where focus is on image.

Concepts like "selfhood" and "authenticity" became problematic associations related to achievement—social and economic—and image, as best captured in early newspapers, magazines, and the cinema. Aesthetically, intellectually, and historically the human condition was characterized by the "modern absolute" (Williams, 1986, p. 38), and its assumed permanence led to feelings of anxiety—a constituent of modern self-realization. Thus we have the postmodern identity crisis—selves fractured by the double bind of positivist/essentialist/rationalist thought and the socially constructed masks that are simultaneously performance and posture.

In the movie *To Die For* (1996), Suzanne Stone's character played by Nicole Kidman is iterative of the flat, television-made identity characteristic of the social milieu of contemporary culture. Image is everything. All the stereotypes are in place. Identity is truly a series of masks and performances.

Suzanne had known since early childhood that she wanted to be on television—after all "television is how we learn who we are . . . [because] what's the point in doing something if nobody sees it." As Kellner (1995) suggests, television seems to have replaced myth in terms of playing a role in helping to structure identity, that is, "integrating individuals into the social order, celebrating dominant values, offering models of thought, behavior, and gender" (p. 237).

Suzanne marries Larry Maretto, played by Matt Dillon. The Marettos are an "ethnic" family, as Suzanne puts it; her father suggests she is marrying beneath her status and that her husband's family could be connected to the mob (indeed, we learn by the end of the movie that her husband's family is connected). While honeymooning in Florida (a place her family wonders about since tanning the skin is not good for television), she schmoozes with the rich and famous. Her entire identity revolves around being a television personality. Aggressively, she convinces the local, small-town television station to hire her; she settles for being "the weather girl."

In her quest for opportunities to advance her career, Suzanne decides to do a documentary about local high school students—a documentary about identity, a movie she's orchestrating with her as the star. She superficially connects with a couple of students who agree to accompany her as she interviews students about small-town life, their futures, and so on. They become her project—her victims and victimizers, her alibi as she plots to kill her husband, who she perceives is trying to interfere with her rising stardom.

To Die For is itself filmed largely in documentary style and is more image than story, flashing images of desire, opulence, power, and violence dotted with the fairy-tale story of a small-town girl becoming a star—at her own funeral (as it turns out, the mob steps in to avenge the family's murdered son). Fracturing the modern code whereby identity marked an association with work, role, or function in society, Suzanne's masquerade pushes ever on the boundaries of postmodern discourse, where looks, sex appeal, and high fashion make you who you are. As is typical in the postmodern theater of identity, Suzanne's locus of control lies not in moral decisionmaking but in winning the game. She doesn't want to be merely "a player"; she wants to be a winner—so badly that she virtually sells her soul, creating a symbolic morality play in her demise. In Kellner's (1995) words, "The player 'becomes someone' if she succeeds and gains identity" (p. 243).

The value of *To Die For* lies not in teaching the body, or, as de Certeau (1984) puts it, "making the body tell the code" (p. 148); the value lies in the opportunity for viewers to make a variety of meanings respective to the process of identity-making/marking. It is valuable in its suggestion

that identities are not fixed, that subjectivities fluctuate, that self-knowl-
edge is a process, that social actors have agency despite webs of confusion
and constraint.

Like Madonna's frequently criticized self-documentary *Truth or Dare*
(1991), *To Die For* (1996) widens the lens on meaning-making and multiple formations of identity. Although *To Die For* is mockish in its appeal to
"all-American" and "feminine" ideals, *Truth or Dare* is mockish in its reen-
actment of a heterosexist "norm" in a stereotypically homophobic manner.
Both are, nevertheless, invitations to imagine different versions of "self."
Yet what is strikingly problematic about both movies is the suggestion that
one can consummate relationships of difference (sexual, ethnic, class,
etc.) and not be radically altered. Playing around with difference is neither
subversive nor lasting.

The simultaneity of masking and unmasking identifies the body in
both films and, perhaps not coincidentally, reveals the mythologies from
which its masks derive. For example, Madonna's "in-your-face" portrayal
of sexist and heterosexist mythologies might be an example of what Anzaldua means by "making face." Anzaldua (1990) says, "*Face* is the surface of the body; [it is] the most naked, most vulnerable, exposed and significant topography of the body . . . that is the most noticeably inscribed
by social structures, marked by instructions . . . tattooed with the sharp
needles of experience" (p. xv). It is the sharp needles of experience that
viewers see in the sexually explicit documentary *Truth or Dare*.

Truth or Dare is a concert documentary. It takes you backstage as
often as front stage, but it always shows the theatricality of performance.
Madonna's doting on her "emotionally crippled" dancers and her quipping
about "those girls' singing" is not only brutally telling respective to who
Madonna thinks she is; such slurs have the effect of evoking little to no
ethos or pathos as the documentary takes the audience from concert to
concert and reunion to reunion with performers and parents and siblings
who mostly seem to want to meet the "infamous" Madonna.

Throughout Madonna's music videos, and in this film in particular,
there is the suggestion of a supposed desire to break through the masks of
culturally repressive forms of female sexuality. What the film actually
shows, however, is a reproduction of those forms in heterosexist ways,
reinscribing male desire. Madonna seems to neither short-circuit the system nor shatter patriarchal mirrors; instead she appears to reinscribe what
Lorde (1978) suggests is a plasticized, sensationalized version of sexuality.

Yet Madonna sets the contemporary standard for a more aggressively
sexualized female personae. From a "material girl" to a bawdy woman
who stands with a whip in one hand and man (often a black man) under
one foot, Madonna's prowess overshadows that of the objectified Marilyn
Monroe or Jean Harlow of film screens past. But does her version of sexu-

ality reclaim agency, or is it simply another form of objectification? Madonna's continual reinvention and representation of herself seems to mark a double inscription of sexual economy, one that exploits women's sexuality as it simultaneously suggests other ways of being.

Despite this critique, the opportunity for multiple readings permeates Madonna's work, and so with each new set of images, Madonna constructs a new identity. Again, as with the Metallica example in Chapter 3, changes in identity are perceived to be connected to particular fashions and images. Unfortunately, however, from this vantage point identity is a mere series of tropes one can put on and take off. Struggle is reduced to wardrobe decisions instead of political affiliations; value is replaced by consumerism. The both/and of a self-in-other/other-in-self identity is of fleeting interest at best, for the image Madonna leaves with us is a world in which you either do or are done to.

Critics approach Madonna's work from a variety of perspectives. Kellner (1995) argues that Madonna's chief success comes from her marketing brilliance. He deploys an analysis of cultural production and political economy to suggest Madonna is always in *control* of her own images and thus of her own "effect." Kellner describes her as a border-crosser who "appropriat[es] the pleasures of both cultures and multiple relationships" (p. 271); further, Madonna is as much a cultural icon for black and Hispanic females as she is for white females—all fantasize about being her or being like her.

bell hooks (1994), in contrast, problematizes Madonna's interracial relationships as slices of sexual commodification woven into a white-supremacy narrative. She charges that as a cultural icon Madonna is "dangerous." hooks says Madonna uses sex to "express right-wing anti-feminist sentiments" (p. 18) while selling her feminist friends on the idea that feminism is about having the choice "to dominate or be dominated" (p. 22). hooks disagrees, however, saying that feminism has never been about women gaining the rights to be "dicks in drag"; again she says that we should insist "we want an end to domination" (p. 22).

Finally, hooks (1994) characterizes Madonna's identity in terms of sameness and difference, that is, as the "young Italian girl wanting to be black" and as the essential "white female beauty" (p. 20). Yet beneath these images, hooks suggests, lies the representation of colonial imperialism—the narrative of domination and control.

With respect to representing identity, Julia Kristeva (1986b) suggests that when women enter the symbolic order (patrilineal time) so their voices can be heard, they enter into a world that uses a form of logic that is shot through with patriarchal ideologies. She says such identification leads to double-penning messages that continue repression/oppression. Identification in this manner often creates a double bind, says Kristeva.

In a media-culture course where students had read previously Kellner (1995) and more recently hooks (1994) (see description of course in Chapter 3), I showed clips of *Truth or Dare* (1991). I placed my own students in somewhat of a double-bind, asking them to recall Kellner's cultural production analysis in light of hooks's critique in *Outlaw Culture* (1994). After asking the class to divide into three groups, I asked one group of students to attempt an analysis of the political economies at work in the film (i.e., to discuss marketing strategies and production techniques, to say how those strategies/techniques contributed to a commodification of Madonna's artistry, and finally, to suggest how these strategies/techniques are a part of a wider culture-industry). I asked the second group to do a text-reception analysis (i.e., to say how they as an audience received the text and what other possible meanings audiences might make, to say what if any impact those meanings might have on cultural practice, and finally, to discuss the text as a wider public script and say what if any resemblance it bore to universal narratives about women and men). I asked the third group of students to do an ideology critique that would go beneath hooks's analysis of race and sexuality (i.e., to discuss the representations, images, narratives, and myths within the film and suggest what wider ways of thinking they align with, to suggest what ideological apparatuses—church, school, state, even family—and their rhetorics are suggested in the film, and finally, to discuss the wider implications of hooks's race/sexuality critique). Separating these three analyses from a positioned audience response, I finally asked each group to take up and write a brief position statement on Madonna, in general, as a cultural icon.

Group one responded more generally by agreeing with Kellner that Madonna was "all image" and "marketing" and that she knows "sex sells" and so makes "big bucks" from it. These students also disagreed with Kellner that Madonna was in complete control. They believed consumers dictate what they want to see/hear and that producers provide it. For example, they believed part of Madonna's popularity came from audiences wanting to know "what she'd do next"; so from a production/consumption perspective, students suggested producers and directors would continue to push Madonna to make changes whether she wanted to or not.

Group two suggested that its response to Madonna was much like hooks's response. These students liked the way hooks characterized her as a "dangerous" feminist and didn't perceive that Madonna was actually subversive of anything. Most of them announced that they were just happy to finally read something that agreed with how they felt about Madonna. Only one student in the group said that if she had a daughter, she'd make sure she saw Madonna's videos and film so that she might see that she didn't have to be subservient. Other students wondered why her daughter might have to learn this from Madonna and not from her. The student responded by saying that she believed young girls looked up to "stars" for this kind of perspective on "the ways of the world" more than they listened to parents. Several students followed: But what kind of message does Madonna really send girls? And might there not be better "role models"? (Time did not permit further brainstorming for role models.)

Group three had a mixed response to *Truth or Dare*. First, several students suggested that the gay dancers were portrayed in a very stereotypical manner, saying that they did not disrupt any "myths" about "homosexuality and dance or the theater." Second, other students in this group agreed with hooks's "narrative of domination" theme, both from the perspective of Madonna's roles in the concerts and backstage with her troupe. Only one student perceived that Madonna was a "disruptive force," unmasking "feminine constructions of identity" in a "positive" manner.

Only two of the three groups took a position respective to Madonna as a cultural icon: both shared views that suggested some positive and negative aspects of Madonna as a "figurehead" or person in "the public eye" who garnered lots of "power." One group saw Madonna's identity as a "dance" that "moves between what is considered the norm and what is an assumed deviation." In this respect, both groups said this showed Madonna's ability to move between "multiple audiences" and that that could be good. Yet each group could see ways in which the multiple portrayals of self might not reveal inner subjectivities but more "glitz and glamour," in which case they weren't sure how that would play, especially to younger audiences who were looking for "someone to look up to."

Despite the fact that no group responded to all parts of its prompts and lacked sufficient time to discuss Madonna as an icon, it seems that the activity did offer some positive ways of examining "the Madonna phenomenon" (Kellner, 1995, p. 268) that could help students resist the easy oppositions maintained within essentialist ways of viewing media culture. It remains important to find ways to help students produce a variety of readings respective to human actors and their activities. Though many students' responses matched the rather bipolar responses offered in the two readings (hooks and Kellner), it goes without saying that it takes frequent critical practice to resist the politics of essentialism. This course, like this book, is one attempt, but much more work of this nature is needed.

What appears to remain perplexing to my student audience (and often to me) is that it is difficult to know whether Madonna constructs herself out of the desire to dismantle or whether she is herself seduced by the power she has attained and thus plays out on stage. Either way, the result may be the same. Power is not disrupted; indeed, Madonna's "phallus substitute" seems to be a "phallacy" (Benstock, 1991). Although she characterizes an opposite role for women, she does not appear to stand in opposition to what violates women, and the relations of power that violate remain intact. Power has been merely shifted but not disrupted. And thus what appears to be a "border identity" (McLaren, 1993, p. 220), or one that opposes dominant forms and fights the failure to see the self in other, is not all that it seems to be. The performative dimension or what appears of Madonna's identity suggests to me the layers of masking about which Anzaldua writes and the potential for art to masquerade rearticulation of particular phenomena, in this case power.

Regardless of the possible critiques, what seems readily apparent to me is that Madonna reveals the varying levels of intentionality and stance-marking in the performance of identity. What can also be learned is that one's identity is, indeed, changeable regardless of how one defines identity or how fixed one perceives her or his life. Madonna shows that identity is a project that is as much about appearance as about what is real. It is impossible from studying Madonna (or anyone I know) to say if what is outside is what is inside. For the ambiguous project of constructing a narrative about one's identity is slippery and often revealed only in the empty "husks" left behind.

This idea may seem overly obvious and simple. Yet in a world in which power relations seem to dictate actions and interactions, I perceive that imagining multiple ways of being that resist fixity and essentialism is actually not obvious at all. In any case, imagining and actually resisting are very different modalities: the former is merely ambitious, the latter a constant struggle.

If what is outside is not necessarily what is inside (a function of the masquerading "effects of power"; Butler, 1993), then examining the effects of power on the social body seems crucial in the late twentieth century. The multiple inscriptions that "interface" (Anzaldua, 1988) between the masks are not reducible to privilege and marginality. Indeed, neither privilege nor marginality exists in isolation, and each exists in relation to time and space.

When I was a child I was poor; today I earn more than my father earned in twelve and a half years of work. Everything is relational. Because identities are never fully constituted, they shift, slide together, and overlap. In other words, identity not only forms in relation to location and position but also remains in flux over time. Beneath my masks are many selves, and not all of them are referential to bloodline.

Identity, then, is a performance (Butler, 1990) acted out daily in the "theater of identity," where, as Kristeva (1992) puts it, "People [wear] masks to convey what [is] essential, [even] though masks serve only to confuse." She continues: "Break the mask of conformity. Delve down to your roots . . . but deeper still—to the level where there are no roots left, where everything is eradicated. [There] you might find a counteridentity . . . and realize how utterly strange it was to contemplate . . . [the mask]" (pp. 146–147). In the "game of power," however, both Trinh (1991) and Kristeva (1992) are careful to note: if the act of unmasking has liberating potential, then there are times and circumstances in which masking has a similar effect. Kristeva suggests this counteridentity serves to both reveal and conceal simultaneously (p. 146); Trinh suggests its necessity depending on the context (p. 151).

That identity is a performance fraught with masking and posturing may be true. What I perceive to be most interesting is what happens between the masks, where the unquiet self attempts "to crack the mask and thrust out" (Anzaldua, 1990, p. xv). This chapter calls into question the "project" of identity-making/marking as a self-reflexive, self-referential moment, historicizing it against readings that suggest the most likely "place" of identity practice is between the masks, a place characterized by psychic more than social fragmentation and a subjectivity that is unquiet.

The Unquiet Self

If mythologies that suggest a unitary history do violence, then surely those that suggest unitary ways of being are equal in their volitional, destructive capacities. Creating a break that attacks dominant ideology is like "attacking the giant." Borrowing from Anzaldua (1990), this work occurs best when art (a soulful project) and intellect (a mindful project) unite with a spirited body to perform deliberate acts aimed at subverting the status quo. To Anzaldua, political art or activism is "a sneak attack while the giant sleeps, a sleight of hands when the giant is awake"—a creative move on which survival depends (p. xxiv).

Though I borrow the notion of the "giant" from Anzaldua, I understand this play on words to underscore the necessity to struggle to make and mark identity against all the apparatuses of culture and ideology. Although this chapter focuses on the masks in film and literature, it further suggests the linkage-making struggle to reconnect the selves displaced behind the mask, the struggle to make every identity-making act an activism, thus exposing the unquiet self.

According to Kristeva (1986a), this linkage occurs best in the semiotic or in the material body, in drives, the unconscious—a "zone of meaning before meaning," as Michael Wood suggests (1995, p. 17) that is always examined in relation to language, meaning, and power (the symbolic). The obverse of the semiotic, the symbolic, according to Kristeva, is based on ideological assumptions about the way the world *should* work. Because the semiotic (meaning before meaning, dreams, drives, and so forth) is, for Kristeva, a place in language between the "not yet" and the "not that," Wood suggests that the semiotic may be "our best bet against the tyranny of the symbolic" (1995, p. 18).

For both men and women to change in relation to the symbolic order, then, I perceive it is necessary to relearn the body in order to reclaim the colonized mind. Charlotte Perkins Gilman's The Yellow Wallpaper (1973) provides a powerful example of the semiotic that disrupts the symbolic by relearning the body. In what might approximate de Certeau's (1984) de-centering move that "displaces the proper," Gilman's narrator moves to-ward a "politics of place" (p. 55) in an unquiet self.

The narrator, a silenced woman whose body language signifies "those killing ideals of gender" (Butler, 1993, p. 125), a woman trapped in her gender-normed body and a marriage to a man who does not legitimate her creative efforts to "[re-]write her body," dramatizes her prisonlike existence by peeling the paper from her bedroom walls. Behind this paper she sees "creeping women" with "strangled heads and bulbous eyes and waddling fungus growths [that] shriek with derision" (Gilman, 1973, pp. 34–35). She wonders if they come out of that wallpaper as she believes she did. Escap-ing from behind the wallpaper during the day to free those creeping women, she perceives that at night she will "have to get back behind the pattern." Outside she says things are green instead of yellow, but inside, in the yellow wallpaper, she has to creep smoothly on the floor and along the wall so she won't lose her way. Her creeping and peeling gestures free her and she exclaims, "I've got out at last, in spite of you and Jane. And I've pulled off most of the paper, so you can't put me back" (p. 36).

The hard lessons of school and society—especially those that stem from essentialist instruction on ways of being, for example, how women should be feminine and men masculine and each always heterosexual—may result in particular ways of living day to day while the psychic dam-age that such ideals produce is repressed and shows through a variety of body languages/forms. It is then in the body that anger and repression are stored, casting shadows that mimic "the killing norms." Despite the body's potential to dislocate traditional meanings—because the body/text that embodies through signification is also inextricably bound to the social and ideological that coexist with the symbolic—the body may also rein-force dominant, Western, ideological customs/codes.

Critically, Gilman's story is told as a woman's descent into madness—one of the body's postures during a crisis (of identity/legitimacy). It is Gilman's (then Charlotte Stetson) own story. But examining the body lan-guage of the narrator reveals more than the actions of a madwoman. In-deed, the narrator's actions seem to mime her circumstances in ways that go beyond madness to reveal her own insights respective to the prisoner that society has made of her. In this regard I perceive the narrator stories an example of the both/and that functions within the literacy of the body. That is, she reads and acts even as she was read and acted upon. She im-posed meaning and meaning was imposed on her. The patriarchal meanings imposed on her created a psychic violence, but the desire to strangle the woman behind the paper seems an act of resistance more than of violence. That is, by killing the woman and her gendered norms, she perceives she might free the imprisoned woman within herself.

The narrator functioned as more than metaphor to symbolize a sick society; she functioned mimetically (to show through the body or body language) in order to mimic what society had made of her—but also to signify that she could not be restrained by its codes either. She was not merely the construed object as per any denoted interpretation or "truth" by another outside herself, and she was not merely posited or positioned in subjective meaning. She was her own "subject of enunciation," signifying through the body, breaking the thesis that had been assigned her for identification purposes (to identify her as mad). Additionally, through this break that served to rupture assigned meaning, she was no longer constrained to voicing her resistance through linguistic forms. Indeed, her experiences in language had perhaps taught her that grammatical locution was normed in precisely the same manner that she had been normed. By choosing to mime, the narrator chose to denounce language as the processor of meaning, and through the ambivalence of her performance she dissolved both the meanings attributed her as object and as subject.[1]

In Lynda Hart's and Peggy Phelan's collection of essays titled *Acting Out: Feminist Performances,* Elin Diamond (1993) discusses what Luce Irigary (1974) and Julia Kristeva (1986a) theorize as the transgressive potential of mimesis (mimicry or mime) through "manipulation of referentiality" so that the political may be broached. Diamond's thorough examination of concepts of mimesis from Plato and Aristotle through modern realism suggests representation has a "festishistic attachment to the true referent . . . thereby concealing historical contradictions, while reaffirming or mirroring the 'truth' of the status quo" (p. 366). In the essay Diamond explores the double inscriptions given mimesis. First, she asks whether it is possible for women to get along in this society without traditional imitative performance, then whether a transgressive notion of mimesis can dislodge "women from their prisonhouse." Though not referring to the woman in *The Yellow Wallpaper* (Gilman, 1973) per se, Diamond questions whether the body can "signify and also escape signification" (p. 377). She concludes that acting is necessary in any case, because the sex and gender codes that women are forced to acquire simply have no ontological basis. Julia Kristeva's (1986a) theorizing of a "true-real" signifier in the body (often marginalized because it is described as hysteria)[2] creates a place for transgressive performance or acting out.

Other bodies in literature have also signified imprisonment. For example, the overcoded bracelets Lily Bart wore to attract men in Edith Wharton's *The House of Mirth* (1979) could be read as representing Lily's reflection of the male gaze. Yet since the symbolic order is language and, as I perceive it, is steeped in patriarchy, a semiotic reading that requires the body in its physicality/sensuality to signify meaning might suggest that with Lily's every movement the clinking bracelets tell a story that signifies both desire to please and desire to resist her chains of containment, identifying a disparity between the word and the world.

My point here, however, is not to particularize women's bodies but to suggest the way in which I perceive bodies read and are read and how this reading becomes a political terrain for helping students interrogate and potentially rearticulate their own normed bodies. In the ambiguity or uncertainty marked by a "play" of appearances in the drama of the body, the white-masked, biracial/ethnic person can turn "confusion into a strategy of political subversion" (Bhabha, 1994, p. 62). Here masks become a convenient way of surviving a ritualized "theater of identity" (Kristeva, 1992, p. 147). Playing roles, stance-marking, passing: these are all important elements in the drama of identity.

Nella Larsen's *Passing* (1929) reveals perhaps what is the most widely misunderstood mask—the masquerade of multiple subjectivities that do, indeed, mask an unquiet self. Larsen centers on the desire and resistance of two women; the "whiteness" of "blackness" in this novel details the pain of racially polarized bodies. In the legally inscribed necessity in 1927 to be nonblack in a "white" establishment, both women approach their bodies and the looks they exchange as if reading hieroglyphs. Clare—who passes for white in her marriage, with her friends, and in everyday situations—seems to find relief in the speculative gaze of a similarly racialized woman, who she discovers was a childhood friend. Irene, in contrast, is all the more conscious of her body because she senses Clare's alluring gaze is the "colonizing white gaze."

Lauren Berlant (1991) writes in response to Larsen's characters that what the two light-skinned African Americans want in bringing each to "mutual crisis" is "relief from the body." Her critique focuses on the "imitation of life," a life Clare and Irene have because they can afford to buy it. Berlant asks whether Irene's desire for Clare is mutually erotic or whether she simply wants "to wear [Clare's] way of wearing her body, like a prosthesis, or a fetish" (pp. 110–111).

Irene's self-styled identity appeals to the "norm of good taste" while Clare wears the exotic mask of privilege: Irene's mask renders the body invisible while Clare's exoticizes visibility. Both are, however, equally capable of "passing" through public sites that would otherwise be off-limits. What seems clear is that both women live between masks in their racialized "white American" identities. Hortense Spillers (1987) suggests that American gender identity can be nothing less than racially inflected as the drama of identity is performed between the masks.

The tension between race and identity is also present in much contemporary multiethnic literature. For example, in Janet Campbell Hale's (1993) autobiographical *Bloodlines*, which Hale admittedly fictionalized, the narrator, who like Hale is from the Coeur d'Alene tribe in northern Idaho, describes trying to bleach her hands white to match those of the white man she married. In the Richard Rodriquez (1982) autobiography of Mexican American assimilation, *Hunger of Memory*, he writes that he once tried to slice the outer layer of his skin to see if he was pink underneath like his white friends. And in Christina Garcia's (1992) *Dreaming in Cuban* (a story of generational response to the Cuban revolution), Ofelia rub's whitening cream on her face and wonders, "Who am I whitening my skin for?" (p. 41).

What must be interrogated in the illustrations here is the relational context. Humans are not merely receivers but producers of meaning within a context—one that is political, economic, and fraught with cultural prescriptions. The question, then, is not who is inside and who is outside of any cultural "norm" at any given moment, but rather how all people can subjectively own the images of themselves so that they are not rendered objects of those representations. Here as elsewhere in the several media, even when people align themselves as outsiders against the status quo, a demonizing, essentialized version of culture is often projected that suggests society is the fixed domain of particular subjects. What, I wonder, does this suggest about the process of growing up today? How can members of youth culture especially reclaim and define a "generational referent" that articulates a sense of who they are and their vision without co-opting or being co-opted (Giroux, 1996, p. 31)?

Julia Eklund Koza (1994) recalls the "we/they binary [as] seen in a scathing criticism of rap fans" by journalist Jerry Adler. She writes that Adler described rap fans as "working class" and "underclass" youths "who forgot to go to business school in the 1980s." Koza offers another example of the negative characterization of rappers—both fans and performers—in George F. Will's sentiment that "rappers are lower animals" (pp. 9–10). Clearly Will and Adler see themselves as what Bhabha suggested in his construction of a "We," aligning with a dominant narrative.

The categorizing of humans and their experiences amounts to what Foucault (1972) has suggested is an act of power, yet it seems impossible to talk about issues related to descriptions of human conditions without invoking the "context of categories." Foucault extends this problem in *Language, Counter-memory, and Practice* (1977) when he states that the trick is to think of categories as spaces where what is true can be distinguished from what is false. He writes: "Within categories, one makes mistakes; outside of them . . . one is stupid. . . . Thus we court danger in wanting to be freed of categories . . . we risk being surrounded not by a marvellous multiplicity of differences, but by equivalences, a levelling uniformity" (pp. 188–189).

I perceive it is not necessarily categorical thinking but the devastating effects of the hierarchical positioning of power on persons in relation to particular sites that results in their categorical reduction and then dismissal. My aim here is not to further polarize by invoking categories of race, gender, or ethnicity or by suggesting universal Beingness in coded categories; it is rather to complicate such categories by thoroughly interrogating how power circulates in, around, and through. Again, my purpose is not to evade the discussion of categories but to interrogate their appearances by making visible what lies between the masks so as to open up questions of cultural affiliation, revealing the interfaces and their complexities.

On the Limits of *Bodies That Matter*

Though the body signifies both physical and shadowy psychic ills through an important mind/body connection, in many instances the body is merely functional. For example, to the medical community a body serves to further medical practice. With the exceptions, perhaps, of more holistic practices, the body itself, in science, is a political question that provides both scientists and physicians the opportunity to be heroes in a society with a John Wayne complex. Under the hero metaphor, healing is a matter of finding a cure instead of preventing illnesses. Thus the status accorded the medical community, for example, is not similarly accorded chiropractors and massage therapists, who also do body work. If the body is capable of signification, might it not also be capable of acting beyond the boundaries of the colonized mind?

Indeed, bodies matter. They are written and they write. They read and are read. Bodies house the classed, raced, and gendered identities that mark the stories lives tell. Indeed, there seems little doubt that our bodies house the meanings words impose to represent identity, but relatively little attention is paid to the way in which bodies also produce meaning—a form of literacy for reading, writing, and constructing worlds.

As mentioned in Chapter 3, de Certeau's (1984) view of signification suggests that social codes are written on the body—as if by tattooing or branding with a hot iron. I am suggesting that bodies are not merely receptacles for social inscription; they also sign. They are not only spectacles; they also participate in the writing of culture—not so much as passive spectators but as actors in the social drama of life.

The latter suggests the body can transgress normalization and produce its own set of signifiers; this view of meaning-making (and thus showing knowing through the body's language) suggests a literacy of the body, even though markers of the body's literacy often bear the scars of the relations of power reproduced in and through the body. The body politic, such scarring suggests, renders the body almost untheorizable respective to its own capacity for signification. Yet theorizing body literacies as the struggle to unmask essentialist identities suggests the body is "always already caught up in multiple networks of conflicting ideologies" and seems to unconsciously deploy shifting markers that would "unsettle" any conceptual framework or containable category (Moi, 1985, p. 162). Since it is impossible to distinguish what is and what appears, bodies seem a rather suitable terrain for contesting regulatory inscriptions that render the body a series of monolithic categories of identity. Despite the contradictory nature of social and linguistic codes that mark and isolate particular attitudes and practices—what results in particular representations of identity and the set of power relations from which those representations derive—showing what is known through the body may foreclose that which language tends to mask.

In the "drama of the body," however, transgressive ritual often masks layers of dominant representations and mythologies (Bakhtin, 1965; 1984), and bodies often signal the scars of mediated social behaviors. Ethnographic observations confirm Turner's theories of performative ritual as I notice the "appropriately" but "cautiously" dressed students in my classes in contrast to the young people who meander up and down the sidewalks or who gather in the coffee shops across the street from campus. Outside my window, the tattooed, pierced, and sometimes chained bodies tell an important tale. They are not silent bodies; they are screaming their resistances.

Inside my classroom, however, students are performing "the docile body" routine that Foucault (1972) refers to: they appear to have a transcendental anonymity as regards voicing that reveals positionality (pp. 20–122). He says instead of speaking as an individual subject or even as some kind of collective consciousness, students speak with the kind of anonymity that suggests the multipositioned nature of the speaking subject. Indeed, my own students often speak a "jargonized" objection to social codes of behavior, yet their bodies hesitate. Appropriate but cautious talk fills the room in nearly all discussions, even in discussions of the most confrontive texts. Their bodies attempt to remain silent—ankles neatly crossed, thighs together, arms folded across their chests. Yet even the appearance of silence is noisy as it foreshadows possible repressions, resistances, and a range of other body signatures signaled by the masks worn in this classroom drama of identity.

My students have learned to play the game called school all too well. They may resist what I'm teaching, or their seemingly closed postures may suggest that repression motivated their resolve not to respond when, for example, during a course on autobiography and gender, we read some of Virginia Woolf's letters that allude to her bisexuality (Woolf, 1979). The young people across the street, in contrast, who may or may not take classes at the university, suggest that they too recognize the game and have decided on a different way to play it. The classroom is one context for my students; from this gaze they seem to perceive themselves as "insiders." Young people in East Lansing, Michigan, however, situated in relation to the conservative university life across the street, set up a completely different context: they may be "outsiders" in the eyes of Michigan State students, but these young people are insiders within the peer groups that distinguish themselves from the "properly" dressed university crowd who they perceive are on the outside. Both groups have masks in common.

For Bhabha (1994) the process of "identification . . . is always a question of interpretation." For my students, especially, this appears to be a dual process, a performance that doubles or splits the subject. As spectators among themselves and spectacles when braving the busy street that separates the coffeehouses from campus, my students seem to affirm their own fetishistic perceptions as they dismiss, as culturally outlawed, persons who chain themselves to lampposts or spike their orange hair and shave "fuck you" on one side of the head and "MSU" on the other. This splitting of subjectivities, then, seems to lead to a kind of spectator/spectacle relationship—a doubling, according to Bhabha, evident in the "play" of illusion over appearance—a moment that marks both the possibility and impossibility that the mask could render the subject invisible. To crack the mask threatens to expose, it threatens to render privilege "missing" in the "play" of illusion. This "dialectical hinge," however, seems to be what creates a critical site for interrogation (Bhabha, 1994, pp. 51, 64).

Frame of reference and contextual relationship operate within the dialectic and initiate both the strategic and the contingent. The hinge, however, can be a bridge from which something begins to mobilize in the "slippage" between the presence/absence of everyday life—in the interface between the masks.

It seems to me Fae Myenne Ng's 1993 novel *Bone*, about the drama of identity in a first-generation Chinese American family, makes the issue of complexities abundantly clear. Moreover, the tension between blood and bones strikes me as a bridging place in the text—a place where worldview and context mark both the strategic and the contingent, revealing the complexities of what interfaces masks. On the one hand, the novel seems fixated on returning the cremated bones of grandfather Leong to ensure that Chinese tradition will continue. (It would cost $5,000 to send the bones back to China, his last request. Over and over, the question of where to get the money for returning Leong's bones enters the story.) On the other hand, the novel focuses on the stories three sisters' lives tell, suggesting the dilemmas respective to how they (Leila, Ona, and Nina) each represent Chinese American identity.

Appearing unsure as to which mask to take up, each sister tries on a different identity. Leila, the oldest sister, is conscientious about not corrupting Chinese ways but is simultaneously trying to survive in San Francisco; she understands the Chinese community is watching her as they watch each other for slips in custom, and all are constantly observed by those passing through to eat and shop in Chinatown. Leila often feels the most co-opted and is in conflict with Nina, the youngest, who dared to live with her boyfriend, moved to New York, and seems happy with her Americanized life, choosing anonymity over connection. Neither Leila nor Nina understand Ona, the middle sister, who is most confused by the complexities of constructing an individual and cultural identity that will not render the body a spectacle. As she observes Nina and Leila, psychic distress leads to attempts to anesthetize the pain. Ironically, Ona shifts from being a spectator into a spectacle as she jumps to her death from the Nam building. Each wonders whether blood or bones prescribe identity. Bones in this context signify the uncertainty of tradition (the family doesn't have the money to return grandpa's bones), which is historic, cultural, and under construction; of course, blood signifies race. On the first page readers learn about Ona's suicide, and a few pages later they learn about the cultural/historical implications of a proper resting place for the bones—how one's fate could be divined by the weighing of bones. Ona's suicide, however, mixing blood and bones, becomes a bridging place in the novel.

Sau-Ling Cynthia Wong (1994) writes that in works like Ng's *Bone* the uneasy union of habitation and spectacle makes the novel highly problematic in that living under the "white" gaze (wearing a mask for survival and profit) confuses the psyche and creates a new cultural product. This new cultural product amounts to being a "sign-stealer," Wong says, as those who habitate and are spectacle work with prescribed signs already bearing traces of their own subjugation. Wong agrees, however, that in the three sisters' very different generational approaches to conflict, Ng shows greater awareness of individual and incidental complexity.

As the novel unfolds with discussion of why Ona committed suicide, a presencing begins, hybridity initiates—what Wong argues is a problematic cultural product. On the one hand, this presencing marks something new for everyone in the story; on the other, it suggests the end of a way of life, capturing, of course, the precise notion of complexity Wong articulates. That Ng complicates the notion of a cultural pastiche and community ethos is to her credit.

I perceive Ng's novel was the sort of untelling Trinh refers to (1991). The work of displacement and in(ter)vention is long and difficult, for it must break open the monolithic nature of categories (like blood and bones, for example) that appear one way or the other. In *Bone* Ona's death became both the displacement and the in(ter)vention; the mixing of blood with bones on the pavement literally marked a rupture of family categories. With respect to self-authorized identity, like the beginning presencings from Ona's in(ter)vention, for example, Bhabha writes that representations of identity should not be read as reality because the dual-entry process of "displacement"—the family's questioning and differentiating after Ona's death—within a binary system renders such representations shadowlike at best. And, indeed, Nina and Leila are not fully constituted at the end of the novel, as they would not be in life. The idea of "absence/presence" respective to particular representations of identity conveys the notion of a not-fully constituted identity. For the "representation/repetition . . . the image of identity is at once a metaphoric substitution, an illusion of presence, and by the same token a metonym, a sign of its absence and loss" (Bhabha, 1994, p. 51). What began to present itself from the borderline or bridge was conceived in Leila and Nina's loss and Ona's absence. I perceive this is what Bhabha (1994) means by a dual-entry performance within a binary system: "From this edge of meaning and being, from this shifting of boundary of otherness within identity . . . hybridity initiates" (pp. 51–52, 64). And it is hybridity that marks the untelling of essentialized identity or the telling of a different story—a story of difference that makes a critical difference (Johnson, 1987, p. 15).

Ng's novel further suggests to me the tension between referential meaning and relational meaning, that is, how especially referential meaning can be abstracted and normalized as in the connection between bones and traditional bloodlines. Bones became a reference point in the novel, but the relational context in which Ona mixed blood with bones suggested a different story. It is not, then, abstraction in the text that marks identity; rather it is a "meaning-event" (Foucault, 1977) particularized only within the context of the story.

If one of the problems of race (and gender and class) in U.S. culture is ideological abstraction, then the fetishizing of an essence of "Americanness" that serves to maintain borders is one of the directions in which that compulsion leads. As one student from Colombia pointed out, "Latinas/Latinos are Americans, but we aren't Westernized Americans." As she spoke I couldn't help thinking of all the icons within media culture that suggest "whiteness" and "American-ness" go hand-in-hand. (Of course, in that representation abstraction leads to distinction so that it isn't just the white American who is legitimately privileged, it is the white, male American of upper- or middle-class distinction). Indeed, "whiteness" is so much the "norm of reference" that rarely in common speech do people talk of the United States as anything but America, making it clear that "white America" perceives that the United States is the navel not only of the Americas but possibly of the world. In Westernized dress, actions, attitudes, idioms, values, schools, churches, governments, and so on, a co-constructed notion of "American-ness" and "whiteness," equaling a "selective tradition," is so prevalent and simultaneously so submerged that it is noted simply as an artifact of everyday experience, a fact of life (Williams, 1977).

Kellner also associates "boundary maintenance" and the "legitimation and mystification of social reality" with abstraction. He writes: "A cultural studies that is critical and multicultural must therefore carry through a critique of abstractions, reifications, and ideology which traces reified categories and boundaries back to their social origins and which criticizes the distortions, mystifications, and falsifications therein" (1995, p. 62).

Masked in nostalgic images that allege family values and "the good old days," "the politics of innocence" in the media message easily conceals an ideological matrix of racism, sexism, heterosexism, classism, and so on (Giroux, 1994, p. 43). Here media serves to bind a culture's perceived need for a common center (Fiske and Hartley, 1978). Of course, alongside this "normed" version is a more complex alterity beginning to surface within the "machineries" of representation.

In ethnicity, sexuality, dress, speech, values, attitudes, and the like, some are making a concerted effort to dismantle the master narratives scripting culture. In her 500-year map of the *Almanac of the Dead,* Leslie Marmon Silko writes that ancient prophecies warned of "white settlers" who would take over tribal lands; that same prophecy also foretells that indigenous peoples will rise up against "white settlers," reclaiming their places (1991).

Many narratives are themselves embodied signs of resistance, signifying the body's relationship to its identity, resisting the classified, flat, or monolithic identities that have marked much of the emphasis on contemporary identity politics. A semiotic approach that understands the place of the body and critically engages difference in narrative may be a useful opening onto the untelling of essentialism. For even though words and conversations can be rendered silent, the body speaks, reads, and writes regardless of the subject. The body, as Kristeva (1986a) suggests, can be both the object of enunciation and the subject of enunciation. Though bodies often appear silent, the body that appears silent utters as well. In other words, the body in pain, through whom no words are mouthed, may signify its pain through silent scars that both foreshadow and shadow as easily as the body that overtly attempts to conceal pain or that which iterates joy. The body is always a text through which a tale is told; it speaks, reads, and writes in addition to being inscribed and to representing how it is coded. The body that expresses resistance openly is no more or less a text than the body that is docile or that which crouches and creeps.

Body narratives reveal body boundaries in media and in literature (Martin, 1992); they reveal similarly the transgressive potential when ritual performance becomes transformative and social contradictions result in what Turner calls the antistructure of resistance (1982). Breaking norms while simultaneously appearing to adhere to them (Benstock, 1991) and wearing masks that simultaneously reveal and conceal (Kristeva, 1992) are among the problematics of cultural recovery.

Part 3 begins a discussion of performative bridgework. Chapters 5 and 6 suggest interventions with the goal of reflexive performance to critically engage difference.

Notes

1. See Kristeva, *The Kristeva Reader* (1986a, pp. 113–123), for an in-depth discussion of mimesis. Also see *Desire in Language* and *Revolution in Poetic Language* for an in-depth discussion of metaphor, metonymy, and mimesis in the semiotic matrix of referent, signifier, and signified (especially when dealing with identification).

2. Judith Butler (1990) reads Kristeva's (1986a) notion of the true-real in a negative light as regards the implications that sexual difference marks a moment of madness or hysteria, suggesting that a thoroughgoing analysis of the power relations embedded within sexual difference would render a different reading. Kristeva's psychoanalytic reading of sexuality depends on the mother-child split, and Butler argues that this leads Kristeva to a nonpolitical understanding of sexual difference. I do not, however, read Kristeva as celebrating the true-real of hysteria.

Part Three
In(ter)ventions: Performative Bridgework

5

Acts of Cultural Recovery

In *Marxism and Literature* Raymond Williams (1977) fosters a notion of art/writing as the reproduction of culture that passes through dominant, residual, and emergent phases with an alternative view of art as social practice. His critique of tradition clearly positions art/writing in a particular milieu that suggests its potential to shape culture by subverting those philosophical and political categories that function materially on our bodies and minds. His notion of an alternative view of art as social practice that contradicts tradition suggests art can be a catalyst pushing culture through emergent phases by overlapping textual spaces (conscious/unconscious meanings) with cultural spaces (conscious/unconscious practices) in an attempt to displace essentialist categories that render culture a fixed and maintainable social order.

The desire to objectify art, to render it something other than experiential or performative, according to Williams, is a conscious desire to remove art from the material conditions of production. Yet as he reminds us, writers, painters, sculptors, and dramatists remain attached to the physical and material aspects of production. Therefore, Williams writes, "The inescapable materiality of works of art is then the irreplaceable materialization of kinds of experience, including the experience of the production of objects, which, from our deepest sociality, go beyond not only the production of commodities but also our ordinary experiences of objects" (p. 162).

Here Williams agrees with Mikhail Bakhtin (1993) respective to the extent to which material "reality" can be understood through aesthetic experiences. In raising the question of language and reality, Williams draws attention to both the representational and presentational aspects of art, that is, he proffers the socially constructed nature of the world. (The Italian philosopher Giambattista Vico raised this question earlier in response to Descartes, proposing that "we can have full knowledge only of what we can ourselves make or do"; paraphrased in Williams, 1977, p. 23.)

Williams writes that "language is a constitutive faculty . . . a human opening of and . . . to the world" (i.e., he suggests that we believe we can understand the world because we have made it, not in any scientific sense but as regards experience). For Williams the activity of language is central. These arguments, however, were at the fore of a distinction between that which was thought to be human (the humanities) and science (positive knowledge) that Williams sought to address in his notions of the overlaps between history, culture, art/literature and science.

Bakhtin (1993), in contrast, addresses this overlap in a slightly different manner. He seems to find artistic forms that rely on language somewhat problematic in that they are part of what he calls "the phenomenology of the lie," which suggests words are implicated in the ritualized practices that govern the everyday. Despite the performative nature of language, the grammatical lexicon seduces language users, according to Bakhtin, into believing that words give access to objective reality and that by naming or categorizing reality it is possible to *know* what is real. What is real here implies objective truth or absolute truth. Bakhtin writes: "We have conjured up the ghost of objective culture, and now we do not know how to lay it to rest" (p. 55). And thus begins the premise on which meanings, practices, and therefore identities are thought to be fixed.

Yet Bakhtin (writing with or as Volosinov, 1973) also suggests language is always communal—word is a two-sided act—and therefore identities are always communal, obtaining "the highest degree of sociality" (Bakhtin, 1984, p. 287). Kristeva refers to this communal identity as a "subject in process" (Guberman, 1996, p. 190) incapable of being fixed. Thus, according to Kristeva, as the plural identity evolves it appears as fragments of characters. It is the site, as Lester Faigley (1995) states, "of overlapping and competing discourses . . . a temporary stitching of a series of often contradictory subject positions" (p. 9).[1]

Gloria Anzaldua (1988) elaborates on these notions of the material/experiential overlap within the constitutive nature of language, the sociality of identity, and the conscious production of art. She describes art that is performative as a social practice that does not separate the sacred from the secular or art from everyday life. Despite this theorized overlap in the production and reproduction of society, however, I presume the stories that lives tell are still tenuous and fraught with potential for perpetuating dominant interests.

Shari Benstock makes explicit this relationship in *Textualizing the Feminine* (1991, pp. 92–97). She says some of the narrative forms that we are so apt to encourage today (journals, letters, autobiographical narratives) often challenge proprietary order but, in defying this system, also encode its power. Benstock offers the case of letters as a more precise example of a form that produces emergent meanings and practices but also reproduces the past. Particularly in the case of "women letter writers who invented their lives and inspected their suppressed desires through letters," to use Benstock's words, expression of the forbidden circulates, "properly speaking, under the stamp that taxes the exchange of desire within a phallic economy" (pp. 97, 100).

Though Benstock's ideas seem to sidestep issues of human agency, her words suggest a set of problematics in acts of cultural recovery. Transformative rituals that transgress the decree of this stamp, then, are crucial to cultural recovery, as is "a space for change" posited by Paulo Freire and Donaldo Macedo (1987, p. 126).

Body/texts such as those Benstock (1991) describes respective to inventing the self through letter writing follow Allen Feldman's (1991) argument that events/experiences are not what happen so much as what is narrated and *enacted* with/in the site of the body. Phelan (1993) reminds us, however, that "performance's challenge to writing is to discover a way for repeated words to become performative utterances, rather than . . . constative utterances . . . to remark again the performative possibilities of writing itself" (pp. 148–149). Thus performative narration—an act of doing—can be a site in which the multiple guises of the body act out various interpretations or readings on contentious situations. As the squirming, signifying body repositions itself over and over under the mask, performing becomes a sorting activity. This rearticulation sometimes requires fighting our way out of the abyss, looking beneath the mask, confronting the face (Anzaldua, 1988).

Like Anzaldua, day in, day out, I sit before my computer staring into that black hole of a screen, trying to type the words that match my visions, my dreams. Tearing at the layers of masks I wear is exhausting work—work that does not leave me ready to sleep when I close my eyes at night. Breathless and filled with anxiety, I rush from my bed, searching for the door, for a window, for air. Images like hallucinations plague my half-sleep.

Over a beer one afternoon, I tell my Mexican psychotherapist friend about feeling like I'm on the edge of an abyss and that waking breathless is what prevents my falling in, tumbling forever into nothingness. He tells me I've read too much Freud. I say, no, there are palpitations; my chest feels like a heard of elephants is sitting on it, and I'm not asleep. But I can't wake up either. He says, "It must be depression."

I say, "Always the excuse, heh!"

He says, "That'll be 90 dollars, please."

We laugh, leave. Nothing changes. I sit again. Write again. I know it's me underneath, squirming. Tearing away at the masks.

In her book *Refuge*, Terry Tempest Williams (1991) writes: "I was taught as a young girl not to 'make waves' or 'rock the boat.' 'Just let it go,' Mother would say, 'You know how you feel, that's what counts.' For many years I have done just that—listened, observed, and quietly formed my own opinions, in a culture that rarely asks questions because it has all the answers. The price of obedience has become too high" (pp. 285–286). The price has, indeed, become too high!

Anzaldua writes of the sorts of transformations Terry Tempest Williams addresses—transformations that come only through the body, like Aztecan blood sacrifices. She says that "only through the body, through the pulling of flesh, can the human soul be transformed. And for images, words, stories to have this transformative power, they must arise from the human body—flesh and bones" (1988, p. 40).

What remains in this chapter is a discussion about the ritualization of the word (particularly within education) and the potential for transformation through the material body that may rupture the decree of the stamp (Benstock, 1991), the Laws of the Father (Kristeva, 1986a), and so on. Foucault (1972) describes the ritualization of schooling to which I refer in the next section. He writes: "What is an education system after all if not a ritualization of the word; if not a qualification of some fixing of roles for speakers, if not the constitution of a (diffuse) doctrinal group; if not a distribution and an appropriation of discourse with all its learning and powers" (p. 227). Ritualized classroom performances can be altered, but not generally without risk-taking and experimentation. I experimented with theater.

Earlier, work in autobiographical tale-telling taught me that students engaged in personal narration sometimes need a push to move beyond their egocentered positions. In other words, self-conscious narrative that is not also self-critical can lead to celebrating the victim, which (in my opinion) is not very helpful. Reflexive narrative, however, that looks beyond the self and critiques and, in fact, works to recast universal narratives that tend to script experience can be a productive and very useful activity. For such activities I have turned to concrete dramatizations—to what my students often think of as *play*(ing).

Though my goals have not been therapeutic but rather a search for methods of collaborating that promote archaeological digging, solidarity/ collectivity, and definitely a move away from the ritualized practices that have often heretofore governed my classes, the upshot of these activities has often been what Augusto Boal (1995) has referred to as "therapeutic theatre."[2] Boal suggests that theatric psychotherapies consist of posing alternatives. Since theater itself always raises many more questions than it answers, it has proven a suitable medium for my teaching goals.

My teaching project has been risky to say the least. From my perspective, identity work that helps students unearth the multiple ideologies that have guided their practices is worth the risk. What students have risked, however, has been much greater.

In opening a place for the sort of critical reflection required for acts of cultural recovery aimed at providing a window on the multiple locations from which voice and identity derive, students engaged in sometimes threatening possibilities. They often discovered that looking deeply revealed hidden differences and a variety of masks they were not prepared to deal with. My role as encourager and listener was seldom satisfactory to students who wanted answers; nevertheless, it seemed to facilitate a kind of solidarity among peers that my greater involvement may have prohibited. Of course, I had to take a more direct role in pushing students to ask harder questions. In so doing I sought to teach students to engage in self-critical reflection in an effort to prevent their narrative explorations from ending in solipsistic self-indulgence.

Ritual Performances and Transformative Rituals

Play, as opposed to ritualized practice, has a kind of transformative power (Boal, 1985; Kristeva, 1986a; Turner, 1982).[3] Play(ing) can disrupt ritualized performances of schooling as well as the essentialized mythologies that tend to guide "common sense" understandings of identity. In the scenarios described in the next two sections, students and I are playing with content and pedagogical form—our play may or may not be ritual.

Victor Turner (1982) insists that play breaks with ritualized behavior because it occurs in an "antistructure" or transitional location by which all other sites and/or categories are destabilized: "Play can be everywhere and nowhere, imitate anything, yet be identified with nothing. . . . [Play exists] betwixt and between all standard taxonomic modes, . . . [is] liminal, . . . interstitial, . . . elusive" (Turner, 1983, pp. 233–234). In *The Future of Ritual: Writings on Culture and Performance,* Richard Schechner (1993) produces a reading of Turner's work that shows contradictions "between Turner's theories of playful liminality and the ethological-neurological propositions" he forwards late in his career—contradictions Schechner says Turner himself recognizes (p. 256). Though Schechner admits to admiring Turner's perceptions of human experience and its "not-yetness" and agrees that Turner's vision of ritual performance is more like the process of deconstructing accepted texts to reconstruct new ways of doing/being than the specific ways of acting that mark particular cultures, he nevertheless reads Turner as dichotomizing ritual and play. Additionally, Schechner states that Turner's desire to find ethological-neurological connections between all cultures does not recognize the "genre-specific" ways that, for example, "[a] kathakali performer, a ballet dancer, [or] a noh shite" is marked by "genre-specific ways of moving, sounding . . .

being" (p. 257). Schechner also argues, "Hopi mudhead clowns . . . are also antistructural, but [are] always in the service, ultimately, of reinforcing traditional ways of doing and thinking" (p. 258).

Though I would argue that Turner does not dichotomize ritual and play so much as he suggests that play transforms ritual (it alters but does not necessarily invert)—that is, play transforms ritual performance into transformative ritual—and even though I too perceive that everything is relational if not connected, Schechner does make some important points respective to Turner's notions of play and to his sense of globalization. His rebuttal is this: "Isn't love-play or foreplay necessary to procreation? Doesn't play educate? And isn't the play of ritual clowns—like the playing of the superbowl [sic]—carefully orchestrated rather than 'freewheeling'?" (p. 25). Additionally, he points to some problematics associated with what Turner refers to as the "free-wheeling" nature of play. These are summarized as "play acts," which Schechner measures against six templates: "structure; process; experience; function; ideology; and frame" (p. 25). Schechner raises some interesting questions associated with these templates.

Perhaps most interesting is the question of ideology: "What values do play acts enunciate, propagate, or criticize either knowingly or unknowingly? Are these the same or different for every player?" (p. 25). A postcolonial critique of globalization would find any assumptions of unification political and therefore problematic.

Schechner's questions around ideological concerns might also be applied to Peter McLaren's (1986) study of schooling as a ritual performance and to the disruption of the ritual of "making Catholics" vis-à-vis what McLaren says is students' resistance articulated as play that occurs in Turner's "antistructure." Although McLaren addresses the ideological, he does not address the precise questions around play acts that Schechner does. (See Chapter 6 for a more in-depth discussion of Turner's and McLaren's works).

Previously, I have argued that performance narratives can be as much a part of ritualized classroom practice as any other aspect of schooling (Brunner, 1994, 1996, 1997). In this section I show some examples that I perceive suggest performance narratives per se are not transformative; rather it is the performative element of transgression in an "area of risk and salvation" (Kristeva, 1986a, p. 217), a free-wheeling and often playful element, *that can change the ritual of performance into a transformative ritual* (my interpretation of Turner's relationship of play to ritual).

The most important aspect of this section, however, is that the examples show individuals speaking from lived experiences and *not for entire communities,* resisting "the indignity of speaking for others" (Foucault, 1977, p. 209). I agree with Kobena Mercer: it is only when "strategic cultural and political choices . . . [are drawn from] experiences of marginality . . . [that] critical insights and interventions are made possible" (1994, p. 214). Mercer's cultural critique of the "restricted economy of representation," which essentializes difference by reducing minorities to a category of sameness, suggests that "critical dialogism," or what Cornel West (1990) has called the new "cultural politics of difference," calls for a "critical response that reopens issues and questions" instead of merely *celebrating* differences (pp. 214–215).

Moreover, West (1990) writes that "the new politics of cultural difference" is not intended to simply contest the status quo. Instead, "they are distinct articulations" made by those who would align themselves with disenfranchised peoples for the purposes of "social action" and, whenever possible, "to enlist collective insurgency" in the service of freedom. "The intellectual challenge," however, he writes, "is how to think about representational practices in terms of history, culture, and society" (p. 94).

Philip Auslander's (1997) work in performance theory addresses the representational practice of artistic production and its supposed antidote: performance. His conceptualizing of a nondichotomous relationship is not unlike Gloria Anzaldua's (1988) idea that "invoked art" can combine in powerful ways.

Despite the poststructural tendency to suggest everyday performances are presentations and not simply representations (Auslander, 1997, drawing on Derrida), my aim in the courses under discussion was to open places for a deliberate representation of history, culture, and society through what I am calling here *reflexive performance,* that is, performance that transforms ritual through critical reflection on everyday practice, performance that cannot escape narrativity and its preoccupation with time, performance that is played out against a backdrop of history, culture, and power. Auslander (1997), for example, discusses several arguments respective to theatricality as performance and theater as art form. Auslander cites work by Michael Fried (1967) and Josette Feral (1982) that suggests theatricality can bring forth a presence, the discovery of something new ("performance explores the under-side of theatre"; Feral, p. 176), whereas theater can only represent (Fried takes the position that theatricality is the enemy of art because of its presentness). Performance groups like Split Britches and the Wooster Group may be said to retain a "presentness" and explore the "under-side" of theater.

Likewise, in a discussion of visibility politics and the theater, Phelan (1993) claims there is power and value in that which cannot be represented, in that which remains "unmarked." Moreover, she says, "performance implicates the real through the presence of living bodies. . . . Performance clogs the smooth machinery of representation necessary to the circulation of capital" (p. 148). Yet Auslander (1997) is not so quick to dichotomize theater and theatricality that presents because of the "apparent collusion between political structures of authority and persuasive powers of presence" (p. 62).

Auslander's point is precisely the caveat that bears mentioning here as regards the everyday performances of schooling: what must always be considered is that the political nature of school makes all attempts to present something new a bit tenuous. In fact, it is never wise to discount that much of what students might offer as a presentation already lies in their "political unconscious" (Jameson, 1981a) as a learned representation of the world. The following scenarios, then, are not meant to "make the case," as it were, for performative transformations but to suggest some alternatives to traditional classroom interaction that may, if approached as possibilities for beginning the process of critical reflection, pique both the curiosity and interest of students toward the goal of recovering self-in-other/other-in-self, especially in terms of the interplay of history, culture, and power.

Classroom Contexts

The several courses described in this section shared topics and some of the same readings. Though readings reflected what might have been perceived as a survey course on diversity (i.e., readings were by African Americans, African Caribbeans, Asian Americans, Asians, Cubans, European Americans, Mexican Americans, Native Americans, one short story by a Scotswoman, etc.),[4] my intent was not to celebrate these authors (though they were worthy of celebration). My intent was to open tough issues and ask hard questions. One of the key questions in each of the courses, which Mercer (1994) suggests is key for our time, "concerns the cultural construction of whiteness" (p. 214).

A focus on the body and on the co-construction of race and gender underlined talk in both courses. In an attempt to focus attention more specifically on issues of race and ethnicity in the graduate course, I began class with a reading of Toni Morrison's *Playing in the Dark: Whiteness and the Literary Imagination.* Although the undergraduate course focused more on a kind of narrative inquiry respective to understandings of self with/in other and had as a primary component an end-of-semester theatrical production, the graduate course addressed topics of inquiry through writing. Topics of inquiry explored in both courses included the following:

- How is our perspective of "whiteness" constructed through literature?
- How do perspectives of "otherness" help construct our sense of Americanness?
- What "selective traditions" (from Williams, 1977) in literature help us define "whiteness"?

At first students in both courses seemed unaware that the question of "whiteness" was worthy of being a semester-long topic of inquiry. In many students' minds "white was white—what else was there to discuss?" In the undergraduate course, more than one student on more than one occasion asked why we were reading so many people of color when the class was mostly white (there were two young black women, and a graduate student sitting in or auditing was from Turkey). In the graduate course, one student apparently became so disenchanted with our conversation during the semester (as some of his early written work revealed) that he stopped attending class but never officially dropped the course. He did the same in another class—a literature course developed entirely around the writings of Toni Morrison. In both classes he could not recognize (or accept) the "many colors of blood" (McWilliam, 1993) residing in the construct of "white American."

Because white represents a cultural exchange that is predominately ideologically driven and naturalized through the effects of racism, students have seldom theorized "whiteness" as an ethnic identity. To do so is a difficult endeavor, as I learned. Yet as Mercer (1994) suggests, "The real challenge in the new cultural politics of difference is to make whiteness visible . . . as a culturally constructed ethnic identity historically contingent upon the violent denial and disavowal of difference" (p. 215).

This work is situated, then, in a diversity of attitudes among undergraduate and graduate students regarding the nature of their sexed, raced, and gendered identities (most are white women, only a small percentage are men and students of color, many are first generation college students, and many are prospective and experienced teachers). The undergraduate course was an elective course in the English Department; it was one among many courses offered to fulfill students' requirement for a diversity course within the literature curriculum. The graduate course was elective for students in the general literature master's program and required for students in the Critical Studies in the Teaching of English master's program (there were four students from the critical studies program and five from general literature).

Issues of racial or ethnic identity arose most often in the context of particular readings in both courses. Discussions were frequently tension-filled, challenging students and me to revise our understandings of what a multicultural curriculum ought to provide. Molefi Kete Asante's (1991) suggestion guided our thinking:

> Multiculturalism is [not] a matter of anecdotal references to outstanding individuals or descriptions of civil rights. . . . Neither acknowledgment of achievements per se, nor descriptive accounts of the African experience adequately conveys the aims of the Afrocentric restructuring. . . . From

> the establishment of widespread public education to the current empha-
> sis on massaging the curriculum . . . we are more likely to reach [a com-
> mon culture] when we allow the full participation of all ethnic groups in
> a quest for a usable curriculum. In the end, we will find that such a cur-
> riculum, like inspiration, will not come from this or that individual model
> but from integrity and accuracy (pp. 269, 272).

Thus I pushed students for a different sort of engagement with the curriculum—not one that left us smiling and speaking politely, but one that
led to lively debates and, unfortunately, sometimes dissolved into anger
and hurt feelings.

I wanted students' deliberate excursions into their own pasts to help
them begin to rewrite relationships between difference and power as reflected in their own experiences, assessing and attempting to disrupt institutional politics that tend to isolate, fragment, and marginalize. Such a
project, Henry Giroux (1994) suggests, ought to do more than "promote
self-understanding and understanding of others, it must work to create the
institutional, political, and discursive conditions necessary in which
power and privilege are not merely exposed or eliminated but are 'consciously rendered reciprocal' (and put to good use)" (p. 50). In suggesting
the recovery of meanings and practices over relationships of difference,
however, I did not want to suggest what Chandra Mohanty (1994) calls
"benign variation" or diversity that represents a culture of harmony or an
"empty pluralism" (p. 146).

Respective to whiteness and race/ethnicity as well as to sexuality/gen-
der, the central issue for these courses was not merely acknowledging difference but situating the question of difference politically as a struggle that
includes, as Stuart Hall suggests, "the 'play' of history, culture, and
power" (1990, p. 225). Difference as defined by Mohanty (1994)—"asym-
metrical and incommensurate cultural spheres situated within hierarchies
of domination and resistance"—is the understanding I tried to help students realize through the complex web of readings offered in each of the
courses that sought to bring to question issues of racial and ethnic identity
as well as sexual identity (p. 146). Building solidarity and/or collectivity
in such classes was a matter of struggling to develop alliances that were
pedagogic, agential sites where ideas could be "produced, reinforced,
recreated, resisted, and transformed" (Mohanty, 1994, p. 146). Narrative-
performative inquiry became such a site.

Both here and in my teaching, I apply Judith Butler's (1990, 1993) notions of the performative and Bakhtin's (1965, 1984) drama of the body to
link concepts of narrative performance with the notion of masks that layer
and mirror dominant representations inscribed by and in bodies, masks
that often scar both signature and soul. Butler's (1990, 1993) work de-

scribes a set of practices that takes place in the performance of identity where the ambiguous place of masquerade can as easily be a threshold or nexus for perpetuating status quo interests as for contesting it. Though Butler describes the masquerade as having ambiguity, she names performance as the subversive location for resignification or rearticulation. Seeing the performative as beyond binary codes, Butler suggests performance acts outside language as a means of displacing authority.

Yet Foucault (1977) warns that such spaces are like categories that are theoretically fluid; their fluidity can prevent fixity and simultaneously give the appearance of fixedness, spinning "false" stories (p. 185). This is why I perceive it is impossible to assume that all performance narratives mark a transformation of ritual.

For purposes of this discussion, I draw both on students' reflective writings and how they seem to perform and on students' dramatizations. Writings are often produced in response to particular pieces of literature; some student writings are autobiographical in nature and are used to script narrative theater productions.

Students' responses suggest both the potential and the limitation of performative-narrative inquiry to unearth the repressed shadows of students' individual and collective struggles to consider, critique, and possibly rearticulate identities. Because I study and teach the political nature of language as a terrain for contestation, I argue that multipositioned speaking subjects often speak, as Bhabha suggests, "with forked tongues" (1994, p. 54). That being the case, then, I perceive that much of what is said during class discussion is bound up in the very political nature of schooling.

Attitudes like "America is supposed to be a melting pot where, no matter what, you are American" prevailed. But occasionally another voice was heard: "If humans were raised with unrestrained sexual freedom and no gender roles, I bet labels like heterosexual and homosexual would not exist, or if they did there would be no negative connotations attached to either."

Strategies

In both courses I strategized with students ways into the readings. Though the sensitivity of some of the readings challenged students' sense of self, most reactions could be considered part of a ritualized response. For example, after reading an ethnobiography called *Growing up Gay in the South* (Sears, 1991) in the undergraduate course, one student, who was appalled at the age of some of the interviewees in the study, blurted out, "How did these informants know they were gay? They didn't even give themselves a chance to be heterosexual."

One strategy was a timeline with focal points at ages three, six, twelve, and fifteen. I asked students to try to recall what they were reading, watching, and listening to in each period on the timeline. Also, I asked them to say who they identified most with in their community, from books and from media. One student said she "grew up reading romance novels even though no one she knew lived in such a fantasy world." Another student sang the praises of talk-show host, Oprah Winfrey. The timeline was one attempt to move students to an examination of some of the means by which social and cultural messages are transmitted.

In another class period I asked students to "name their forbiddens." One student wrote that she would be "forbidden to have some of our course texts on her shelf at home." Another student commented vaguely on the overidealization of race in U.S. culture. This activity provided yet another attempt to focus on who we invest with the power to determine codes of behavior. Both activities were used as a lead-in to discussion of course material. Although most responses to the timeline and naming-forbiddens activities were somewhat predictable, often what followed in class discussions showed students struggling with their own predispositions toward issues raised in particular texts.

In the graduate course, after several weeks of twenty-minute introductory lectures on border intellectuals, one student referred to border-crossing characters in three novels as "witches" (Eriko in *Kitchen* by Yoshimoto, 1993; *Sula* by Morrison, 1973; and Fleur in *Tracks* by Erdrich, 1989). He said that he referred to these characters as witches because they "transgressed societal conventions in a very uncompromising manner." This student stated further that "subversive 'supernatural' characters are representative of the struggle all 'multiculturalists' are engaged in." In linking the ability to transgress social codes with a kind of supernatural power, this student disclosed his own logic respective to the fixity of status quo practices. Furthermore, in suggesting the supernatural had representativity with multiculturalism and discussing this notion around the writings of three nonwhite authors, he skirted the subject of racial identity while he seemed to betray his own unimagined relationship to race and ethnicity.

Yet several students' comments suggest the possibility that the texts, activities, and conversations in both classes had opened a *grappling place*, as speech-acts had produced a drama of interrogation (Bakhtin, 1986). One afternoon after class, a student confided, "I felt like a gaping wound that had been open for a long time had finally begun to heal."[5] And another student wrote in her journal, "Narratives of race should be complicated if they are going to be honest and if they are going to serve any purpose in terms of helping to articulate race in our culture." Still another wrote that "these books present the rough areas." Other responses from journals or in-class discussions were less profound but did seem to indicate awareness of an unlit corner.

Subject as Pedagogical Site

A pedagogy to deal with oppression uses the stories of the people involved as a rehearsal for more social action. The "theater of the oppressed" is a series of dramatic techniques for breaking up ritualized, mythicized forms—for social activism. Because teaching/learning and art are political acts, they necessarily involve inner subjectivities, drives, and desires that if nurtured can lead to moments of symbiosis. Drama workshops in which students do warm-up exercises and perform some of the techniques suggested by Boal (1985, pp. 127–156)—knowing the body, making the body expressive, theater as language, and theater as discourse—are places where the symbiotic can be seen.[6]

Boal suggests using story vignettes in performance or "narrative theater" to move beyond initial resistance to oppressive structures. He suggests dramatizing one's plight in order to find a voice in which to frame ideas, feelings, and protests.

The staging technique in the following example is "image theater." Boal suggests three parts to this technique. The first is to mime the actual image, the second is to mime an ideal of that concept, and the third is to suggest a transitional image, showing how one might represent images carrying out a change from one reality to another.

As a prelude to discussing Lorene Cary's *Black Ice* in the undergraduate course previously noted, I read a segment of Cary's text in which skin-shedding becomes the central metaphor for Libby's life. *Black Ice* is a coming-of-age story that details a young black girl's schooling experiences in a prestigious, mostly white boarding school—experiences that include a near date rape, an attempt to run away, and an eventual coming to terms with the impact of racism on past and present experiences as a person of color. As skin and skin-shedding are implicated in the turn of events in the protagonist's life, I invited students to begin to consider what central metaphor might be implicated in the major turn of events within a particular period of their lives.

After reading and discussing *Black Ice*, Shirley Muller, a former doctoral student, helped lead the miming technique of image theater. At the beginning of class we asked students to list three to five themes they saw running throughout the Cary text. Students listed these items on individual sheets of paper, and I tabulated them while Shirley listed on the chalkboard the five most commonly recurring themes from students' jotlists. The five themes were fear, alienation, sexual awakening, learning to trust self, and freedom.

Next we asked students to divide into five groups, and each group was asked to take a theme and discuss how the abstract theme could be concretized by acting. Shirley gave students about five minutes to discuss possibilities, then she asked them to think about how they might mime their ideas. We told the class that each group would have an opportunity to mime their word twice. During the first mime, groups were to mimic something from the text that related to Libby's life. The performing group was asked not to reveal the theme from which they were working in order to see if they could, without words, interpret the theme in such a way that the class could recognize it. After each group had an opportunity to mime something that depicted Libby's experience, they were asked to mime again—this time drawing on their own backgrounds of experience.

As students mimed their themes, they showed me—without their even knowing, I think—the nature of their oppression. The group that tackled the liberation theme attempted to mime their sense of Libby's escaping to freedom. Even in the first acting segment, when students were depicting Libby's experience, I sensed what Anzaldua (1987) has called a "crossroads," where cultural and political forces collide (p. 79).

In this scene Libby climbs out of her bedroom window to freedom. Throughout our discussions most students had claimed not to have known oppression, yet as their mime showed some had great difficulty as they pushed walls forward to find freedom; others found walls easier to move. Still other students held their hands over their heads to the ceiling in a gesture of carrying the weight of the world.

The series of demands placed on students at this interpretive juncture appeared to lead them to infuse their own understandings of escape to freedom with those of Libby's. It was unnecessary, however, according to the text, to show the degree of oppression that perhaps lay behind their modes of escape—hands trembling as they pushed on walls, arms betraying a kind of entrapment as they pushed forcefully upward at the ceiling. From the discussion that followed this acting segment, it would appear that students unconsciously placed themselves in the experience that was to be Libby's and in doing so exposed some of their own shadows through mime.

In the discussion period that followed this activity, some students seemed somewhat surprised by what Shirley and I along with many of their peers suggested we saw. The group that had performed maintained an ambivalent attitude with respect to their actions; even now I am unclear about what that ambivalence suggests. Nevertheless, I do perceive their ambivalence was somehow important. If the place of performance is an ambivalent one fraught with cultural collision, do performers always already stand ready to interpret what such ambivalence means? I suspect not. It is largely for this reason that I suggest that much of what happens even in the most out-of-the-ordinary teaching moments can at best only begin the process of critical reflection that may lead to further rearticulations. Yet it is relatively clear to me that what Bhabha calls this "third space" acts as a bridge from which something does begin to presence

(1994). In any case, the same culture (of which schools are one) that already (always) seems structured to prohibit transgression nevertheless can produce occasions for ambivalence that can lead to the desire to violate status quo ways of being and seeing the world.

Historically, formulations that systematically other all that is outside and privilege that which is status quo have flourished because of an assumption that there are certain acceptable ways to be, that other ways are perverse, and that truth (when we can find it) is absolute. Because dominant culture has based this assumption in its own brand of absolutism, ideas, language, and phenomena (as in concepts of discipline) are naturalized to seem "just the way things are."

Between the Masks

The undergraduate class, its final project a dramatic performance of narrative theater, moved directly from the Boal workshop to working with individually produced student narratives for purposes of scripting. We read only one more book during the semester, and that just prior to our performance at the end of the term. The weeks that followed were entirely given over to turning individual narratives into a class script. Though the process seemed somewhat painful to students at first, they soon became invested in the project so much that many of their differences of opinion during earlier discussions seem to fade into the background as they worked to produce a play.

By this time in the semester students naturally gravitated to the nearest people, those with whom they had been *sharing secrets* all term. The task was to strip-mine individual narratives for related parts that would fit together to form a single script. The class elected to form five groups; this grouping eventually became the structure of a two-act play (Act I with four scenes and Act II with only one scene).

When each student in a group had selected a portion of text with help from the group, the selected vignettes told a story, not a chronological story but one that held the vignettes together through a particular theme, motif, person, important event, and the like. In other words, their pairings needed to be cogent but not necessarily chronological.

The week after students began working with their scripts I was away for a conference, and I asked students to continue to work on the play with their groups. When I returned I was amazed at the amount of work the groups had accomplished. Scenes had been developed from the scripts with transitions written where needed, and students were ready to decide music and choreography, costumes, and sets.

My job at this point was that of technical director. For example, when the cutting and pasting was complete, I Xeroxed copies of each group's script so that everyone had a copy with which to work. When time came to arrange a location, I acquired a stage (for classroom purposes there was no cost). When students were ready to advertise, I produced flyers that they distributed around campus. I reserved spotlights, typed and Xeroxed the programs, made sure the required furniture props were available, and contacted the campus Instructional Media Center for the sound system (the cost of equipment, flyers, and programs was covered by the English Conference Fund). Students did everything else.

Students were consistently nervous about the production and occasionally lapsed into whining about their lack of know-how. For the most part, however, whatever they lacked in acting ability, the students made up for it in energy and imagination.

The collective auto/biomythography, now a play created from parts of individual narratives, had drawn the class together in ways I had not imagined through the goal of a common project. Of all the years of trying to teach for cooperative learning, this experience epitomized the spirit of collaboration like none I'd witnessed heretofore. Not the individual narrative but the collective one was important, and not for what it confirmed but for what it questioned.

Students titled the play *Healing to Wholeness*, which they performed on stage before an audience of parents and peers. I perceived the title especially appropriate since the experience did seem to mark a bringing forth of something new. Despite the fact that the play marked a kind of closure since it occurred in lieu of a final and was a summarizing activity, it seemed almost an opening instead, an awakening of sorts that issued from a sense of connectedness; it seemed to be a regenerative moment. Their performance, though assigned, was constructed in a place of freewheeling play, largely without my intrusion; students were my teachers in this instance. And their work seemed to transform what had been heavily ritualized classroom talk into a bridging act of cultural recovery.

Using a variety of performative styles—mime, dance, and some traditional acting with dialogue and the like—students dramatized self-discoveries through a coming-of-age motif. Choosing from among the themes jotlisted for their Boal workshop, the play articulated a series of trials. Trials were expressed as scene titles. Act I had four scenes: "Fear and Loneliness," "Becoming," "Needing Someone," "Faith." With only one scene, Act II was titled "Refugees—A Story of Awakenings."

The lines extracted below, spoken only by women, ended Act I, scene IV ("Faith") and seemed to suggest a kind of re*sign*ation, to use Butler's word, resignifying one's own understanding of self as woman—a signification that challenges traditional representations of sexuality. That is, by coming to terms with one's own gender/sexuality, the texts under discussion, and perhaps some shadows, students may indeed have begun to "break the mask of conformity," as Kristeva suggests (1992, p. 146). Here they spoke of the psychic pain of fragmentation and of having "pulled out the hurt and struggled":

> I tried to be like them but their being was heavy on my woman and my eyes shut tight and sealed them so,
> blind, I tried to be them, wanted them, couldn't.
> The degeneration of growing, my whole is in pieces, chunks and slices struggle to reform as I'm being pulled apart from the inside.
> And it escapes me, the freedom my desperation has afforded is not a freedom I have.
> I thought big, thought I was big got tired of trying to have the hurt bruised out of me and pulled it out myself and struggled (Healing to Wholeness, 1994).

One student's narrative (printed in Chapter 6) was the impetus for the title of Act II, "Refugees—A Story of Awakenings." A poem recalling a near rape experience ended Act II. With the cast forming a circle around another student, she read what may have been a prelude to transformation. The poem tells of the sickening silences that can surround the compression of spirit and the voice that fights back:

> Heart lays exposed, beating, shivering, outside my chest.
> What a fear it is to think I have internalized my mother's teachings.
> Huge, cavernous, black abyss swallows my soul and my anger mutely.
> I hear her rebuking my justified outrage, rebuking my absolute need— DESIRE—to fight back, hot and unrestrained, rebelling against ignorance and self-satisfying cruelty.
> Summer sky, age of 5, very strawberry curls, everything's turnin' upside down.
> Mommy, mommy, mommy . . . everything's crashin' round.
> Mother is afraid. Afraid of gossip and shame.
> Secrets, sickening, silences, surround, encompass, compress, the spirit.
> Mother is afraid, of me and for me because of my anger, my VOICE. She serves condemning rebukes because "You have no sense (child)," should "choose your fights wisely," and "Jesus turned the other cheek; always, ALWAYS, turn the other cheek."
> Fuck that.
> Never again.
> Innocent, trusting, child, I hate this. Curiously wandering, laughing, easily held captive—ated.
> Never. Not to me or my children. Keep your silence. I have work to do.
> Again (Healing to Wholeness, 1994).

Because students perceived this task as outside the usual (both the task and the stage literally created a new classroom dynamic), they may have been more capable of acting outside accepted modes of being. *After all, it was acting and acting is perceived as different from "real" life.* The literal stage and the metaphoric dimension here allow for wearing a different mask or no mask at all (but clearly suggest a mask could be worn); it allows for social commentary to be produced outside that which is understood as a *given* or taken-for-granted, and it allows for the disembodied, violated body to be reembodied and united with the spirit—a kind of liberatory symbiosis that can mark a transformation of shadows produced by both school and society.

As Thomas Moore (1992) suggests, "Shadow qualities may ultimately bring [us to our] proper, if mysterious and unpredictable, home." He continues by suggesting the importance of dealing with "the shadow" so that experiences are whole. Moore says that if "violence is the repressed life force showing itself symptomatically, then the cure for violence is care of the soul's power[s,] . . . [that is,] eccentricity, self-expression, passion" (pp. 89, 135).

In that regard, then, I perceive we need to assess how much of our work in the institution called school creates shadows and to what extent we are willing to create places for potential transformation. Indeed, how is such work valued in our departments, our universities, and by our colleagues?

Though I do not perceive that Butler assumes performance is transcendent or produces a complete alternative to the social and politically naturalized body, I do perceive she assumes a site that suggests a reassembling of resources regardless of how impure. Therefore, this ambivalent place of loosening and change may be paradoxical if and when it occurs with/in a system that typically perpetuates dominant discursive practices. Yet even if privilege is only tilted and not upturned, perhaps through protest and imagination we can begin to subvert dominant consciousness and break through our politically regulated social realities and see possibilities for change (Marcuse, 1978).

Here Anzaldua's (1988) concept of "invoking art" that revolutionizes is useful. Art that is by and for the people, that is, dynamic rather than static, that belongs to the performance not to the museum, can begin the process of cultural recovery.

No one was prepared for the response to the play; we were astonished at the supportiveness among parents, grandparents, and peers (the play was held during graduation weekend). Although many seemed surprised at the language and its explicitness in sensitive subjects, each of us was most affected by the emotional responses, which ranged from joy to pain. It suggested to us that the range of experiences presented in the play were not isolated; students sensed they were not alone in their feelings and experiences. For many it seemed the experience of the play may have opened topics for discussion that had not been broached before. This was both frightening and encouraging to my students. For most students, the performance and the collaborative work of preparing for it raised many questions about behaviors and attitudes.

I too am left with a number of questions from experimenting with narrative theater. Several are similar to those that Butler (1993) asks. For example, how does such work enable the "reformulation of kinship" (p. 240)? And how can a redefinition of home, which may include a reasoned consideration of one's identity, serve as a marker of *agency* and not a consequence that functions within traditional power structures (Butler, 1993)?

The work of the courses discussed in this chapter aimed at challenging racial, ethnic, and sexual representations that can lead to essentialized notions of identity. In the heteroglossia of conversations around body/texts, I saw students wrestling with their own myths of the represented "functional" body, firmly entrenched in institutionalized modes of being. Yet it was not only conversation but also miming that joined students in the common project of the drama of the body, a reflexive drama that attempted to defeat representation. The playfulness of mime, it seems, "form[ed] a bridge between . . . sharers which [became] the basis for understanding much of what [was] not shared . . . and lessen[ed] the threat of their difference" (Lorde, 1978, p. 5). Mimetic transgression, then, became the bodies' means of signifying, between the masks, the scars, and often the joys.

I perceive that radical praxis is possible through activity that begins the process of critical reflection, what I perceive is the first step in resisting fixedness. In fact, I proceed with the assumption that particular intersections of pedagogy and content can create a site through which ordinariness may be recast and through which shadows may be unmasked in order to recover what has remained suppressed. Again, I perceive this place to be what Bhabha suggests is a third space (Rutherford, 1990), where perpetuation of dominant practices may occur but where contestation is also possible and might eventually result in resignification. And although I do not agree that all performative *tasks* create engaged, critical negotiation or that all tasks that require negotiation are performative, I do perceive that when a particular space in a particular time includes the restaging of the drama of the body it may, indeed, reside with/in that which is performative.

I assume the potential for transformative, even revolutionary moments occur each time we create a place for imagining the unimagined, saying the unsaid, being that which has not been—re-signifying our politicized subject identities. *But success is never guaranteed.* For the drives, the passions, the subjectivities that might lead to revolution seem, with little doubt, in this society the least valued and most often silenced.

I want to make clear here that although some students in both classes seemed to overcome their initial resistance to discussing race and ethnicity in terms of what they perceived their own whiteness meant, and although most of the undergraduate students eventually seemed to enjoy the dramatic tasks, such assignments pose risks not only to students but also to teachers. It is frightening to self-disclose, and teachers must be prepared to deal with what such disclosure unleashes. For many teachers these risks may outweigh the potential gain that such a moment may offer.

If the work of performance, then, according to Auslander (1997), is to defeat representation, then the job of reflexive performance is not to simply restate the original formation but to make a genuine critique. The problem associated with such critical practice, however, is stated in Derrida's (1982) *Margins of Philosophy*. He writes: "To attempt an exit . . . without changing terrains . . . one risks ceaselessly confirming, consolidating . . . that which one allegedly deconstructs. . . . [But] to change terrain . . . by placing oneself outside, and by affirming an absolute break . . . [one risks] inhabiting more naively . . . [that which] one declares one has deserted" (p. 135). The blurring of distinctions that Derrida claims holds the possibility for radical revision requires something more than suggesting alternative cultural formations or simply identifying with an*other*. For collusion between performer and presentation cannot sidestep the power relations implied by particular identifications: "the postmodern theatre of resistance must therefore expose the collusion of presence with authority and resist such collusion by refusing to establish itself as Other" (Auslander, 1997, p. 63).

Useful critique, then, requires a kind of border literacy. As Trinh (1989) writes in *Woman, Native, Other*, "Trying to find the other by defining otherness or by explaining the other through laws and generalities is, as Zen says, like beating the moon with a pole or scratching an itching foot from the outside of the shoe" (p. 75). The job of reflexive performance is to resist the politics of essentialism.

Notes

1. Faigley's notion of stitching here recalls the contradictory nature of the ego-self created by Dr. Victor Frankenstein in the novel by Mary Shelley (1969/1818). In *The Annotated Frankenstein* Leonard Wolf (1977) claims the story is one of greed and pride, reflecting a "creator" syndrome. Wolf's reading is typical of meanings ascribed by other critics and is especially warranted given the book's perspectives drawn from myth (Prometheus created people from clay) and science fiction. Another reading, however, might suggest that the story is also reflective of Shelley's own life as a writer, shadowed if not displaced by her husband's (Percey Bysshe Shelley) writing life, making her creation in the novel a "polyphonic" rendering of her own *stitched identity*, which allowed her to talk about herself, escap-

ing the boundaries of her own perceived identity while integrating "the imagined rejoinders of others" (Bakhtin, 1984, p. 52).

2. In *The Rainbow of Desire* Augusto Boal (1995) describes many dramatic techniques. I have modified and used a number of the techniques he describes, but the one that comes closest to the type of experimental theater I refer to as narrative theater is his "cops-in-the-head" technique. This particular technique retells a particular story through the voices of a protagonist and antagonist. The audience (or what Boal calls *spect-actors* to indicate that they are active/acting spectators) interprets the actions of the role players, and someone from the audience volunteers an interpretation. Two spec-actors are selected from the audience to become the "masks" that the protagonist and antagonist revealed in their first role-playing. The spect-actors mask the behaviors they observed, then two more spectactors become masks to show what they observed within the second team of actors. This process continues until a variety of masks are revealed. The next step is to replace the spect-actors who have seen a number of masks (some of which have presented alternative ways of viewing the particular conflict) with the original protagonist and antagonist. The goal of this latter part is to see if the conflict changes and/or resolves dues to the new levels of awareness contributed by the audience of spect-actors. Though the specifics of Boal's therapeutic technique are different, the results of both techniques are similar; both have therapeutic value in that they combine memory and imagination in a psychic process. The effects of this process on the body and on the consciousness of the protagonist is that she or he becomes both subject and object simultaneously, both self and other simultaneously, aware of self and of actions. The decentering act of seeing the world from perspectives not one's own can be both liberating and exhausting. Yet this reflexive moment helps individuals to become more empathic; spect-actors "become empowered to penetrate into [the protagonists] lived experiences . . . feeling his[/her] emotions and perceiving analogies between their own lives and [the protagonists], when they exist—and they almost always do (only then will there be genuine *sym*-pathy and not mere *em*-pathy)" (p. 28).

3. The concept of "Play" is thoroughly discussed in Chapter 6.

4. See, for example, Maryse Condé (1992); Louise Erdrich (1989); Christina Garcia (1992); Kaye Gibbons (1987); Janet Campbell Hale (1993); Candia McWilliam (1993); Toni Morrison (1973); Fae Myenne Ng (1994); Jacqueline Woodson (1991); Banana Yoshimoto (1993).

5. That the student draws an analogy between "a gaping wound" and our narrative-performative inquiry, according to Peggy Phelan (1997), is because the theater invokes questions on the body: "The depth of the drama of the human body is made literal in . . . the hole in the body [that] is the physical mark of the separation between one and the Other" (p. 32). In *Mourning Sex: Performing Public Memories* Phelan argues that a focus on trauma through the analysis of different injuries (e.g., performances of Anita Hill and Clarence Thomas during senate hearings) can create a fusion that erodes the distinction between art and theory. She refers to this as the catastrophe of embodiment or living (in) skin.

6. I led students in a variety of "drama exercises" that placed emphasis on the physical/material body (exercises are suggested in Boal, 1985). The exercises of the "know your body" stage provide a method for physically interpreting differ-

ence. In other words, in the "slow motion race," I invited students to run the race in slow motion with the aim of losing. The last to finish was the actual winner. Finding balance in this race is largely reliant on the racer's ability to adapt muscles to the new task of not competing to get ahead; it's a matter of changing one's center of gravity. In the "cross-legged race," I asked students to rely on each other's combined third leg (two people stand side-by-side and entangle the center legs to form one leg). This movement requires trust and dependence on one's partner. In this position, if one student tries to move the legs independently, both fall to the floor. In an effort to move students to accept out-of-the-ordinary phenomena, the "hypnosis" activity required that students find partners and face each other. One participant places her or his hand about an inch away from the partner's nose without touching. This exercise requires complete concentration because while the participants are in close proximity they are not allowed to make physical contact, and in order to remain hypnotized, the responding participant must follow her or his partner, maintaining the original distance from hand to nose. Physically this activity loosens the body and requires positions that are out of the ordinary. In order to "make the body expressive" students have to abandon more common movements in favor of new ones. Here, I asked students to role-play different birds or animals and, without making a sound, mimic the movements. For example, the student playing the hummingbird made frenetic movements with her hands to mimic the rapidly moving wings as the hummingbird moves from flower to flower. Additionally, I encouraged students to make up their own activities that helped them loosen the body's musculature and express through the body. The goal of the "theater as language" stage was to open up the roles of spectators and performers and use them interchangeably, to create spect-actors. Boal proposes three stagings: the first is "simulatenous dramaturgy," a sociodrama in which a central conflict is acted and different resolutions are proposed by the audience, which takes turns acting out various solutions. The audience and actors continue to switch roles and act different solutions until all the solutions, suggestions, and opinions are offered in theatrical form.

Border Literacies, Body Literacies

Home is no longer the place I go to feel safe.
Home is no longer inside me.
I breathe in and feel blue sky on a crisp day rush into me,
only to exit like a sunny summer porch.

—*from a collaborative student script titled*
Communities and Boundaries: Places We Have Been,
performed May 1996

As a child I wanted to dance, but my working-class parents not only couldn't afford lessons but also didn't value dance, so I had to pretend. Up and down the front porch of my house, across splintered boards, I'd twirl on toes. I came to see that pretending was like rehearsing; like imitating, pretending is a form of knowing, that is, showing knowing through the body. I'd choreograph great ballets in my head at age five, but by age ten school and society, which was by then my world, taught me that since I hadn't taken dance I couldn't dance; since I wasn't a dancer and really didn't know classical music I hadn't choreographed anything. At twenty-nine I took dance for the first time. I imagined much that I couldn't do. But the dance was still in my head, in my senses. The sense-memory my body retained added much to my study, but too many years and too much flesh had created limitations that didn't allow me to match with my body what I thought/felt I could do. So today running has replaced dance and teaching/writing has replaced other art forms. But the lessons of child-hood play and schooling experiences have taught me much about how and under what conditions we imagine ourselves.

I have learned, for example, that I imagine myself—that is, I resist the essentialized, constructed identity that accompanies my academic life—best not necessarily in unexpected moments but in spaces, into which I am deliberately drawn, that nurture creative impulses (i.e., pondering the earth and its tenuous ecology while hiking, composing in my head while I run, interloping in another world while snorkeling). Yet I am not suggesting one cannot be creative amid routine or participate with/in the struggle against containment in everyday sites and situations. Indeed, I both problematize and think through possible solutions often in moments as mundane as folding laundry or washing dishes.

As E. Paul Torrance (1979) and David Perkins (1981) suggest, creative activity works to dislocate boundaries, and it is more often than not a conscious effort. I am suggesting, then, that how and when such moments occur is not fixed, and neither is the kind of identity one might construct in those places. Rearticulating identity may occur, indeed, with/in different sorts of disruptions; I do assume, however, that disruption is necessary for revision.

Stories of Albert Einstein's breakthrough or epiphany respective to the theory of relativity as he stepped onto the platform of a train, for example, have led many to decide that such moments just happen.[1] I don't assume such moments just happen or that Einstein's discovery did *just happen*. Einstein nurtured his creative genius, constantly working on formulas, theorizing, expanding accepted scientific principles to imagine other possible explanations for the time-space continuum (Schwartz and McGuinness, 1979). That an answer came to him like turning on a light bulb is not unusual. When work is constant, any break may create just the sort of disruption needed for re-seeing. Leaving and later returning to ideas is how many discoveries are made. And, possibly, the fact Einstein could communicate his ideas clearly was all that stood between him and a psychiatric ward. To the scientific community Einstein was an oppositional identity formed against traditional relations of power that valued particular scientific knowledge. He expanded the script Isaac Newton had formulated, extending scientific principles beyond what had gone before. He ruptured the code, disrupted contained boundaries, and suggested a new way to imagine and understand the universe even as many thought his ideas wrongheaded and his eccentricities a sign of lunacy (Gardner, 1993).

In a discussion on schizophrenia in *Steps to an Ecology of Mind,* Gregory Bateson (1972) theorizes that a break in logic—what he calls a quantum leap—is necessary to overcome the double-bind. Bateson suggests the double-bind is often created when children constantly receive mixed messages, a problem for persons of all ages. Bateson states, however, that the *way out* for those affected by the double-bind is to create *another* logic—what Bateson calls "unlabeled metaphor." This *other* way is, perhaps, analogous to a reasoned rupturing of codes or what the symbolic order means and how and what it represents, which, according to Kristeva (1986b), is an act that requires resistance to assuming prescribed roles and/or identities. (Though I do not necessarily intend an association with the pathological by drawing on Bateson here, those who aim to preserve dominant interests might suggest that anti–status quo attitudes such as those suggested in this book are a blight or pervasive disease on society.)

I do not intend a one-to-one correspondence between Bateson's unlabeled metaphors and the kinds of disruptions I suggest may re-present identity, though I suspect some of the metaphors needed to suggest other ways of being may be seen like out-of-the-ordinary discourse (because, of course, what is ordinary is dominant discourse). My point in drawing on Bateson at all is to suggest that an unlabeled metaphor suggests a displacement of dominant logic—that is why it is unlabeled. Indeed, to suggest anything contrary would seem unlabeled. For when we speak in terms of something being like one thing or the other, I perceive we mean that something is one way or another.

When students and teachers, however, create places for interrogating the kind of taken-for-grantedness that seems to occur naturally in representations that define and identify, then time-out disruptions—as when Einstein proffered a theory of relativity that extended scientific thought respective to quantum physics—may occur in ordinary classrooms through particular curricular moments. Imaginative moments that shape and have the potential to represent identities may occur in classrooms as well, especially through participatory art forms like filmmaking, dancing, dramatizing. Again, disruption seems fundamental to the ongoing process of identity-making and perhaps especially to constructing border literacies.

Butler's (1993) masquerade, which she theorizes is capable of rearticulating identity, and Kristeva's (1984) theorizing of the semiotic to disrupt the symbolic order seem to connect with Bateson's (1972) notion of a quantum leap. Change, however, may actually occur only rarely in quantum leaps and, perhaps more likely, occur in smaller steps and over a period of time. Despite this assumption, if and when change occurs that is so momentous as to call it a quantum leap it may relate to the sort of metaphoric thinking that can occur when worlds collide, rendering problematic all that is and allowing one to see in new ways, revising and spinning possibilities. Such a disjunction can, I perceive, create a moment of clarity or brilliance that engages the social imagination, that critiques what is, and surfaces possibilities for what might be.

Perkins (1981) spoke of it as an epiphany; Torrance (1979) suggested it in *The Search for Satori and Creativity.* Whatever one chooses to call it, I perceive it is suggested in the activity of re-vision, or seeing and seeing again (Berger, 1977). Whatever allows us to make sense of the double messages that inscribe bodies and borders is the meaning that comes closest to the disruption I attempt to articulate here.

In its sensuousness and artistry, then, performance showcases the signifying body, its drives and desires, the body's literacy: "the grammar of the body," writes Phelan (1993), works by metonymy. Although metaphor "works by erasing dissimilarity and negating difference . . . turn[ing] two into one[,] . . . metonymy is additive and associative; it works to secure a horizontal axis of contiguity and displacement" (p. 150). In this way performance, according to Phelan, is "capable of resisting the reproduction of metaphor," and the metaphor she is interested in resisting is gender (p. 151).

When performance is an act of cultural recovery, then, body literacies may morph into border literacies, rearticulating the ideological. Yet as a signifier of meaning, the body, inextricably bound to social and ideological codes/customs that coexist within the symbolic, *may* at once *reinforce* dominant ideologies. Body literacies/border literacies suggest identities that reside between the masks, walking between two worlds simultaneously—struggling always for memory against forgetting (hooks, 1990).

Evidenced in the desire to consume popular art forms is, I perceive, the desire to walk between two worlds, to derail time, to see the self in someone other and someone other in the self. That events in music, film, literature, and theater have the capacity to shift foci is indeed part of their seduction.

Though border literacies come through the body, performative disruptions are constructed in time-out-of-time moments. Such moments can derail sameness and create a place for otherworldness, a place in which the self reflected in the other and the other in the self does not negate the self-other but suggests instead a reappropriation of the very terms by which self and other are inscribed.

Similarly, and perhaps more interestingly, this means that no understanding of identity is complete unless perceived in both spatial *and* temporal terms. Suggesting, for example, that identities reside between the masks is a figural statement that connotes both temporality (in the between movement from mask to mask) and spatiality (in the concept of mask as a container or boundary marker of identity).

In other words, how my identity forms when I am not masquerading as an academic can be very different from how I identify at other times. This is precisely why I perceive that re-presenting identity is a performative activity (spatial and temporal), occurring between the masks. At times, for example, I identify as a hurried, frazzled mother trying to keep pace with a busy work schedule, looking for time to share a sensitive moment with my sixteen-year-old daughter. On other occasions, I identify as an eccentric who prefers isolation for my habits of mind.

I speculate on work time and try to work in, through, and around perceptions of time and space that allow imaginative energies to flow. I presume that if the corporate world wants automatons then it has found the best way to produce them: slot people into rushed schedules where no one has time to think; the result is conformity, possibly higher profit margins (productive stress, they call it). Nevertheless, such schedules can create perfect little worker bodies. The corporate university has discovered this as well. But at what price? And for whom?

Thus eccentricity is a luxury I sometimes give myself—not that I can really afford it, however. In any case, the body that acts perceiving boundless capabilities may, indeed, assume an identity that is inscribed in possibility, signing difference between the masks.

To unlearn "individualism" is also an important part in discovering moments for the release of border literacies. If we can link possibility to social imagination, we can link identity to community. Rearticulation of identity and collective action—an action aimed at putting an end to domination—may release community-oriented individuals for public life. Where the goal is social action in the wider context, fully present persons may identify private and public life as being a self-in-other relationship in the service of struggling for freedom.

In order, however, to unlearn "individualism," to link identity with community, recovery of the material body is necessary. In *Bodies That Matter* Butler (1993) articulates why bridgework is possible when a focus on body literacies is prevalent. By distinguishing linguistic self-disclosure (language governed by grammars) from performative foreclosure (language governed by the body), Butler links the sociocultural with the physical to establish a counterpublic sphere in which recovery of identity becomes recovery of the body and spirit. For Butler, recovery begins with the premise that the phallological order pathologizes bodies, and healing occurs when we can learn to construct identities through which new meanings and possibilities arise. Because gendered bodies, both male and female, according to Butler, are taught to perform (to define, to mean, and to practice) from a basis of white male privilege, foreclosure especially involves the embodied act of resisting domination in the lives of individuals. Indeed, in Butler foreclosure suggests denying the phallus, breaking the rule of mythologies that govern sex, race, and gender; it also means denying language that violates through its power to define. Foreclosure seeks to undo, for example, the violent marking of identity through images that are conjured in language and reproduced in the various media, miming killing norms (Butler, 1990).

Butler uses the word *foreclosure* also to distinguish a body literacy from literacy as a purely linguistic phenomenon. She says subject positions/identities are produced in language through "regulatory" acts, which define and therefore repress because "what is refused or repudiated in the formation of the subject [read: identity] continues to determine that subject [always read: in relation to object]" (1993, p. 190). Butler concludes that the masquerade that signifies what *appears* rather than what necessarily *is* may be the site most likely to permit subjects to transgress their social and political realities (Butler, 1990).

According to Butler (1993), then, although political signifiers designate subject positions, they are not descriptive; therefore they "do not represent pregiven constituencies, but are empty signs which come to bear phantasmatic [or appearance] investments of various kinds" (p. 191). The relationship, then, between subject positions or subjective identities designated by political signifiers and the performative function of the masquerade seems to lie precisely in what appears to be the promise or potential for openness, for bridging borders and literacies, for the signification of new meanings and possibilities—for political re*sign*ification.

The political resignification that is possible through performative bridgework offers the potential, then, for persons to signify a reality that is not one half of a subject/object, fact/value, true/false dialectic. The plasticizing effects of language that can violate reducing persons to essentialized, isolated, and fragmented images objectify the body not as a body but as a discourse about it. If the plastic force of language reveals the political, and the political reveals mythologies that assign women and men to essentialized categories, then the cultural and historical reveal the material.

"There is nothing more coded than the body," suggests Philip Auslander (1997, p. 91), quoting Herbert Blau (1983, p. 458). Bodies are as much spoken as speaking. Performance theory that denies the material body—the body that bruises, scars, eats, drinks, sweats, defecates, copulates, and so on—jeopardizes the body's ability to expose "the ideological discourses producing it" (Auslander, 1997, p. 92). Under the assumption, then, that the body's own literacies produce signifiers, the body that writes itself opens possibilities for resignification as a radical alterity—not of previous possibilities.

The goal of narrative-performative inquiry in my classes, then, has been to serve as a potential catalyst, rhythmically comprising likenesses and differences, sparking a desire for revolution, both for the rearticulation of identity and for the reformulation of kinship. Such a rearticulation is produced by both body literacies and border literacies. Indeed, as Butler (1993) states it best, it redefines home in *other* terms, "not solely that of whiteness or heterosexual norms, and in all its forms of collectivity" (p. 240).

Negating activities like those around performative moments establish a bridge, according to Bhabha (1994), "where presencing begins because it captures something of the estranging sense of the relocation of home and the world—the unhomeliness—that is the condition of extra-territorial and cross-cultural initiations" (p. 9). Moments such as those described here are what Bhabha calls "unhomely moment[s] that creep up on you stealthily as your own shadow" (p. 9). Displacing essentialism, then, is an unhomely moment when "the borders between home and world become confused, and, uncannily, the public and the private become part of each other, forcing us into a vision that is as divided as it is disorienting" (p. 9).

Performance negotiates border literacies, body literacies restage ritual and power in a range of "transhistorical" sites (Bhabha, 1994). Such reformulations are a marker of agency in spite of powerful strategies. Such a move seeks to forge "a future from resources inevitably impure" (Butler, 1993, p. 241) and to find symbiosis among individuals despite layers of difference.

The temporal nature of the aforementioned moves and formulations also has the spatial/temporal aspect I will discuss In the next two sections as an *antistructure*, or unbounded, uncontained place. I am never sure if teachers can promote such a structure since so much of our training suggests we do the opposite. I am fairly sure, however, that we must give ourselves a kind of conscious permission to "undo the proper" (de Certeau, 1984). I am also fairly sure such a change will require continual renegotiation. I never perceive that rearticulations occur easily, and I do not perceive they are necessarily singular acts. I do assume, however, that classrooms, which are not generally sites of collectivity, must be continually renegotiated as places for critical, reflective, even narrative-performative activity if the intersections between words and actions are to render *answerable signatures*. On the contrary, border intellectuals may emerge in spite of the system. If, however, classrooms are to operate on the verge, as Maxine Greene (1988) suggests, if they are to work at the crossroads (Anzaldua, 1988), then rearticulation of how we understand school must change.

The "Aesthetics of Curiosity" in the Theater of Resistance

In the theatre of resistance there is an "aesthetic of curiosity" (Mulvey, 1992), a curiosity that leads to looking for secrets that sometimes lie at the crossroads of desire and "the machine." Like the curiosity that fosters imagination in the growing-up spaces about which Bachelard writes in *The Poetics of Space* (1964), the theater of resistance relies on a similar curiosity—a playful, free-wheeling, socially imaginative space-time.

Free-wheeling play occurs in precisely the sort of unbounded space-time that Turner (1982) calls *antistructure*, the sort of place Kristeva (1986a) refers to as a threshold through which meanings are both made and contested. It is light and ambivalent; it can dupe those who take its meanings too seriously and in so doing play can transgress all manner of boundaries. Play occurs in the uncontainable semiotic space-time as an altering or thetic dimension (as Kristeva theorizes, 1986a). A willingness to play with arranged ideas, preordered structures, and presumably fixed institutions is the wellspring from which critical activity occurs between the masks, between the performance and masking places through which status quo rituals are transformed. Play occurs both in the "beyond and between," says Turner (1983), drawing on Bateson's (1972) work on the ecology of mind. For this reason, Bateson says play can evoke a metalanguage.

Three students combined lines from individual scripts to explore their unquiet, playful selves. Their project became an unmasking of surfaces as they located the nexus to their own theater of resistance. Following are some excerpts from their May 1996 script *Communities and Boundaries: Places We Have Been*, which explores everyday masks:

> My storied self speaks with more than one mouth. . . . I chose the mask out of fear, fear that I'd fall short of people's expectations of me if they knew of the "bad" things; fear of not being loved; fear I wasn't "good enough, not smart enough. . . ." I have lived my life with two faces: "the perfect child," the girl who puts on the bright face, covering over despair, the one who has the appearance in public of following all the rules but who breaks even shatters them in private. . . . Early on I got the message that love and silence were intimately connected. . . . But I no longer want to be quiet, polite, proper. I am angry, wild, loud, strong.

In spite of words that appear in opposition to silence, the theater of resistance here is not conceived in terms of a margin/center binary but instead is conceived as a place of relationship between contraries (spaces, modalities, etc.). Semiology is key in developing an alternate mind on what would otherwise be conceived as either/or. Similarly and despite scholarship that suggests differently,[2] Kristeva (1986a) posits the semiotic as an "illicit" place and the symbolic as the space of sanctioned Laws of the Father, yet she reads these locations relationally as a means of guarding against ideological *fixity* or the sort of containment that resistance seeks to disrupt.

Everything is relational in this analysis. If, as Foucault (1980) suggests, power circulates differently in different spheres of influence, then a relational reading of culture prompts the asking of questions such as those Trinh (1991) poses: She says we should always ask, Marginal in relation to who and when and where? Thus in spite of the fact that an alternate location would seem by its very design geared to subvert the supposed center, it is important to remember that thresholds or crossroads are places of critical activity, which is to suggest, as McLaren (1986) does, that meanings are affirmed and simultaneously denied, that practices are contested and perpetuated.

Such places are necessarily, then, both/and. Like Mulvey's (1992) mythic box, which contains powerful secrets that may reinforce a binary reading of culture (i.e., the release of "incivility" or "evils" that threaten to change the center), curiosity and imagination that leads to unmasking may provide, as Mihai Spariosu (1997) suggests, "a playful opening" (p. xii), or, as per Mulvey (1992), an "enigma." The place of resistance, therefore, is not conceived as marginal but simply alternative (even though the mindset of those with dominant interests might perceive any resistance a threat to center); it is a place of both/and that resists fixed margins and centers because it is a space-time of agential control with/in the circulation of power.

Moreover, Turner (1982) writes that "liminoid" production (or resistant activity) occurs in a critical space-time because it is outside of the binary work/leisure; it occurs in a free space-time as an ambivalent, free-wheeling activity. He says that even though universities are spaces of symbolic interaction they are also settings for experimental behaviors. This is not to say, however, that liminoid productions have no political significance just because they exist in antistructure space-time. Furthermore, Turner attempts to make clear the connection between play and liminality in order to further distinguish the liminoid from the liminal (the *liminoid* is critical production that takes place during *play,* as conceived here; the liminal is suggested in those who, or that which, easily pass[es] between particular borders).

McLaren (1986) also discusses liminality in "the care-free abandonment of students at play." Here in the antistructure, resistant students "undermined the consensually validated norms and authorized codes of the school" (p. 147). He writes:

> Organized resistance to school policy in the form of student unions or grievance committees is largely the preserve of the children of the ruling class. . . . Resistance among working-class students rarely occurs through legitimate channels. . . . This is because they are resisting more than just a formal corpus of rules and injunctions: they are resisting the distinction between the "lived" informal culture of the streets and the formal, dominant culture of the classroom. . . . Resistances were, in Turner's idiom, "liminal" experiences; they occurred among students who had begun to traffic in illegitimate symbols and who attempted to deride authority by flexing, as it were, their countercultural muscles (p. 147).

Students in McLaren's study were engaged in "liminoid production." In other words, they were not just passing between bordered codes and territories; they were mimetically transgressing the dominant order of the school. Classical mimesis, mimicry, or mime, according to Kristeva, is precisely noted as "the construction of an object . . . according to . . . verisimilitude" (1986a, pp. 109–112)—having sameness. In most ideology critiques, however, the word has come to signify "mastery of the narrative code" as in pure imitation (Fiske, 1978, p. 86). Nevertheless, mimetic, transgressive play in Kristeva's linguistic analysis of poetic discourse suggests a space for the mime to function as a corrupter of the symbolic order (in which the grammaticality of the sign-system functions). Mimesis can also mark the transposition from one sign-system to another (what is often called *intertextuality*) and in this regard suggests the displacement of single meaning and thus of representability. Mimesis and poetic language (what Kristeva refers to after Bakhtin as *multivocalic language*), then, *can maintain and simultaneously transgress*, questioning the "very principle of the ideological because they unfold [its] *unicity* . . . (precondition for meaning and signification) and prevent its theologization [read: as sacred dogma, the Law of the Father]" (Kristeva, 1986a, p. 112). In other words, poetic language and mimesis both reveal and conceal, both protest and are complicit in what they argue against, but in their complexity they unfold a practice through which "the signifying process joins social revolution" (1986a, p. 112).

Augusto Boal (1979) also notes the revolutionary potential of theater as a language. Among the artistic languages available for literacy instruction, Boal includes with theater photography, puppetry, films, and journalism. And because Boal insists on theater as language, he suggests it requires no special talent: "theatre as language [is] capable of being utilized by any person" (p. 121). In particular, Boal's work is in the service of the oppressed. Using theater as a vehicle for revolution, Boal works to teach oppressed peoples to express themselves. The main objective in what he calls the "poetics of the oppressed" is to help people change themselves from "passive beings in the theatrical phenomenon . . . into subjects, into actors, [into] transformers" (p. 122).

In a class where all the assigned readings were autobiographical renderings of a sort (letters, memoirs, ethnographic interviews, fictionalized autobiography, etc.), I asked students to explore some aspect of their previous growing-up experience (students were third- and fourth-year undergraduates).[3] I encouraged students to select what Cornel West (1993) refers to as a "conversion" experience (not in the biblical sense but as it applies to any life-changing experience).

The assignment followed a reading of Lorene Cary's *Black Ice* (1991). Cary's novel takes the reader inside the head of Libby, the central protagonist, to show how she internalized a near rape experience and racial abuse. We discussed this novel of transformation in terms of "the skin we're in."

One of the few males in the class (all male students were white) responded to the assignment through a series of metaphoric language plays. He wrote about a "special homecoming" and his own struggle with the skin he's in:

> I knew I had to go home, there where my parents wanted me. . . . I needed them, not just for financial support but for moral support too. Well, I'll tell you about moral support and about homecomings. Here's your fucking moral support. I saw Jesus sitting on the side of the road this afternoon. He was wearing glasses and a white shirt and white pants and he was talking to himself. He said, I am Jesus, and I'm here to save the few souls left in this world who are pure, who aren't choking on sin like vomit. He said, I'm here to destroy all liars, sinners, and blasphemers. Are you listening to me? What do you think would have happened if he'd gotten his wish? Do you think there'd be anyone left? Thank God they dragged him away by his fingernails, screaming, and took him to a loony bin. There's your moral support for you.

Though his narrative alludes to myth, is written metaphorically, and seems to mask his own place in the story, he does, I perceive, make clear his lack of support at home and the moral indignation with which his words are met. His larger piece was titled "Refugee."

This student's story reminds me of Audre Lorde's (1978) suggestion that the power of a common project can transcend differences. Sometimes the only community or "home" students can find or redefine is the one they find with each other over common projects. And sometimes, as in the particular case of this class, students learn that understanding who they are can be as oppressive as it can be liberating. Yet by exposing fictions that help construct the masks by which lives are often identified, sometimes commonplace taken-for-granteds are recast.

The homecoming story also illustrates the performative nature of playful language to disrupt "common-sense" narratives. The language here is mimetically transgressive, displacing if not corrupting the representability of the narrative of "home" as a safe place. His intertextual allusions transpose meaning to both reveal and conceal, to both protest and share complicity. In their complexity, these few words from the homecoming performance narrative unfolds into a "signifying process" that aligns him with "social revolution" (Kristeva, 1986a, p. 112).

Boal (1985), however, carefully distinguishes between fictions and lived experiences. He agrees that while performance in itself may not be entirely revolutionary, it can be a rehearsal for revolution. And even though theatrical action may be a fiction, it is nevertheless action, and change requires action. Mimetic play, then, according to Boal (1985), Kristeva (1986a), and Turner (1982), can disrupt ritual.

From Ritual to Play

Like Turner states explicitly and Boal implies, Kristeva (1986a) suggests that playfulness can render transgression. She says that the aesthetic realm of art functions primarily as a site of transgression for disrupting the ritualized symbolic order: in fact, "crossing that boundary is precisely what constitutes 'art'" (p. 120). The artist at play, as if a child at play, is the most transgressive element in society (Bakhtin, 1990; Kristeva, 1986a). Artists, then, are positioned in the place that Benstock (1991) and Williams (1977) refer to as the overlap between textual spaces and cultural spaces.

Likewise, hooks and West (1991) suggest that the Western preoccupation with power might be upended through Play, with a capital *P.* They suggest that perhaps the most threatening thing unquiet activists can do is laugh (the regenerative, profaning carnival laugh that Bakhtin suggests; 1984) in the face of power structures. They suggest that the spirit of Play "serves to mediate the tensions, stress, and the pain of constant exploitation and oppression" and may be our immediate hope for derailing the pathological linearity of corporate America and its bottom-line mentality (1991, p. 77).

Play is the dance of the body, when the self-in-other and other-in-self is most fully achievable. In this way play transgresses the sort of thought that perpetuates divisiveness (Bakhtin, 1993). Playing is an event that changes, that transforms rather than conforms. Play is a place of imagining rather than imaging. In this sense play does not seek to imitate so much as to create; it does not seek to represent so much as to present. Play, unlike, art is not answerable to the status quo; it may be answerable, therefore, to a completely different set of rules, to antirules as it were (Bakhtin, 1990).

The following is an example of the sort of Play that intervenes and shows the ordinary in a new light, Play that is answerable to a different set of rules. It is why I suggest that border literacies are interconnected with body literacies.

I teach an academic-year doctoral seminar that is a topics course in critical studies in the teaching of English. Students in the course are usually experienced teachers. Performative/narrative inquiry was the topic for the 1994/95 school year. Teachers attending this seminar performed radical theater as cultural intervention (Kershaw, 1992) for their 1995 year-end project. We met on a Sunday morning in the middle of the foyer in Morrill Hall, the building where the English Department is located. Students arrived early, and over the entry they draped brightly colored tapestries of African cloth for decoration. Several students were beating coffee cans tightly covered with pieces of leather. The words of an African song was taped to one wall, and a student from Swaziland was teaching us the words to chant to the beat of the coffee-can drums. In the center, where group members who were not beating drums sat, an altar was created with burning candles.

Articles such as lipstick, a bra, and cards with words like POWER, SEXISM, RACISM, and the like were placed around the altar. Lifted up in their text were passages or cycles of life that are often marginalized, especially women's passages (out of eighteen students, two were white men, two were African American women—not counting the African woman from Swaziland—and the rest were white women). Students invested these places with childhood memories, men's and women's memories, memories of love and loss, of pain and happiness.

From seeing the first douche bag to experiences caring for a mother or grandmother who had become ill—marking a role that is often the duty of a daughter—the narrative rendering of the script in vignettes was only loosely connected with this recurring phrase read in unison: "This train is about to derail." Sentences like "Just forget laundry. If you do wash them, the smell just gets sealed in; the rustling clothes send their messages" and "I tremble for I too have lost my home" were interspersed between the unison cry, "This train is about to derail." Chantings and quiet speech marked lines like "I look at people's eyes and wonder if they know what my eyes have been through" and "I would like to speak to the eyes of the child that stares at me with sadness" and "I use my power and then sometimes stand contrite as I scratch the rust off corroded memories and discover reasons for who I am," always concluding with "This train is about to derail."

In the eighteen-page script sliced from individual vignettes are the terrifying and sometimes prophetic visions teachers need to remember in order to recognize themselves beneath masks that both protect and deny. Here the ordinary and the extraordinary frame the stories lives tell and add meaning to the communal struggle for change.

If the bias in artistic production is the ideological representation of signs, then the reflexive performance of teachers struggling to recall can be seen as a presentation—a bridging or bringing forth, an uncovering. Not that these experiences were not drenched in everyday representations that mark ideological difference and theatricality; they were. But here difference was examined, turned on itself, and rendered a special instance instead of common experience. Here, as in the homecoming narrative and the combined script about moving beyond silence, difference marked a presencing of something new, something with the potential "to destroy the binding or absolute status of any representation" (Jameson, 1981b, p. 112).

In the disruptive moment of Play with African drums and chants in the background and students encircling an altar with burning candles, one of my colleagues walked by. The next week, at faculty meeting, this same colleague said, "So you're doing pagan rituals with your classes now!" I said, "No, we were doing experimental theater" (Boal, 1985). He replied with a question: "There's a difference?"

Teachers shared more than their lives as they experimented with theater. Teachers demonstrated once more that the complexities of life and work necessitated their being intellectuals, not in the sense of academics or because they had special intelligence but because they found it necessary to be activists for the children they taught.

Who, then, cuts the border? Many can and will, but I especially perceive that teachers must. That special group of people with whom I most often work, English teachers, must be intellectuals (Giroux, 1988), that is, teachers must be intellectuals in order to displace all of the systemic social and administrative deterrents to teaching and learning. Displacement is necessary because social and administrative issues/concerns/agendas are seldom the same as teachers' concerns. In other words, administrators serve many interests other than the best interests of students and teachers, and teachers must advocate on behalf of students. There is little, then, that a teacher whose greatest concern is the welfare of her or his students can do but be an intellectual. That, of course, does not mean every teacher will immediately contest hindrances that interfere with teaching and learning. Yet I have every faith that teachers who have students' best interests in mind will eventually find a way to help students question the taken-for-grantedness of language, school, and society. A critical pedagogy of narrative-performative inquiry can help teachers displace interests that do not serve the best interests of all children, and it can help them interpret social and academic issues for wider public spheres of influence.

The following is an excerpt from a script performed at the close of another doctoral seminar on critical studies in the teaching of English (May 1996). Texts in this seminar focused on issues of race, gender, and ethnicity and worked toward a critique of "whiteness" in school as an institution. Readings for the course were almost entirely narrative and written by indigenous peoples, mostly women. One student combined this script with others in a small group to perform with masks what were "threads, webs, disjointed poems, stories, a weaving together of lives":

> Our teaching templates are etched by "white" design, and political correctness oozes from every pore of the system. This perplexes me: Do I endeavor to lead kids to the hard questions, to help them unearth the "grit"

of our fractured ideologies, to expose them to the faces of pain and injustice—to "the real stuff"? . . . The big-picture—that of spirit and self and finding one's collective place in the world—is scrapped in assemblages of packages, of things to do. Prospective activities which trivialize the real task of learning about what it is to be human. To be a good person. School remains a place of and for programs not students, for classroom not in the world. It's about appearances and how kids score and where the money's coming from. And it continues to be about separations: administrators and teachers, teachers and students, schools and communities. Sometimes I catch myself wanting to blurt out, "Oh, get real! Speak in plain language and tell the truth!" ("Threads, Webs, and Tales of Woe," 1996).

Mark Twain urged us to tell the truth. He said it will confound your enemies and amaze your friends.[4] Often dramatists and other artists perform for the purposes of legitimating the prevailing order (Turner, 1982), but here students were not seeking to legitimate but to critique, to displace, to liberate. They were liminal subjects participating in liminoid production, to use Turner's phrase (pp. 41–44), that is, they did not "invert or profane reality [through] myths and folktales" (as one might possibly read the homecoming narrative to have done). Teachers sought to tell the truth, not Truth as in something absolute but what for them and their students' practical situations was *truth*. They sought not the "reversal . . . of workaday socioeconomic structure or . . . a rejection of 'necessities,'" but the liberation of human capacities of cognition, affect, volition, creativity, etc., from the normative constraints incumbent upon occupying a sequence of social statuses, enacting a multiplicity of social roles, and being acutely conscious of membership in some . . . group [/faculty]" (Turner, 1982, p. 44).

Students chanting repeatedly "This train is about to derail" may have signified the same urgency as my student's "Get real." All seemed to recognize the need for something profound to change, to liberate human capacities. And yet as with any truth, if it is not *the* presumed Truth, it might not only confound but also confuse, distort, and anger. Any truth in the academy, I perceive, may indeed be disarming.

Signifying through Play, then, does not mean trivializing various hardships caused by economic and political strife; as hooks and West (1991) suggest of Play, it is one of the body's coping strategies. It may be a way of articulating that which is not possible through purely linguistic means; it may be a way of recognizing the "architectonic" wholeness of a life that cannot exist for-the-self-only but whose daily advocacy is with others (Bakhtin, 1990). It may be in this theater of resistance that the unquiet self Plays, experiencing a timeout in which conversion, as West conceptualizes it, becomes possible (1993)—not a religious conversion but a renewal of the human spirit that gives one the capacity to reinvent/re-present one's self-in-other. I perceive this conversion lies in the imaginative and in the performative—an agential place of space-time that is always open, a place where neither time nor truth is linear, with a discourse that short-circuits the hardwired systems of thought that bind traditional ideologies.

In this place "the sacred and the sensual . . . live very near one another in the psyche, for they are brought to attention through a sense of *wonder* [also read: curiosity], not from intellectualizing but through experiencing something . . . that for the moment or forever . . . takes us to a pinnacle, smooths out our lines, gives us a dance step, a whistle, a true burst of life" (Estes, 1992, p. 342). The unquiet self, I perceive, can be discovered; indeed, it already always resides in the body's own literacy, where performative action may give way to transformative, critical reflection—the critical move from ritualized performance to transgressive ritual or Play.

Notes

1. This story was told by E. Paul Torrance in 1983 at the University of Georgia in a course on creative thinking.

2. Mihai Spariosu (1997), for example, suggests both Turner and Bakhtin discuss liminality in terms of movement between margin and center, "with the margin either reinforcing the center or undermining the center" (p. xii). I especially do not agree with Spariosu's judgment in the case of Bakhtin, whose entire corpus of philosophical inquiry insists, as strongly as Kristeva's suggests, the need to resist containment, to resist a single "truth," to resist a singular perspective on human characteristics/behaviors. Also respective to Turner's work: in *From Ritual to Theatre* (1982) Turner discusses liminality in relation to binary structures but suggests play that can escape binarisms because it is defined as not "mattering" or "irrelevant" (p. 29). (I suspect, in fact, that "irrelevant" is how students' resistance to the orthodoxy of the Catholic Church was considered in McLaren's (1986) ethnography.) In *The Wreath of Wild Olive*, however, Spariosu does make an intelligent argument for undoing the margin/center positioning of literatures by suggesting an alternative place that is neither margin nor center but a "a playful opening toward alternative worlds that are incommensurable . . . or passageway from one historical world to another" (p. xiii)—a borderland, a place where, as Bakhtin suggests, "the most intense and productive life of culture takes place" (1986, p. 2). He rejects the artificial categorization of canonized Western literature as center and what has been termed "third world" literature as marginal. He describes criticism as play in a "no-man's land" (p. 302) He is accurate, I perceive, in naming this a problem of modern thought or Western discursive practices more than literature. I do not agree, however, that it is possible to remove issues of power from language and practice or that a countermemory of "primordial peace" escapes the circulation of power; rather, I perceive Mariosu's question and my own to be a matter of relationships betwixt and between issues of power, history, and discursive practice.

3. This is the undergraduate class under discussion in Chapter 5.

4. I have no idea where I read or heard this, so I cannot give credit where I am sure it is due—one of the best and worst artifacts of the collective nature of language. My apologies.

Coda
Critical Teaching
and Theatricality in Everyday Life:
A Reflexive View of Performance

In *Masks of Conquests* Gauri Viswanathan writes that the Western literary curriculum is as much about things unseen and unsaid as it is about interpretation (cited in Marshall, 1996). According to R. H. Marshall (1996) of Featherstone High School in London, England, the Western canon is a culture site first developed in colonial times to reinforce claims of the superiority of Western cultural hegemony. This debate over the English curriculum, then, is as much a "space issue" or one of boundary maintenance as it is a "text issue," says David Sibley, in *Geographies of Exclusion* (1995): "Difference in a strongly classified and strongly framed assemblage [read: Western canon] would be seen as deviance and a threat to the power structure. In order to minimize or to counter threat . . . spatial boundaries would be strong, . . . a consciousness of boundaries and spatial order" (pp. 80–81).

Spatial organization (especially read: as boundary maintenance) suggests questions of what counts and who decides. Spaces are not empty or innocent, although they do often give the impression of fixity. Time, in contrast, can suggest movement, a dynamic, the possibility of change—an opportunity to cross borders and extend boundaries.

Spatiality and temporality conceived as space-time or place between the masks in this text, then, is important in the multicultural revision of knowledge and curriculum. Though I assume teachers can teach students to read the world between the lines regardless of the literature by offering new readings that resist easy oppositions and by exploring the complex and diverse relations within those texts, multiethnic literatures and media materials can provide many contemporary and relevant opportunities to engage difference in terms of community rituals in other crucial houses of knowledge that make and mark identities. Likewise, performance pedagogies that connect and reframe disciplinary "homes" (Dolan, 1993) can also mark a crucial location for the revision of knowledge and curriculum.

I agree with Laura Perez (1995), who suggests that the knowledges of a culture are both embodied in and produced through the community rituals of schooling and the popular culture. Indeed, Perez suggests it is an irony that the same conditions that create and thereby contain particular visions also make possible potentially liberating practices. She refers to this "fertile compost" paradoxically as a "borderland fund" that can simultaneously function to contest dominant culture even as it so often reinscribes the mental and material practices that ensure a single vision of society.

Because universities (and, in my particular case, English departments) are often perceived as crucial sites of knowledge where the initiated uncover, recover, transmit, and reproduce, educators who resist the domination of traditional paradigms can invoke transgression and the deliberate evasion of dominant codes that can assist in the revision of a multicultural/multiperspectival curriculum. Instead of valorizing Western logic as *the* single perspective—one that works through much of Western literature—I perceive that culture studies and performance studies offer a timespace disruption, that is, they create an opening through which to cross borders and extend boundaries.

Culture studies and performance studies conceived in this manner distinguish high culture from low but are based on the premise of producing readings over a range of crossdisciplinary texts from print to film to music to theater event, and so on, using a range of methodologies from Marxism to post-Marxism to feminism to postcolonialism to semiotics.[1] The hybridity of the discipline itself, then, is a site for critical practice in which students from all disciplinary fields bring significant cultural experiences on which to draw. This interstitial opening, which may be perceived as a "crack" to traditional boundary maintenance, may promote the rupture of sexist and heterosexist, racist, and classist images (Brunner, 1995) and other ideological biases in order to connect, to reciprocate, as Stuart Hall (1990) suggests, in spite of incommensurable differences and social logics. A critical pedagogy or "problem-posing" education that takes peoples' "histories as their starting point" (Freire, 1970, p. 65) along with creative in(ter)ventions such as those described in the performances in this text can place classrooms on the very threshold of change, where anything can happen—what Maxine Greene (1988) calls the "verge."

But critical projects of schooling need to make clear the teacher/researcher/author's own agenda and complicity in institutions based on hierarchical structures that dominate and thus can disenfranchise. To "act naturally," especially in the school, is perhaps to simply conform to ritualized, expected behaviors; to "fantasize" the possible, in contrast, may involve our deepest impulses (Shepard, 1984, p. 8). To recover one's life through story and performance is, indeed, a dramatic moment.

The theatricality in such moments may deny dominant representations, bringing forth something new, or it may, as Auslander (1997) suggests, simply expose the collusion between action and political/economic relations. Despite the reflexive view of performance discussed throughout this text, reflexivity in and of itself is not an "access to truth" (Auslander, p. 84).

This reflexive view of performance demands one to consider the rhetorical problematics of performance, and it requires examination of the institutional practices that both affirm and deny experience. For example, Conquergood (1991) suggests[2] it is especially important to ask: "What kinds of knowledge are privileged or displaced when performed experience becomes a way of knowing, a method of critical inquiry, a mode of understanding"—such as in the proposed narrative-performative inquiry of this book. Also: "What are the conceptual consequences of thinking about culture . . . as unfolding performative intervention instead of a reified system. . . . What happens to our thinking about performance when we move it outside of Aesthetics and situate it at the center of lived experience?" With respect to performance and hermeneutics, he asks: "What are the range and varieties of performance modes and styles that can enable interpretation and understanding?" Moreover, respective to the politics of performance, Conquergood asks: "What is the relationship between performance and power? How does performance reproduce, enable, sustain, challenge, subvert, critique, and naturalize ideology? How do performances simultaneously reproduce and resist hegemony? How does performance accommodate and contest domination?" (p. 190).

A reflexive view of performance forces me to admit that although many dramatic moments unmask, they do not all seem liberatory; neither does critical teaching always feel empowering—at least not at the moment in which a negative function of ideology rears its head. Earlier in this book I quoted Trinh's (1991) charge to always ask about marginality and privilege relationally; likewise it would, I perceive, be wise to do so in this instance. In other words, perhaps one should always ask: Libertory for whom and empowering to whom? And when? And where? Perhaps one should seek to understand the silences created by such moments as well as the outbreaks? If a "performance paradigm" (Conquergood, 1991) is to be truly useful as a way of understanding classroom/

cultural enactments, then it must offer a way of critiquing inscribed textualisms.

Many years ago Elizabeth Ellsworth (1989) wrote in *Harvard Educational Review* that critical pedagogy didn't feel empowering in a situation in which a single voice took over her class; there was much debate over what strategies she might have used to displace the single voice who took up all the speaking space. I have since encountered a similar experience, but I find in that moment it is not necessary to abandon my longtime, comfortable approaches in order to call a timeout and say enough is enough (e.g., seminar format discussion, allowing everyday experiences to enter the discourse of the classroom, encouraging students to question course reading materials, inviting disagreement, and providing an agenda through readings and additional course materials that call the question on status quo interests and threats to critical thinking).

Though I agree this call smacks of authoritarianism, I have no qualms about admitting that a degree of authority already always exists in my classes, even when my approaches aim for critique and free speech. Although students set the agenda for discussion through leadoffs[3] and discussion topic generation, I select the readings. I am, indeed, often complicit in the power structures I rail against (perhaps I even needed to write this book in order to recognize how difficult it is not to lapse into essentialist habits of mind); but this does not seem to preclude or interfere with critical teaching anymore than if I didn't recognize the illusive nature of authority. Indeed, I would say the latter may be construed more as hypocrisy than naïveté.

Like Greene (1995), I teach for openings. Sometimes those openings are confrontive encounters that result in chaos. Sometimes, I perceive, those openings can plant seeds of change.

In this particular moment, drawing on a critical approach instead of abandoning, leads me to try to understand the position from which the student speaks, to use this moment in my frustration as a bridging or presencing of something else (Bhabha, 1994). If, indeed, critical teaching begins where the student is, with the student's own history, then the challenge in such moments is to suspend judgment and work strategically.

The dramatic moments that occurred in a recent composition theory course (populated by experienced teachers), when a student lashed out by digging in heels conservatively against the class, suggested new opportunities for critical action. When a student turned on his classmates over a discussion of multicultural education and began to hammer out a position against affirmative action that used up nearly two hours of the three-hour class, it became clear to me how unaware this student was of his own social construction. Like Althusser's "constitute[d] concrete individual," his rhetoric functioned to ensure his compliance in a hegemonic system that recognizes no human agency (1971).

Here a working-class, white male perceived his inability to get what he defined "regular" teaching jobs as the fault of affirmative action. He could see no connection between his own subject positioning and the rhetorics or discourses and discursive practices that he deployed and allowed to self-define. He did not see how the church, the school, even the state prison system—for which he now worked as a teacher—were all ideological apparatuses with specific rhetorics. Furthermore, in a composition theory course where much time was given to the discussion of rhetorical traditions from a theoretical perspective, he could not see that the purpose of theory is to ask how discourse is received and what are its motivations.

The anger and angst that filled the room during this dramatic performance—his own and the students', who must have felt under attack (women and other ethnic minorities)—created a place, however, for a series of critical conversations (between him and me and among the other students in the course and him) about politics and university studies, about students' rights (his own and others'), about change that displaces rather than simply inverts, and, most importantly, about multiperspectival approaches to pedagogical content. Although it is never clear how much unmasking occurs in such dramatic moments, it is clear, to me at least, that none of us walks a clear line. In other words, we live between a variety of masks, many of which are so seamlessly sewn together that we do not recognize them as masks.

By the end of the course the student was still angry—not so much with the class or me but with the world in general. And I did not discourage this, even though I did not agree with the source of his anger. For there is, indeed, much to be angry about, and anger is generally a marginalized emotion. Although he very much disliked the literacy politics of Paulo Freire and Donaldo Macedo (*Reading the Word and the World*, 1987)—primarily, I think, because they announce themselves as socialists—he did seem to understand that the difference between having a functional literacy and a critical literacy was the ability to use language to get things done in the world, as evidenced by editorials he had written and diatribes he had voiced in the class.

Critical teaching does not preclude my sense that there is no place for fascism in the classroom. I will not allow students to beat up verbally on one another. Intellectual bullying is far from critiquing ideas. I do want students to know they can disagree with me or with any idea in any text I select for course readings. I will always, however, draw the line when one person's personal agenda, regardless of its content, takes over the class. This position, I presume, does not deny critical teaching but instead in-

serts a reminder that critical teaching is strategic teaching and that pedagogy is as much about ethics and alliance-building as about content.

Tony Bennett's (1986) notion of "strategic alliances" seems appropriate here. In the chapter "Popular Culture and the Turn to Gramsci" he
writes: "New cultural orders . . . [are not simply] imposed mass culture
that is coincident with dominant ideology, nor simply of spontaneously
oppositional cultures, but . . . area[s] of negotiation between the two
within which . . . dominant, subordinant, and oppositional values and elements are mixed in different permutations" (pp. xv–I). Negotiations are
key in Bennett's alliance. I perceive they are key in all alliances. Not con-
sensus, not even dissensus, but continual negotiation. Alliances, like
identities, are sites of struggle where different meanings and values conflict and retreat, shape and are reshaped. They are not unified or harmo-
nious cultures. Referring to Susan Foster's (1986) communitarian view of
performance, Auslander (1997) writes that the "'immanent struggle
within or behind' cultural lines . . . [suggests that the need for] reflexivity
is in fact a symptom" of the need to recover both a place for resistance
and the "democratic vision" to rewrite history without lapsing into nos-
talgia (p. 85).

Forming new alliances, then, is a call to a more humane education. It
requires vision and stamina. It requires critical teaching.

Like performance, then, teaching is a doing thing; it invokes "uncharacteristic" behaviors because it requires that we shuttle between positions
that are usually polarized. But theatricality, like teaching—which involves
uncharacteristic behavior—opens a place to "make ourselves up as we go
along" (Shepard, 1984, p. 8), to unglue the static image of student and
teacher in order to rearticulate a dynamic, uncertain teaching/learning
identity as a body-full dialogic bricoleur (Claude Levi-Strauss's phrase for
the mythmaking collage maker, 1963). Like reflexive performance, critical
teaching requires thought, planning, creativity, the making of knowledge
particular to the subject, and a desire to situate oneself within a culture.

Reflexive performance can create a disruption of the contained ways
students experience curriculum and the scripting of the body. Critical
teaching can create places for Play, as discussed in Chapter 6. Reflexive
performance can rearrange silence as it renders the body problematic,
making obvious the body's literacy and the noticed disparity between the
word and the world. Such curricular moments may help students resist essentialized masks and help create border literacies.

Gloria Anzaldua writes about the intervening spaces between masks,
what she calls "interfacing": "The masks we are compelled to wear, drive
a wedge between our intersubjective personhood and the persona we present to the world. 'Over my mask/ is your mask.' These masking roles
exact a toll. . . . We are all bleeding, rubbed raw behind our masks.' After

years of wearing masks we may become just a series of roles, the constellated self limping along with its broken limbs" (Anzaldua, 1990, p. xv).

Boal's (1985) miming strategies (discussed in Chapter 5) exaggerate the literacy of the body and seem to reveal the masks and interfacings in a theater of internalized oppressions. From reflections on classroom experiences, I now perceive that the performative aspects of discursive practice may have a special capacity to create an interface or a space between two modalities, from which Anzaldua suggests we might "thrust out and crack the masks" (1990, p. xvi).

How powerful, then, is the potential that lies in examining the interface, in "making soul"! "Uncovering the 'inter-faces' where our multi-surfaced . . . bodies intersect and interconnect" might allow for the re-presentation of identity constructed in wholeness (Anzaldua, 1990, p. xvi). How many boundaries might this act alone help to dislocate?

The gray areas *between the masks* worn in everyday performances, then, are where, I perceive, identities reside. I do not refer to precisely the postmodern identity that is theorized as fluid and possibly without center or to a fixed modern identity either. Rather, I perceive intersubjectivities that struggle to unmask essentialist identities and constructed ones, *identities that are more than image, more than what appears.*

Performance is not an answer; it is a *responsive act* to a world in pain. It suggests more than miming killing norms (Butler, 1993); it suggests reappropriating space and time so that the socially responsible body can act with collective others to resist the politics of essentialism.

Theatricality in the everyday life of a critical teacher, then, marks a practice of hope (Giroux, 1997). In Auslander's view the reflexive student/teacher/culture worker must find a way to work at the "surfaces" (read: borders) without "slipping into the reification of those surfaces . . . [and without becoming] slick and fashionable. . . . The danger that this practice can turn into its opposite by reifying the representations it supposedly deconstructs is a danger that must be courted. At stake is the very possibility of political art [and activism] under postmodernism" (p. 85).

Finally, reflexive performance suggests a "wide-awakeness" (Greene, 1978) that insists that socially responsible human beings "answer for a string of personal signatures" or deeds enacted (Emerson, 1995, p. 402). The deeds enacted here take place within the performative, yet the spaces for change signified by performance occur only in timeouts. This space-time, then, discussed earlier as the "place" of disruption in the performance of identity, is suggested in the constant hope that stringing together enough moments will enable human actors to push through petrified social extremes that on the one hand show life as "beautifully-shaped events" and on the other as "raw and shapeless content" (Emerson, 1995, p. 411).

Shifting contingencies of value—which predominate in essentialist thinking—to notions of temporal identities within unfixed frames may make possible ethical projects of artistry in which the body signs differences not forged by mythological giants. Performative bridgework can, I perceive, produce such political interventions in the service of resisting essentialism—a political project that embraces human interests while resisting the reduction of persons, ideas, and phenomena to a single, one-box-fits-all category.

Notes

1. With roots in the Frankfurt School and its fight against fascism under Mussolini and Nazism under Hitler (see Theodor Adorno, Max Horkheimer) and the Birmingham School and its fight against "Fordism" or the new model for mass production introduced by Henry Ford that created increased wages for the British working class but not increased social status (see Richard Hoggart, Raymond Williams), contemporary culture studies inherited a focus on class and power and on interrogating its own ideologies. Such interrogations lay the groundwork for rethinking class divisions and issues of power and hegemony. Williams's notion of hegemony as a process, a "lived system" of meanings and practices (1978, p. 110), is particularly important for contemporary cultural critique. Additionally, Gramsci's notion of the organic nature of ideology extends to Hall's contemporary notion of agency, i.e., unlike the determinism of Althusser, subjects participate in their own making. Williams, Gramsci, and Hall rely on the mutability of humans and culture; they recognize both the possible and the problematic.

2. Though Dwight Conquergood (1991) raises these questions specifically as they refer to performance ethnography, I perceive they apply to classroom application as well.

3. The implementation of leadoff papers in my classes has had its ups and downs (credit is due to Henry Giroux for suggesting leadoffs; personal communication, October 4, 1996). It has, however, had a most profound effect on students' writings. Whereas normally in the course of a semester a student will write approximately three papers to hand in for grades and then weekly journal entries, the process of writing leadoffs minimized the number of student writings to approximately four two-page papers and three larger papers, but the quality of all papers was exceedingly higher. I perceive this is due to the fact that when students write journal entries they are writing only for the teacher. In this instance, however, students had to make copies of their two-page leadoffs to give to everyone in the class for reading before discussion began, a move that, of course, upped the ante in terms of what students were willing to have their peers read. Leadoffs became a way of publishing students' writings. The process was slow in the beginning, but the quality and criticism of later papers in the course far exceeded any journal writings. During discussion students would often quote from leadoffs, and leadoff writers came to enjoy this attention to their words. When it came time for the longer papers, students were comfortable with their writings because their words had already undergone the scrutiny of peers in the wider audience of the class-

room. Thus students wrote more critically engaged, longer papers and with much less hesitation for tackling tough issues. I was not always sure students who were not responsible for leadoffs during a given class were doing their readings carefully, but the quality of all writings was so greatly improved that it led me to think that if the reasons to assign journal writings is to give students more opportunities to write—even if only for surveillance—then in terms of the latter there are definitely quicker, less painful ways. In terms of the former, it seems that fewer meaningful experiences that gave students a larger audience were more beneficial than the quantities of writings students typically produced in response to reading journals.

Appendix

Some ideas related to the "drama of identity" and "narrative/performative inquiry" are published in the following texts:

Brunner, D. D. "The Knower and the Known: Symbolic Violence and the Representation of Women in Popular Music." *Discourse: Studies in the Cultural Politics of Education* 16(3) (1995), 365–375.

———. "Silent Bodies: Miming Those Killing Norms of Gender." *Journal of Curriculum Theorizing: An Interdisciplinary Journal of Curriculum Studies* 12(1) (1996), 9–15.

———. "Challenging Representations of Sexuality in Story and Performance." In James Sears and Walter Williams, eds. *Overcoming Heterosexism and Homophobia.* New York: Columbia University Press, 1997, 169–181.

———. "Between the Masques." In William S. Penn, ed. *As We Are Now: Mixblood Essays on Race and Identity.* Berkeley: University of California Press, 1997, 168–180.

References

Aberley, D. (1993). *Boundaries of Home: Mapping for Local Empowerment.* Philadelphia: New Society Publishers.

Adorno, T. (1946). "A Social Critique of Radio Music." *Kenyon Review* 2, 208–217.

Aisenberg, N. (1994). *Ordinary Heroines.* New York: Continuum Publishing.

Alter, J., and M. Isikoff. (1996, October 28). "The Real Scandal Is What's Legal." *Newsweek*, 30–32.

Althusser, L. (1971). "Ideology and Ideological State Apparatuses." In *Lenin and Philosophy and Other Essays* (pp. 121–173). New York: Monthly Review.

Anzaldua, G. (1987). *Borderlands.* San Francisco: Aunt Lute Books.

———. (1988). "Tlilli, Tlapalli: The Path of the Red and Black Ink." In R. Simonson and S. Walker (eds.), *The Graywolf Annual Five: Multi-Cultural Literacy* (pp. 29–40). Saint Paul, MN: Graywolf Press.

———. (1990). *Making Face, Making Soul.* San Francisco: Aunt Lute Books.

Arendt, H. (1958). *The Human Condition.* Chicago: University of Chicago Press.

Asante, M. K. (1991). "Multiculturalism: An Exchange." *The American Scholar* (Spring), 267–276.

Auslander, P. (1997). *From Acting to Performance.* New York: Routledge.

Bachelard, G. (1964). *The Poetics of Space.* New York: Orion.

Bakhtin, M. (1965). *Rabelais and His World* (Helen Iswolksy, trans.). Cambridge: MIT Press.

———. (1981). *The Dialogic Imagination: Four Essays* (Caryl Emerson and Michael Holquist, trans.). Austin: University of Texas Press.

———. (1984). *Problems of Dostoevsky's Poetics* (Caryl Emerson, trans.). Minneapolis: University of Minnesota Press.

———. (1986). *Speech Genres and Other Late Essays* (V. W. McGee, trans.). Austin: University of Texas Press.

———. (1990). *Art and Answerability* (Michael Holquist and Vadim Liapunov, eds., Vadim Liapunov, trans.). Austin: University of Texas Press.

———. (1993). *Towards a Philosophy of the Act* (Vadim Liapunov, ed., Vadim Liapunov and Michael Holquist, trans.). Austin: University of Texas Press.

Barnes, B. (1985). *About Science.* New York: Basil Blackwell.

Bateson, G. (1972). *Steps to an Ecology of Mind.* New York: Ballantine.

Baudelaire, C. (1964). "The Painter of Modern Life." In J. Mayne (ed.), *The Painter of Modern Life and Other Essays* (pp. 1–40). London: Phaidon.

Baudrillard, J. (1979). *Seduction* (Brian Singer, trans.). New York: St. Martin's Press.

Bennett, S. (1990). *Theatre Audiences: A Theory of Production and Reception.* New York: Routledge.

Bennett, T. (1986). "Popular Culture and the Turn to Gramsci." *Popular Culture and Social Relations* (pp. xv–I). Philadelphia: Open University Press.

Benstock, S. (1991). *Textualizing the Feminine: On the Limits of Genre.* Norman: Oklahoma University Press.

Berger, J. (1977). *Ways of Seeing.* London: Penguin.

Berlant, L. (1991). "National Brands/National Body: Imitation of Life." In H. Spillers (ed.), *Comparative American Identities: Race, Sex, and Nationality in the Modern Text* (pp. 110–140). New York: Routledge.

Berthoff, A. (1978). *Forming/Thinking/Writing.* Rochelle Park, NJ: Hayden.

Bhabha, H. (1994). *The Location of Culture.* New York: Routledge.

Blau, H. (1983). "Ideology and Performance." *Theatre Journal* 35(4), 441–460.

Bloor, D. (1988). *Knowledge and Reflexivity.* London: Sage.

Boal, A. (1985). *Theatre of the Oppressed* (Charles A. McBride, Maria-Odilia, and Leal McBride, trans.). New York: Theatre Communications Group.

———. (1995). *The Rainbow of Desire* (Adrian Jackson, trans.). New York: Routledge.

Bourdieu, P. (1977). *Outline of a Theory of Practice.* New York: Cambridge University Press.

———. (1980). *The Logic of Practice* (Richard Nice, trans.). Stanford: Stanford University Press.

Bourne, J. (1987). "Homelands of the Mind: Jewish Feminism and Identity Politics." *Race and Class* 29(1), 1–24.

Bruffee, K. (1986). "Social Construction, Language, and the Authority of Knowledge: A Bibliographic Essay." *College English* 48, 773–790.

Brunner, D. D. (1987). *Case Studies in Two Contexts: Self-Sponsored Writers' Subjective Impressions of Written Fluency.* Athens: The University of Georgia.

———. (1992). "Dislocating Boundaries: Teaching Cultural Stereotypes." In J. L. Collins (ed.), *Vital Signs 3: Restructuring the English Classroom* (pp. 62–73). Portsmouth: Heinemann, Boynton/Cook.

———. (1994). *Inquiry and Reflection: Framing Narrative Practice in Education.* Albany: State University of New York Press.

———. (1995). "The Knower and the Known: Symbolic Violence and Representations of Women in Popular Music." *Discourse: Studies in the Cultural Politics of Education* 16(3), 365–375.

———. (1996). "Silent Bodies: Miming Those Killing Norms of Gender." *Journal of Curriculum Theorizing* 12(1), 9–15.

———. (1997a). "Challenging Representations of Sexuality in Story and Performance." In J. Sears and W. Williams (eds.), *Overcoming Heterosexism and Homophobia* (pp. 169–181). New York: Columbia University Press.

———. (1997b). "Between the Masques." In W. S. Penn (ed.), *As We Are Now: Mixblood Essays on Race and Identity* (pp. 168–180). Berkeley: University of California Press.

Butler, J. (1990). *Gender Trouble.* New York: Routledge.

———. (1993). *Bodies That Matter: On the Discursive Limits of "Sex."* New York: Routledge.

Cary, L. (1991). *Black Ice.* New York: Vintage Books.

Cassirer, E. (1946). *Language and Myth.* New York: Dover Publications.

Chuck D (1996). "Public Enemy #1." *Rip 3,* 42–50, 78–80.

Clark, K., and M. Holquist. (1984). *Mikhail Bakhtin.* Cambridge: Harvard University Press.

Clifford, J. (1988). "A Poetics of Displacement: Victor Segalen." In *The Predicament of Culture: Twentieth-Century Ethnography, Literature, and Art* (pp. 152–163). Cambridge: Harvard University Press.

Condé, M. (1992). *I, Tituba, Black Witch of Salem.* New York: Ballantine Books.

Conquergood, D. (1989). "Poetics, Play, Process, and Power: The Performance Turn in Anthropology." *Text and Performance Quarterly* 1(1), 82–95.

———. (1991). "Rethinking Ethnography: Towards a Critical Cultural Politics." *Communication Monographs* 58 (June), 179–194.

———. (1993). "Storied Worlds and the Work of Teaching." *Communication Education* 42 (October), 337–348.

Corngold, S., and I. Giersing. (1991). *Borrowed Lives.* Albany: State University of New York Press.

Crownfield, D. (1992). *Body/Text in Julia Kristeva: Religion, Women, and Psychoanalysis.* Albany: State University of New York Press.

De Certeau, M. (1984). *The Practice of Everyday Life* (Steven Rendall, trans.). Berkeley: University of California Press.

Derrida, J. (1976). *Of Grammatology* (Gayatri Chakravorty Spivak, trans.). Baltimore: Johns Hopkins University Press.

Diamond, E. (1993). "Mimesis, Mimicry, and the 'True-Real.'" In L. Hart and P. Phelan (eds.), *Acting Out: Feminist Performances* (pp. 363–382). Ann Arbor: The University of Michigan Press.

Dolan, J. (1988). *The Feminist Spectator as Critic.* Ann Arbor: University of Michigan Research Press.

———. (1993). "Geographies of Learning: Theatre Studies, Performance, and the 'Performative.'" *Theatre Journal* 45, 417–444.

Dorfman, A. (1983). *The Empire's Old Clothes: What the Lone Ranger, Babar, and Other Innocent Heroes Do to Our Minds.* New York: Pantheon.

Ellsworth, E. (1989). "Why Doesn't This Feel Empowering?" *Harvard Educational Review* 59(3), 297–324.

Emerson, C. (1995). "Bakhtin at 100: Art, Ethics, and the Architectonic Self." *The Centennial Review* 39(3), 397–418.

Epp, J. R., and A. M. Watkinson. (1997). *Systemic Violence in Education: Promise Broken.* New York: State University of New York Press.

Erdrich, L. (1989). *Tracks.* New York: Harper and Row.

Estes, C. P. (1992). *Women Who Run with the Wolves.* New York: Ballantine Books.

Fanon, F. (1967). *Black Skin, White Masks*. New York: Grove Press.

Faster Pussycat. (1992). *Smashes, Thrashes, and Hits: Where There's a Whip There's a Way*. New York: Polygram.

Feldman, A. (1991). *Formations of Violence: The Narrative of the Body and Political Terror in Northern Ireland*. Chicago: University of Chicago Press.

Feral, J. (1982). "Performance and Theatricality: The Subject Demystified." *Modern Drama* 25, 170–181.

Fineman, H., and M. Hosenball. (1996, October 28). "The Asian Connection." *Newsweek,* 25–28.

Fish, S. (1980). *Is There a Text in This Class? The Authority of Interpretive Communities*. Cambridge: Harvard University Press.

Fiske, J. (1989). *Reading the Popular*. Boston: Unwin Hyman.

———. (1992). "Cultural Studies and the Culture of Everyday Life." In L. Grossberg, C. Nelson, and P. Treichler (eds.), *Cultural Studies* (pp. 154–173). New York: Routledge.

Fiske, J., and J. Hartley. (1978). *Reading Television*. New York: Routledge.

Foster, S. L. (1986). *Reading Dance: Bodies and Subjects in Contemporary American Dance*. Berkeley: University of California Press.

Foucault, M. (1972). *The Archaeology of Knowledge* (Alan Sheridan, trans.). New York: Pantheon Books.

———. (1973). *Discipline and Punish: The Birth of the Prison* (Alan Sheridan, trans.). London: Allen Lane.

———. (1977). *Language, Counter-Memory, Practice* (D. Bouchard, ed., D. Bouchard and S. Simon, trans.). Ithaca: Cornell University Press.

———. (1980). *Power/Knowledge: Selected Interviews and Other Writings, 1972–1977* (Colin Gordon, ed., Colin Gordon, Leo Marshall, John Mepham, and Kate Soper, trans.). New York: Pantheon.

———. (1982). "Afterword: The Subject and Power." In H. L. Dreyfus and P. Rabinow (eds.), *Michel Foucault: Beyond Structuralism and Hermeneutics* (pp. 208–226). Chicago: University of Chicago Press, 1983.

———. (1985). *The History of Sexuality: The Use of Pleasure*, vol. 2 (Robert Hurley, trans.). New York: Vintage Books.

———. (1986). "Of Other Spaces." *Diacritics* 16(1), 22–27.

———. (1988). *Care of the Self: The History of Sexuality*, vol. 3. (Robert Hurley, trans.). New York: Vintage.

Freire, P. (1970). *The Pedagogy of the Oppressed*. New York: Continuum.

———. (1973). *Education for a Critical Consciousness*. New York: Continuum.

Freire, P., and D. Macedo. (1987). *Literacy: Reading the Word and the World*. New York: Routledge and Kegan Paul.

Fried, M. (1967). "Art and Objecthood." In G. Battock (ed.), *Mimimal Art: A Critical Anthology* (pp. 116–147). New York: Dutton.

Frith, S. (1978). *The Sociology of Rock*. London: Constable.

———. (1988). *Music for Pleasure*. New York: Routledge.

———. (1992). "The Cultural Study of Popular Music." In L. Grossberg, C. Nelson, and P. Treichler (eds.), *Cultural Studies*. New York: Routledge.

Frye, M. (1983). *The Politics of Reality*. New York: Crossing Press.

Fuss, D. (1989). *Essentially Speaking*. New York: Routledge.

Gallop, J. (1990). *Thinking Through the Body.* New York: Columbia University Press.

Garcia, C. (1992). *Dreaming in Cuban.* New York: Ballantine Books.

Gardner, H. (1993). "Einstein." In *Creating Minds: An Anatomy of Creativity Seen Through the Lives of Freud, Einstein, Picasso, Stravinsky, Eliot, Graham, and Gandhi* (pp. 87–131). New York: Basic Books.

Gasché, R. (1986). *The Tain of the Mirror.* Cambridge: Harvard University Press.

Gates, H. L. (1987). *Figures in Black: Words, Signs, and the "Racial" Self.* New York: Oxford University Press.

Geertz, C. (1983). *Local Knowledge.* New York: Basic Books.

Gibbons, K. (1987). *Ellen Foster.* New York: Vintage Books.

Gilman, C. P. (1973). *The Yellow Wallpaper.* New York: Feminist Press.

Gilroy, P. (1992). "Cultural Studies and Ethnic Absolutism." In L. Grossberg, C. Nelson, and P. Treichler (eds.), *Cultural Studies* (pp. 187–198). New York: Routledge.

Gintis, S. B. a. H. (1976). *Schooling in Capitalist America.* New York: Basic Books.

———. (1982). "The Crisis of Liberal Democratic Capitalism." *Politics and Society* 2(1), 51–93.

Giroux, H. A. (1988). *Teachers as Intellectuals.* New York: Bergin Garvey.

———. (1994a). "Living Dangerously: Identity Politics and the New Cultural Racism." In H. A. Giroux and P. McLaren (eds.), *Between Borders: Pedagogy and the Politics of Cultural Studies* (pp. 29–55). New York: Routledge.

———. (1994b). *Disturbing Pleasures.* New York: Routledge.

———. (1996a). *Fugitive Cultures: Race, Violence, and Youth.* New York: Routledge.

———. (1996b). "Hollywood, Race, and the Demonization of Youth: The 'Kids' Are Not 'Alright.'" *Educational Researcher* 25(2), 31–35.

———. (1997). *Pedagogy and the Politics of Hope.* Boulder: Westview Press.

Giroux, H. A., and P. McLaren. (1994a). *Between Borders: Pedagogy and the Politics of Cultural Studies.* New York: Routledge.

Gotfrit, L. (1991). "Women Dancing Back: Disruption and the Politics of Pleasure." In H. A. Giroux (ed.), *Postmodernism, Feminism, and Cultural Politics: Redrawing Educational Boundaries* (pp. 174–195). Albany: State University of New York Press.

Gramsci, A. (1971). *Selections from the Prison Notebooks* (Q. Hoare and G. Norwell-Smith, trans.). New York: International Publishers.

Greene, M. (1978). *Landscapes of Learning.* New York: Teachers College Press.

———. (1988). *The Dialectic of Freedom.* New York: Teachers College Press.

———. (1995). *Releasing the Imagination: Essays on Education, the Arts, and Social Change.* San Francisco: Josey-Bass.

Grossberg, L. (1986). "Teaching the Popular." In C. Nelson (ed.), *Theory in the Classroom* (pp. 177–200). Urbana: University of Illinois Press.

———. (1988). "Rockin' with Reagan or the Mainstreaming of Postmodernity." *Cultural Critique* 10, 123–149.

———. (1994). "Is Anybody Listening? Does Anybody Care?" In A. Ross and T. Rose (eds.), *Microphone Fiends: Youth Music and Youth Culture* (pp. 41–57). New York: Routledge.

Guberman, R. M. (ed.). (1996). *Julia Kristeva Interviews.* New York: Columbia University Press.

Guns 'N Roses. (1985). *Appetite for Destruction.* New York: Asylum Records.

Hale, J. C. (1993). *Bloodlines.* New York: Harper Collins.

Hall, S. (1990). "Cultural Identity and Diaspora." In J. Rutherford (ed.), *Identity: Community, Culture, Difference* (pp. 222–237). London: Lawrence and Wishart.

Hart, L., and P. Phelan. (eds.). (1993). *Acting Out: Feminist Performances.* Ann Arbor: University of Michigan Press.

Haymes, N. (1995). *Race, Culture, and the City.* Albany: State University of New York Press.

Hebdige, D. (1983). "Posing . . . Threats, Striking . . . Poses: Youth, Surveillance, and Display." *Substance* 37/38, 68–88.

———. (1988). *Hiding in the Light.* New York: Routledge.

Heidegger, M. (1993). "Building Dwelling Thinking." In *Basic Writings of Martin Heidegger* (pp. 323–339). New York: Academic Press.

Hofstadter, D. R. (1979). *Godel, Escher, Bach.* New York: Basic Books.

hooks, b. (1990). *Yearning: Race, Gender, and Cultural Politics.* Boston: South End Press.

———. (1992). *Black Looks: Race and Representation.* Boston: South End Press.

———. (1994). *Outlaw Culture: Resisting Representations.* New York: Routledge.

———. (1995). *Art on My Mind: Visual Politics.* New York: New York Press.

hooks, b., and C. West. (1991). *Breaking Bread.* Boston: South End Press.

Horkheimer, M., and T. Adorno. (1972). *Dialectic of Enlightenment.* New York: Seabury.

Hulme, P. (March 1980). *Hurricanes in the Caribbees: The Constitution of Discourse of English Colonialism.* Paper presented at the University of Essex Conference on the Sociology of Literature, Essex.

Irigaray, L. (1974). *Speculum of the Other Woman* (Gillian C. Gill, trans.). Ithaca: Cornell University Press.

Jameson, F. (1981a). *The Political Unconscious.* Ithaca: Cornell University Press.

———. (1981b). "'In the Destructive Element Immerse': Hans Jurgen Syberberg and Cultural Revolution." *October* 17, 99–118.

Johnson, B. (1987). *A World of Difference.* Baltimore: Johns Hopkins University Press.

Kellner, D. (1995). *Media Culture.* New York: Routledge.

Kelly, G. (1970). "A Brief Introduction to Personal Construct Theory." In D. Bannister (ed.), *Perspectives on Personal Construct Theory* (pp. 2–12). New York: Academic Press.

Kershaw, B. (1992). *The Politics of Performance: Radical Theatre as Cultural Intervention.* New York: Routledge.

Kotz, L. (1992). "The Body You Want: Liz Kotz Interviews Judith Butler." *Art Forum* (November), 82–89.

Koza, J. E. (1994). "Rap Music: The Cultural Politics of Official Representation" (unpublished manuscript).

Kristeva, J. (1984). *Revolution in Poetic Language* (Margaret Waller, trans.). New York: Columbia University Press.

———. (1986a). *The Kristeva Reader* (Toril Moi, ed., Leon S. Roudiez, trans.). New York: Columbia University Press.

———. (1986b). *About Chinese Women* (Anita Barrows, trans.). New York: Marion Boyars.

———. (1992). *The Samurai.* New York: Columbia University Press.

Kuhn, T. (1970). *The Structure of the Scientific Revolution.* 2nd ed. Chicago: University of Chicago Press.

Kundera, M. (1994). *The Book of Laughter and Forgetting.* New York: Harper Perennial.

Lacan, J. (1977). "The Mirror Stage as Formative of the Function of 'I.'" In *Ecrits: A Selection.* New York: Norton.

Laclau, E. (1990). *New Reflections on the Revolutions of Our Time.* London: Verso.

Larsen, N. (1929). *Passing.* New York: Knopf.

Latour, B. (1987). *Science in Action: How to Follow Scientists and Engineers Through Society.* Cambridge: Harvard University Press.

———. (1990). "Postmodern? No, Simply Amodern! Steps Towards an Anthropology of Science." *Studies in History and Philosophy of Science* 2(1), 145–172.

Levi-Strauss, C. (1963). *Structural Anthropology.* New York: Basic Books.

Lorde, A. (1978). *Uses of the Erotic: The Erotic as Power.* Freedom, CA: Crossing Press.

———. (1982). *Zami: A New Spelling of My Name (A Biomythography).* Freedom, CA: Crossing Press.

Madonna, T. Clawson, and J. Roewe, prods. B. A. Brown, ed. (1991). *Truth or Dare.* Van Nuys: Miramax Films.

Marcus, G. (1975). *Mystery Train: Images of America in Rock 'n' Roll Music.* New York: E. P. Dutton.

———. (1989). *Lipstick Traces: A Secret History of the Twentieth Century.* Cambridge: Harvard University Press.

Marcuse, H. (1978). *The Aesthetic Dimension: Toward a Critique of Marxist Aesthetics.* Boston: Beacon Press.

Marshall, R. H. (1996, August 1). "Reader Commentary." *London Review of Books,* 5.

Martin, E. (1992). "Body Narratives, Body Boundaries." In L. Grossberg, C. Nelson, and P. Treichler (eds.), *Cultural Studies* (pp. 409–423). New York: Routledge.

McCarthy, C. (1988). *Slowly, Slowly, Slowly the Dumb Speak: Postcolonialism and Postimperialism in Third World Literature.* Dayton, OH: Conference on Curriculum Theory and Practice at Bergamo.

McGee, P. (1992). *Telling the Other.* Ithaca: Cornell University Press.

McIntosh, P. (1988). "White Privilege and Male Privilege: A Personal Account of Coming to See Correspondences Through Work in Women's Studies." Working Paper, No. 189, Wellesley College, Wellesley, Mass.

McLaren, P. (1986). *Schooling as a Ritual Performance: Towards a Political Economy of Educational Symbols and Gestures.* New York: Routledge.

———. (1991). "Schooling the Postmodern Body." In H. A. Giroux (ed.), *Postmodernism, Feminism, and Cultural Politics* (pp. 144–173). Albany: State University of New York Press.

———. (1993). "Border Disputes: Multicultural Narrative, Identity Formation, and Critical Pedagogy in Postmodern America." In D. McGauglin and W. Tierney (eds.), *Naming Silenced Lives* (pp. 201–223). New York: Routledge.

McRobbie, A. (1992). "Post-Marxism and Cultural Studies." In L. Grossberg, C. Nelson, and P. Treichler (eds.), *Cultural Studies* (pp. 719–730). New York: Routledge.

McWilliam, C. (1993). "The Many Colours of Blood." *Granta* 43 (Spring), 197–209.

Meier, D. W. (1996). "Schools for Citizenship." *The Nation* (October 28), 32–38.

Mercer, K. (1994). *Welcome to the Jungle: New Positions in Black Cultural Studies.* New York: Routledge.

Metallica. (1986). *Master of Puppets.* New York: Elektra Records.

Metcalf, P. (1991). *Enter Isabel: The Herman Melville Correspondence of Clare Spark.* Albuquerque: University of New Mexico Press.

Miller, N. (1991). *Getting Personal.* New York: Routledge.

Mohanty, C. T. (1994). "On Race and Voice: Challenges for Liberal Education in the 1990s." In H. A. Giroux and P. McLaren (eds.), *Between Borders: Pedagogy and the Politics of Cultural Studies* (pp. 145–166). New York: Routledge.

Moi, T. (1985). *Sexual/Textual Politics.* New York: Methuen.

Moore, T. (1992). *Care of the Soul.* New York: Harper Collins.

Morrison, T. (1973). *Sula.* New York: Penguin Books.

———. (1992). *Playing in the Dark: Whiteness and the Literary Imagination.* Cambridge: Harvard University Press.

———. (1994). "Unspeakable Things Unspoken: The Afro-American Presence in American Literature." In A. Mitchell (ed.), *With the Circle: An Anthology of African American Literary Criticism From the Harlem Renaissance to the Present.* Durham: Duke University Press.

Mötley Crüe (1991a). "Slice of Your Pie." Music video broadcast on MTV.

———. (1991b). "Sticky Sweet." Music video broadcast on MTV.

Mulvey, L. (1992). "Pandora: Topographies of the Mask and Curiosity." In B. Colomina (ed.), *Sexuality and Space*, vol. 1 (pp. 53–71). New York: Princeton Architectural Press.

Ng, F. M. (1993). *Bone.* New York: Harper Perennial.

Nietzsche, F. (1969). *On the Genealogy of Morals.* New York: New Vintage Books.

Ovid. (1955). *Metamorphoses* (Mary Innes, trans.). New York: Penguin Books.

Perez, L. (1995, April). *Spiriting the Disembodied House of Knowledge: Minority Culture Cures.* Paper presented at the American Educational Research Association, San Francisco.

Perkins, D. (1981). *The Mind's Best Work.* Cambridge: Harvard University Press.

Phelan, P. (1993). *Unmarked: The Politics of Performance.* New York: Routledge.

———.(1997). *Mourning Sex: Performing Public Memories.* New York: Routledge.

Polanyi, M. (1958). *Personal Knowledge.* Chicago: University of Chicago Press.

———. *The Tacit Dimension.* Garden City, NJ: Doubleday.

Pollock, D., and J. R. Cox. (1991). "Historicizing 'Reason': Critical Theory, Practice, and Postmodernity." *Communication Monographs* 58 (June), 170–178.

Postman, N. (1988). *Conscientious Objections: Stirring Up Trouble About Language, Technology, and Education.* New York: Vintage.

Rabelais, F. (1944). *The Five Books of Gargantua and Pantagruel* (Jacques Le Clerq, trans.). New York: Modern Library.

Rage Against the Machine. (1992). *Take the Power Back.* Los Angeles: Retribution Music.

Rodriguez, R. (1982). *Hunger of Memory*. Boston: D. R. Godine.

Rosenblatt, L. (1978). *The Reader, the Text, the Poem*. Carbondale and Edwardsville: Southern Illinois University Press.

Ross, A., and T. Rose. (1994). *Microphone Fiends: Youth Music and Youth Culture*. New York: Routledge.

Rowbotham, S. (1984). "Women Centered Values and the World as It Is." *Dalhousie Review* 64, 650.

Russo, M. (1986). "Feminine Grotesques: Carnival and Theory." In T. d. Lauretis (ed.), *Feminist Studies/Critical Studies*. Bloomington: Indiana University Press.

Said, E. (1991). *Musical Elaborations*. New York: Columbia University Press.

———. (1994). *Representations of the Intellectual*. New York: Vintage.

Samuels, A. (1996, October 28). "Man of Peace: Snoop Rides Out the Storm with a Second Album." *Newsweek*, 80.

Schechner, R. (1977). *Essays on Performance Theory, 1970–1976*. New York: Drama Book Specialists.

———. (1985). *Between Theatre and Anthropology*. Philadelphia: University of Pennsylvania Press.

———. (1988). *Performance Theory*. London: Routledge.

———. (1993). *The Future of Ritual: Writings on Culture and Performance*. New York: Routledge.

Schechner, R., and W. Appel (eds.). (1990). *By Means of Performance: Intercultural Studies of Theatre and Ritual*. Cambridge: Cambridge University Press.

Schwartz, J., and M. McGuinness. (1979). *Einstein for Beginners*. New York: Pantheon Books.

Sears, J. T. (1991). *Growing Up Gay in the South: Race, Gender, and Journeys of the Spirit*. New York: Harrington Park Press.

Shelley, M. (1818). *Frankenstein*. London: Lackington, Hughes, Harding, Mayor and Jones.

———. (1969). *Frankenstein*. London: Oxford University Press.

Shepard, S. (1984). *Fool for Love and Other Plays*. New York: Bantam.

Shields, R. (1991). *Places on the Margin*. New York: Routledge.

Sibley, D. (1995). *Geographies of Exclusion*. New York: Routledge.

Silko, L. M. (1991). *Almanac of the Dead*. New York: Penguin.

Smith, B. H. (1978). *On the Margins of Discourse* Chicago: University of Chicago Press.

Snoop Doggy Dogg. (1996). *Doggfather: Vapors*. New York: Interscope Records.

Spariosu, M. I. (1997). *The Wreath of Wild Olive: Play, Liminality, and the Study of Literature*. Albany: State University of New York Press.

Spillers, H. (1987). "Mama's Baby, Papa's Baby: An American Grammar Book." *Diacritics* 17(2), 77–80.

Spivak, G. C. (1988). *In Other Worlds: Essays in Cultural Politics*. New York: Routledge.

———. (1990). *The Post-Colonial Critic: Interviews, Strategies, Dialogues*. New York: Routledge.

Stewart, S. (1991). *Crimes of Writing: Problems in the Containment of Representation*. New York: Oxford University Press.

Torrance, E. P. (1979). *The Search for Satori and Creativity*. Buffalo: Creative Education Foundation.

Trend, D. (1992). *Cultural Pedagogy: Art, Education, Politics.* New York: Bergin and Garvey.

Trinh T. M-h. (1989). *Surname Viet, Given Name Nam.* New York: Women Make Movies.

———. (1989). *Woman, Native, Other: Writing, Postcoloniality, and Feminism.* Bloomington: Indiana University Press.

———. (1991). *When the Moon Waxes Red.* New York: Routledge.

Trungpa, C. (1987). *Cutting Through Spiritual Materialism.* Boston: Shambhala.

Turner, V. (1979). "Dramatic Ritual/Ritual Drama: Performance and Reflexive Anthropology." *Kenyon Review* 1(3), 80–93.

———. (1982). *From Ritual to Theatre: The Human Seriousness of Play.* New York: Performing Arts Journal Publications.

———. (1983). "Body, Brain, and Culture." *Zygon* 18(3), 221–245.

Van Halen. (1991). "Good Enough." Music video broadcast on MTV.

Van Sant, G. (1996). *To Die For.* Culver City: Columbia Pictures.

Volosinov, V. N. (1973). *Marxism and the Philosophy of Language* (Ladislav Matjka and I. R. Titunik, trans.). Cambridge: Harvard University Press.

Von Glassersfeld, E. (1976). "Constructivism in Vico and Piaget." In E. von Glassersfeld (ed.), *Vico and Contemporary Thought* (pp. 11–15). New York: Norton.

———. (1984). "An Introduction to Radical Constructivism." In P. Watzlawick (ed.), *The Invented Reality* (pp. 1–29). New York: Norton.

Vygotsky, L. S. (1962). *Thought and Language* (E. Hanfmann G. Vakar, trans.). Cambridge: MIT Press and John Wiley.

Walser, R. (1993). *Running with the Devil: Power, Gender, and Madness in Heavy Metal Music.* Hanover: Wesleyan University Press.

West, C. (1990). "The New Cultural Politics of Difference." *October* 53, 93–109.

———. (1993). *Race Matters.* Boston: Beacon Press.

Wexler, P. (1987). *Social Analysis of Education.* New York: Routledge and Kegan Paul.

Wharton, E. (1979). *The House of Mirth.* New York: Penguin Books.

Whorf, B. L. (1997/56). *Language, Thought, and Reality.* Cambridge: MIT Press.

Wigginton, E. (1986). *Sometimes a Shining Moment.* New York: Doubleday.

Williams, R. (1977). *Marxism and Literature.* New York: Oxford University Press.

———. (1989). *The Politics of Modernism.* London: Verso.

Williams, T. T. (1991). *Refuge: An Unnatural History of Family and Place.* New York: Vintage Books.

Winger. (1990). "Baptized by Fire." From *In the Heart of the Young.* New York: Atlantic.

Wittig, M. (1976). *The Lesbian Body* (Peter Owen, trans.). New York: Avon.

Wolf, L. (1977). *The Annotated Frankenstein.* New York: Clarkson N. Potter.

Wong, S.-L. C. (1994). "Ethnic Subject, Ethnic Sign, and the Difficulty of Rehabilitative Representation: Chinatown in Some Works of Chinese American Fiction." *Yearbook of English Studies* 24, 251–262.

Wood, M. (1995, January 26). "Time of the Assassin." *London Review of Books,* 17–18.

Woodson, J. (1995). *Autobiography of a Family Photo.* New York: Penguin Books.

Woolf, V. (1979). *The Letters of Virginia Woolf: 1932–1935*, vol. 5. New York: Harcourt Brace and Company.

Yoshimoto, B. (1993). *Kitchen.* New York: Washington Square Press.

Index

ritual: action, 5; community, 150; cultural, 56, 150; disrupting, 121, 142; dramatic, 12; performative, 100; system, 76; transformative, 105, 111, 114, 119; transgressive, 12, 100, 146; word and, 112
Rodriquez, Richard, 98
role models, 92
Rowbotham, Sheila, 63

Said, Edward, 68
Schechner, Richard, 4–6, 59, 113–14
school, 14; business interests and, 39; funding, 40–41; nature of, 137; performance by, 39; political nature of, 116, 119; privatization of, 38–39, 41; ritual performance of, 112, 113. *See also* public education
scripts: collective, 53; cultural, 56; directive, 58; individual narratives in, 123
seduction, 18, 27, 68, 77
seeing, 68, 75
Segalan, Victor, 11
segregation, 1–2. *See also* racism
self, 3–4, 36, 128n1; unquiet, 94, 146. *See also* identity
self-definition, 32
self-disclosure, 128, 135
self-discovery, 73–74
self-in other/other-in-self relationships, 54, 74, 135
self/other dichotomy, 13, 15–16, 33, 52, 74
self-referentiality, 87
semiology, 138
semiotic, 3, 13, 94
sexuality, 80–81, 89, 124–25. *See also* gender
Shelley, Mary, 128–29n1
Sheriff, Doug, 51
Sibley, David, 149
signs: body and, 7; context-dependency of, 28; dissociation from signifier, 35; mimesis, 140 (*see also* mimesis); political, 136; prescribed, 102; production and, 3. *See also* language
Silko, Leslie Marmon, 104
Snoop Doggy Dogg, 83–85
social accountability, 51
social action, 85, 121, 135
social articulation, 68
social change, 60–61, 63
social construction, 37, 109, 152–53
social forms, critiquing, 73
social integration, 39
social interaction, 3
social order, body and, 67
social theory, 35
Solomon-Godeau, Abigail, 75
space, 7, 149. *See also* place
Spariosu, Mihai, 139
spatiality, 9, 10, 149

spec-actors, 59, 129n2
spectacle, 58, 102
Spillers, Hortense, 97
Spivak, Gayatri, 21n10, 41, 58
status quo: legitimizing, 145; questioning, 133; resisting, 77, 84 (*see also* essentialism); violating, 123
Stewart, Susan, 54
strategic essentialism, 21n10, 41–42
strategies, 37; for approaching readings, 119–20; for disrupting hegemony, 48; narrative-performative (*see* narrative-performative inquiry); networks of, 38; power, 41, 72, 75; for resisting essentialism, 42
students, 33; acceptance of essentialist perspective, 42–43; awakening to self-in other, 54; best interests of, 144; categorizing, 29; reactions by, 17
subjectivity, 6, 59–60, 94, 97
subversiveness, 91. *See also* displacement; disruption
supernatural, 120
symbol. *See* signs
symbolic, 94, 95
symbolic interactionism, 12

teachers, 16, 83, 143–44, 151. *See also* critical pedagogy
teaching: critical (*see* critical pedagogy); critical interrogation, 74, 75; deterrents to, 144; identity work and, 112–13; methods, 79; of the popular, 78–86; as public site, 63; resisting essentialism through, 16–18, 30, 57; strategies in, 37; study of, 33; theatricality in, 56–57, 154, 155
television, 88
temporality, 9, 10, 48, 149; disruption via, 28
text, 36. *See also* language; writing
theater, 5–6, 112, 115–16; as discourse, 121; experimental, 143–44; of identity, 93, 97; as language, 140; narrative, 35, 129n2; as rehearsal for revolution, 59; of resistance, 137–38, 140; students', 123–26; techniques, 121, 129n2, 129–30n6
theatricality, 115–16
theatricalizing activism, 6
thetic, 7, 13, 21n9
time, 7, 115, 149; concepts of, 10–11. *See also* place
timelines, 119–20
To Die For, 87–89
topography, structuring of, 13
Torrance, E. Paul, 132, 133
TPG. *See* Performance Group, The
tradition, 60, 102, 109, 114
transcendence, 61
transformation, 112, 113

About the Author

Diane DuBose Brunner is Associate Professor of English and Director of English Education at Michigan State University.